CRIMINAL W

Gender Matt

Sharon Grace, Maggie O'Neill, Tammi Walker,
Hannah King, Lucy Baldwin, Alison Jobe,
Orla Lynch, Fiona Measham, Kate O'Brien
and Vicky Seaman

With a Foreword by
Pat Carlen
and an Afterword by
Loraine Gelsthorpe

BRISTOL
UNIVERSITY
PRESS

First published in Great Britain in 2022 by

Bristol University Press
University of Bristol
1-9 Old Park Hill
Bristol
BS2 8BB
UK
t: +44 (0)117 954 5940
e: bup-info@bristol.ac.uk

Details of international sales and distribution partners are available at bristoluniversitypress.co.uk

British Library Cataloguing in Publication Data
A catalogue record for this book is available from the British Library

ISBN 978-1-5292-0839-9 hardcover
ISBN 978-1-5292-0841-2 paperback
ISBN 978-1-5292-0842-9 ePub
ISBN 978-1-5292-0844-3 ePdf

Cover design: Nicky Borowiec
Front cover image: tomozina - istock.com
Bristol University Press uses environmentally responsible print partners.
Printed and bound in Great Britain by CMP, Poole

Contents

List of Figures and Table

Figures

Table

Notes on the Authors

Lucy Baldwin is Senior Lecturer in Criminology, Health and Life Sciences at De Montfort University, UK.

Sharon Grace is Senior Lecturer in the Department of Social Policy and Social Work at the University of York, UK.

Alison Jobe is Assistant Professor of Sociology at Durham University, UK.

Hannah King is Associate Professor of Criminology at Durham University, UK.

Orla Lynch is Senior Lecturer in Criminology and Director of Research for the Department of Sociology and Criminology at the University College Cork, Ireland.

Fiona Measham is Chair in Criminology at the University of Liverpool, UK and Director of The Loop (UK and Australia).

Kate O'Brien is Assistant Professor in Criminology and Criminal Justice at Durham University, UK.

Maggie O'Neill is Professor of Sociology and Criminology and Head of Department at the University College Cork, Ireland.

Vicky Seaman is Support Worker with the Cork Alliance Centre and a PhD Criminology candidate at University College Cork, Ireland.

Tammi Walker is Professor of Forensic Psychology and College Principal at Durham University, UK.

Acknowledgements

The authors would like to thank Professor Carlen for providing the inspiration for the book and for writing the foreword. We would also like to thank Loraine Gelsthorpe for writing the endnote, and we thank both for their contribution to feminist criminology.

We dedicate this book firstly to all the women across the UK and Ireland who gave their time to the projects discussed in this book as participants, interviewees, co-researchers and co-writers. We thank you for your time, energy and inspiration.

Secondly, we dedicate this book to all criminalised women to whom we make a commitment to continue to strive for and contribute to positive change.

This book is co-authored by The Criminal Women Voice, Justice and Recognition Network (CWVJR).

Sharon Grace
Maggie O'Neill
Tammi Walker
Hannah King
Lucy Baldwin
Alison Jobe
Orla Lynch
Fiona Measham
Kate O'Brien
Vicky Seaman

Foreword

Pat Carlen

One summer's evening in 1984 seven women met in Central London in response to a proposal by Chris Tchaikovsky, Founder of Women in Prison (WIP), that we form a group to campaign against women's imprisonment. All except me, and the partner of one of the other women, had been in prison. I was there at the invitation of Chris who, having read my recently published book *Women's Imprisonment*, thought that I might be useful to the group, though it was decided that only ex-prisoners were eligible for full membership. So, the campaigning group WIP was born, and several more foundational meetings followed. And it was at one of those very early 1984 meetings that we decided to write a book to publicise both the harms of women's imprisonment and the real-life stories of women sent to prison and thereafter too frequently stereotyped as 'other' – other than real women, other than real mothers and other than real criminals; as women, in short, whom prisons must feminise, domesticise and medicalise.

Four women volunteered to tell their stories, though each wanted to work in a different way. It was agreed that I would be overall editor and second-named co-author for three of the chapters, and that royalties would be shared between the four main authors. Only Chris chose to write her story by herself, and this she did, though we had several shouty arguments at the editorial stage. Jenny Hicks, a founding member of the Clean Break Theatre Company, also elected to write her own story and did so until she felt bogged down by detail in the last third, after which she typed the remainder before we edited together and highlighted some of the recurring themes. Diana Christina decided to tape and re-tape her story with me – alternately inserting commentary she approved of and then deleting it as she later changed her mind. This took hours, then weeks and then months – as several major theoretical arguments erupted and editor and author standoffs occurred along the way; and during which time the whole project was abandoned by all of us more than once. Josie O'Dwyer and I, however, still did days and days of companionable interview sessions, both of us checking and changing what was written as we went along. I don't think any one of the women was ever completely satisfied with her final story, and it was certainly the most difficult book I have been involved with. But at last it was agreed that each chapter was 'good enough' to send to the publisher and *Criminal Women* was published in 1985 by Polity Press. Five reprints, a Dutch translation and publication in the Netherlands followed.

Now, 36 years later, The Criminal Women Voice, Justice and Recognition Network (CWVJR) has produced a varied, informative and stirring collection of narratives from women who have similarly suffered a range of injustices in today's social, criminal justice and penal systems. I would have been very happy if there had been no call for such a book. Unfortunately, the stories here – of Vicky, Ruby, Betsy, Mary and all the others – indicate that the need for governments to rethink social and criminal justice for women in the UK is at least as great in the first quarter of the twenty-first century as it was in the last quarter of the twentieth. What is urgently required is a change in focus from the crimes of the powerless to the crimes of the powerful. Such radical change might result in women's relatively minor crimes and disproportionate punishments at last being seen primarily through the lens of class, racism and gender oppressions, rather than being weighed formally on the scales of a crudely punitive criminal justice. Until, and beyond, that time, autobiographical accounts of women's experiences of the judicial and penal systems will be essential for the ongoing development of a gendered and democratic justice for women.

Introduction

Sharon Grace, Maggie O'Neill, Tammi Walker,
Hannah King, Lucy Baldwin, Alison Jobe, Orla Lynch,
Fiona Measham, Kate O'Brien and Vicky Seaman

The origins of this book lie in collaborative discussions with a group
of feminist criminologists, sociologists and psychologists: the Criminal
Women Voice, Justice and Recognition Network (CWVJR) who came
together to develop research and scholarship which aims to centre women's
voices and lived experiences. This book draws on each co-author's body
of research in their field of expertise and on a range of research projects,
practice and activities. As such the aim of this book is to bring together
a body of feminist research on 'criminal women' that critically examines
women's reasons for engaging in 'criminal' activity and the challenges
they face in 'attempting to become women of their own making' (Carlen
et al, 1985: 1).

The authors were inspired by Pat Carlen's 1985 landmark book made up of
four biographical accounts written with four women – Chris Tchaikovsky,
Diana Christina, Jenny Hicks and Josie O'Dwyer. '*Criminal Women* tells the
stories of four women who, in attempting to become women of their own
making, became deeply involved in crime' (Carlen et al, 1985: 1). Using
the narrative/biographical accounts by the four women, Carlen challenged
both the 'othering' of women who commit crimes and explanations that
suggest women should adapt themselves better to social norms. Following
the work of Heidensohn (1968) and Smart (1978), Carlen analysed women's
experiences, paying attention to 'the complex and concealed forms of
oppression and social control to which women are subject' (Smart, 1978,
cited in Carlen et al, 1985: 6) and explores the possible options and responses
for women in the context of a 'class riven and deeply sexist society' (Smart,
1978, cited in Carlen et al, 1985: 6). Similarly, this book is centred on a
biographical approach to criminology and a commitment to creating space
for women's voices to be heard and shared. Using Carlen's pioneering text
as our starting point, some 35 years later, our aim was to critically examine

the experiences and narratives of women in the criminal justice system (CJS) based upon extensive empirical research and narrative interviews with women. Through exploring the complexities of social disadvantage in terms not only of gender, but of the intersecting experiences and oppressions of class, race and age, we aim to show how unhelpful gendered stereotypes of victims and offenders result in injustice.

Women's voices and experiences are often silenced or marginalised in debates about the CJS, with little attention paid to the perspectives of women caught up in that system as suspects, defendants, prisoners and victims. Traditionally, research has mainly been conducted *on* rather than *with* women who are involved in crime, as both victims and offenders. This book centres instead on women's lived experiences of criminality and victimisation, from a variety of studies focused on drug use and supply, sex work, sexual exploitation and the experience of imprisonment, including self-harm and maternal loss and, more positively, education in prison. The collection highlights that, although much has changed in terms of responses to criminal women since the publication of Carlen's ground-breaking text, concealed forms of oppression and social control remain central to women's experiences of the justice system. The authors and the women's voices in this book make a powerful case that this inequality and injustice must be addressed and rectified, with future research, policy and practice directions considered as a key focus.

Drawing on the expertise of the authors in contemporary fields of study through the use of cutting-edge participatory, inclusive and narrative methodologies, the book updates Carlen's pioneering work for the twenty-first century. As such we hope that it will inform academic research and teaching, policy and practice in a variety of areas affecting 'criminal' women's lives. Most particularly, drawing on a wide range of contemporary examples of 'criminal' women's experiences, it offers readers an understanding of the nature of 'criminal' women's lives through their own lived experience of criminality, victimisation and punishment. The book explores how gender and other social divisions (including intersectional experiences of race, social class and age) exacerbate the oppression and social control of 'criminal' women and how this informs and directs the criminal justice and social responses to their offending and victimisation. It argues for biographical, narrative and participatory methodological approaches as essential to a proper understanding and recognition of the realities of 'criminal' women's lives and the most effective ways to hear them and support them.

Following the foreword from Pat Carlen herself, this introductory chapter offers a brief overview of women's current experiences in the CJS and summarises the substantive content of the chapters to follow. The endnote is provided by another pioneering scholar of feminist criminology, Professor Loraine Gelsthorpe.

An overview of women in the CJS

The differential treatment of women compared with men throughout the CJS has long been a cause for debate, from those who argue that women are treated more leniently than men (the 'chivalry thesis') by virtue of their female status, to those who believe the system is harsher in its treatment of women whose criminality is perceived as a betrayal of femininity. These debates have often simplistically placed women in contrast to men and as a result have frequently ignored wider questions about the particular circumstances and needs of women caught up in the CJS. Historically, female offenders have also been pathologised and treated as abnormal – 'mad not bad' as it is often phrased. In more recent years, our understanding has become more nuanced alongside an acknowledgement that evidence consistently shows that women do not offend as much or as seriously as men. We also now understand that poverty plays a key role in women offenders' lives and drives a great deal of their offending. We also know that many women offenders have a history of unmet needs in terms of experiences of trauma, sexual and violent victimisation both in childhood and adulthood; poor physical and mental health; insecure housing and income; and low levels of training and employment. The Surveying Prison Crime Reduction Survey (Light et al, 2013) found that 31 per cent of women offenders had spent time in local authority care and 53 per cent reported having experienced emotional, physical or sexual abuse as a child. The prevalence of trauma histories have a strong influence in particular on women's involvement with crime; and some researchers have shown that the number of traumatic child events are directly correlated with their lifetime numbers of arrests (Messina and Grella, 2006). In addition, a survey by the Social Exclusion Task Force (2009) found that 28 per cent of women's crime had been financially motivated; and Light et al (2013) found that 48 per cent of women prisoners reported having committed offences to support someone else's drug use (compared with only fifth of men).

What we see therefore is that women's pathways into crime can be seen in some ways as experiences of victimisation, dysfunctional relationships, poverty and marginalisation which has resulted in offending behaviour. This has significant implications in terms of, for example, what interventions or programmes might do to support women's desistance more effectively. It is now generally accepted that treating women offenders the same as male offenders is not always appropriate and yet most interventions or programmes are designed for men.

The Women and the Criminal Justice System analysis from the Ministry of Justice offers us an overview of women's involvement as suspects, defendants and offenders in the system. It shows that women made up 15 per cent of the 698,700 people arrested in 2017–18, and around a quarter of all those prosecuted. Most women are prosecuted for summary offences (88 per cent compared with 76 per cent of men). For more serious offences (indictable offences) men are more likely to be prosecuted than women except for theft offences (48 per cent of women were prosecuted for theft compared with 30 per cent of men). Overall, the number of convictions has fallen for men by 28 per cent and risen for women by 1 per cent since 2007. 11 per cent of women and 25 per cent of men were remanded into custody in 2017 (Ministry of Justice, 2018). However, statistics from the previous year showed that 60 per cent of women remanded by the magistrate's courts and 41 per cent by the Crown Court did not receive a custodial sentence. A third of women (37 per cent) sentenced to custody have committed theft offences; a further 20 per cent summary offences; and only 9 per cent violence against the person offences (compared with 20 per cent, 16 per cent and 15 per cent for men respectively) (PRT, 2019). Overall, 82 per cent of women entering prison under sentence have committed a non-violent offence (PRT, 2019). Statistical evidence also shows differences in sentencing patterns (in large part reflecting less serious offending) where many more women receive short sentences compared with men. This has increased in recent years as in 1993 only a third of custodial sentences given to women were for less than six months – by 2018 this had doubled (62 per cent) (PRT, 2019). In 2015–16 one in four women sent to prison – more than 1,500 – were sentenced to 30 days or less, with almost 300 of them put behind bars for under two weeks (PRT, 2019). Taking into account sentencing rules, which mean that non-violent prisoners are typically released after half of that time, this can result in hundreds of women being in prison for one week or even less. But even such short sentences can put women at risk of losing their children, their jobs and/or their tenancies.

Community sentencing for women has halved in a decade and there is evidence that community sentences have become increasingly punitive (Carlen and Tombs, 2006). Many probation interventions are designed for men and focus closely on offending behaviour and may not be as appropriate for women for whom offending is a symptom rather than a cause of their difficulties (Barry and McIvor, 2010); and for whom 'male-centric' programmes fail to recognise their more complex criminogenic needs (Martin et al, 2009). There are also significant issues for women offenders being able to engage effectively with such programmes and meet their requirements. Some of these issues are practical, for example inconvenient appointment times and places, difficulty arranging childcare or meeting the costs of transport to the probation office (Martin et al, 2009). Women probationers have also described how difficult and intimidating attending probation offices can be – given that they are likely to come across male offenders. This can be particularly traumatic if they have a history of abuse or other victimisation, or if these offenders are current drug users who can persuade them away from their attempts to go straight (RR3, 2012).

As Clarke (2004) points out, if women realise that services are not effectively meeting their needs it is not surprising that they fail to engage with those services. However, this failure to engage can have serious repercussions for women offenders as they may breach their terms and end up in custody – even if their original offence had not warranted a custodial sentence – and there is evidence that breach is increasingly used for further incarceration (Hedderman, 2010). Many women entering prison for breaching their community penalty or licence do so for very short sentences, allowing very little time for constructive work while in prison and doing enormous damage to the already fragile circumstances of the woman's life outside prison (RR3, 2012). As Hedderman (2010) points out, the number of women entering prison for 'other offences' rose by 55 per cent between 2003 and 2009 and around 60 per cent of these other offences were breaches.

As outlined in the statistical evidence above, it can be clearly argued that women are often sent to prison unnecessarily as they frequently present a low risk to the public and most commonly commit low-level non-violent offences (McIvor and Burman, 2011). Just 3.2 per cent of women in prison are assessed as high or very high risk of harm to others (NOMS Women and Equalities Group, 2012). It has been argued that this over-incarceration is partly because of a significant lack of effective community sentences available to women (Carlen and Tombs, 2006); or because sentencers believe that the nature of women's chaotic lives (particularly those involved with drugs or alcohol) mean that they will not be able to cope with the conditions of community sentences (Carlen and Tombs, 2006); or, most worryingly perhaps, because sentencers decide to send women to custody to get the help they need, for example with drug or alcohol misuse, because they do not believe they will get this help in the community (McIvor and Burman, 2011).

Currently, in England and Wales, women make up around 4 per cent of the total prison population. The female prison population in December 2020 was 3,231 compared with a male population of 75,640. However, it is important to bear in mind that there are around 8,000 prison receptions in female prisons in any one year – as women are more likely to receive short sentences, around twice the average female prison population comes into and leaves prison each year. Looking at receptions in this way allows us to see a clearer picture of the number of women who may have been sent to prison, even for very short periods: in 2018, 7,745 women were sent to prison on remand or sentence. Similarly, women in Ireland make up around 4.3 per cent of the prison population and are located in two female prisons: the Mountjoy Dóchas Centre and a female wing in Limerick Prison. The Irish Penal Reform Trust (IPRT) report that most female committals are for non-violent offences and the majority of women receive short-term sentences. In 2019, female committals to prison (including on remand, under sentence and under immigration law) was 1,174 and this number has risen more rapidly than for men. The average number of daily females in custody in 2019 across the two female prisons was 170. According to the IPRT, 16.7 per cent of women were imprisoned for failing to pay court-ordered fines, almost twice the comparable rate for men. Overcrowding is an issue within prisons and a growing concern is immigration-related committals. The IPRT are working towards policy changes that focus upon alternatives to imprisonment.

The overwhelming male dominance of the prison system in both jurisdictions has meant that the needs of women in custody have frequently been hidden and penal policy and practice is most often concerned with the issues that dominate in the male estate, such as violence or security, rather than those that affect women prisoners. Most importantly, the significant damage done by their separation from their children – both to them and the children – can be the most painful consequence for women prisoners to bear (Covington, 2002; Hardwick, 2012). In 2010 more than 17,000 children were separated from their mothers due to incarceration. The Prison Reform Trust (PRT, 2011) estimate that only around five per cent of children whose mothers are in prison stay in their own homes, and only nine per cent of these children were cared for by their father (Dean, 2013).

The evidence of the impact of separation is clear, particularly with regard to high rates of self-harming and self-inflicted deaths among the female prison population which is partly attributed to the problems associated with maintaining relationships with children in prison. A key factor in problems with maintaining relationships with children lies with the organisation of the prison estate and the fact that there are relatively few women's prisons, which means that prison visits are expensive and difficult for family members to organise.

In 2007 Baroness Jean Corston produced a seminal review of women with particular vulnerabilities in the CJS. The Corston review was commissioned by the Home Secretary following the self-inflicted deaths of six women within a 13-month period at Styal prison. Corston's report called for a wide range of radical changes in the way in which the CJS 'manages' such offenders. Most significantly she called for a holistic, woman-centred approach within the CJS that was sensitive to the complex needs of the majority of women offenders; an emphasis on appropriate punishment in the community for low risk, non-violent women offenders; and the abolition of large prisons in favour of small custodial units geographically dispersed widely around the country (Corston, 2007). The Corston review was instrumental in establishing the principle that the complex needs of female offenders meant that equal treatment could lead to unequal outcomes and that differential treatment was necessary. While at the time of publication the government accepted most of Corston's 43 recommendations, we have still yet to see much evidence of the sweeping whole-system reform envisaged by Corston coming to fruition. In 2013, a Justice Select Committee inquiry report welcomed a number of developments since Corston's report but concluded that the female prison population had not fallen sufficiently fast; there had been limited growth in local services to tackle the underlying causes of female reoffending; and that the gender equality duty had not consistently informed government policy.

While the Corston Report is rightly regarded as having raised political awareness about women (House of Commons Justice Committee, 2013), the issues it raised have been well known in academic and campaigning fields for decades. Namely that the vast majority of women in prison have highly complex needs, suffer from multiple disadvantages and that their offending is often directly caused by the impoverished and difficult social circumstances in which they find themselves – further exacerbated by substance misuse, mental health issues and experiences of physical, mental and/or sexual abuse. As the Prison Reform Trust highlighted, it is too easy for women offenders to become trapped in a 'vicious circle of victimisation and criminal activity … worsened by poverty, substance dependency or poor mental health' (PRT, 2013: 337). It seems that despite greater acknowledgement of these facts within criminal justice policy and practice – particularly perhaps since the Corston Report (2007) – women in prison 'have the same social histories of poverty, abuse, lone parenthood, homelessness and poor mental health as they had 30 years ago' (Carlen and Tombs, 2006: 338), and the 'adverse social and economic circumstances of women who are at risk of offending … remains unchanged' (Gelsthorpe and Morris, 2002: 278).

There is also clear agreement in the academic and campaigning fields that prisons are not the best places to help women offenders overcome their difficult life experiences and move onto more fulfilling and happier lives free from abuse, drug and alcohol use and crime (both as victims and offenders) (Clarke, 2004; Carlen and Tombs, 2006; Bartlett, 2007). Indeed, it has been argued strongly that time in prison exacerbates women's problems to the extent that they return to the community in a far worse position that they were in before their sentence (Barry and McIvor, 2010). For example, in 2017–18 37 per cent of women left prison without settled accommodation, around 14 per cent were homeless and four per cent were sleeping rough on release.

Women's options on release are usually narrowed by their time in prison in terms of employment and education opportunities through stigmatization and lowered self-esteem (Carlen and Tombs, 2006) and poor physical and mental health (Plugge et al, 2006). Finding ways to encourage and help women to motivate themselves to resettle and reintegrate, particularly without the motivation of having their children returned to them, can be highly challenging. Under current arrangements in the UK female estate, there is also little opportunity for women to be prepared for release close to home – the average distance from home for women prisoners is 60 miles (WIP, 2012). This results in many women leaving prison homeless, unemployed and without custody of their children. As the PRT (2011) highlight, this can result in a vicious circle developing with women being unable to regain custody of their children because they do not have stable accommodation, but not qualifying for that accommodation without having custody of their children.

Women offenders are also often in a worse position than male offenders on release. It is far less likely that their partners will have maintained a family unit while they have been in prison, and often they are not able to return to their family home, if they have one, due to the risk of further violence (McIvor et al, 2009). This is a key difference between male and female offenders – it appears to be comparatively less likely for women offenders to have pro-social partners to support their desistance. Brown and Ross (2010) highlighted the absence of social support available for women on release, often caused by the fact that their partners might be part of the problem rather than the solution. Persistence in women's offending can be shown to be associated with housing problems and substance misuse (and a lack of treatment to address it) (Brennan et al, 2012). As Gelsthorpe and Wright (2015: 45) argue: 'It is not sensible to talk [about] how and why women persist without looking at the related issue of how and why women do, or do not – or cannot even – desist from offending.'

Overview of the book

The chapters that follow are a homage to Pat Carlen's *Criminal Women* and take up these themes through the authors' combined research and commitment to providing a platform for women to speak for themselves, as experts on their own lives, as well as with academic researchers, with a view to challenging and changing the deep social and sexual inequalities that inform our analysis of *Criminal Women: Gender Matters*.

Chapter 1 by Sharon Grace focuses on the stories of 16 women engaged in drug recovery in two UK women's prisons. It explores their journeys into drug use and crime, their experience of addiction and its associated problems and losses, the impact on their relationships, and on their mental and physical health. The women's need for help and support is explored with a focus on their own priorities for and views on their personal recovery, their plans for the future and the barriers they face in realising those plans.

Chapter 2, by Vicky Seaman and Orla Lynch, explores desistance theory through the concept of 'knifing off' (Maruna, 2001, 2007), highly relevant in the process of desistance, particularly among those who experience or have experienced active addiction, but have never been comprehensively examined among a female population. This chapter presents the findings from a thematic analysis of the life history narratives of women who at one point or another engaged with the CJS in Ireland. Through the lived experience of these women, the process of 'knifing off' is examined in tandem with the role of and nature of social supports sought and utilised by these women as they move away from engagement in offending behaviours through a desistance process. Through an analysis of the participants' relationships before, during and after their involvement in offending, this chapter highlights the relevant gender issues that must be considered in any theoretical framework on desistance for women.

Chapter 3, by Maggie O'Neill and Alison Jobe, centres on participatory research interviews with women who sell or have sold sex and have spent time in prison. There are no official records on the number of women in prison who have sold sex (Ahearne, 2016) and indeed no official records on the numbers of women selling sex more generally in society. The women's life trajectories show that their narratives are 'vivid chronicles of the times' in which they live (Carlen et al, 1985: 11), including experiences of the CJS and leaving prison. In articulating the relationship between private troubles and social issues (Mills, 1970), the authors argue that women's narratives point to future possible trajectories and modes of doing justice with women, working against the grain of what Hudson (2006) calls 'white man's justice'. This is an example of participatory, biographical narrative research as criminological imagination that enables us 'to grasp history and biography and the relations between the two within society' (Mills, 1970: 6; Carlen, 2010; Seal and O'Neill, 2019). In *Criminal Women*, the prison regime is described as being based around the will to 'discipline, infantalize, feminize, medicalize and domesticate' (Carlen et al, 1985: 162), and in the final part of this chapter the authors reflect on the extent to which this relates to women's experiences of the CJS, and how this has changed or stayed the same over time.

Chapter 4 by Tammi Walker highlights that among the women in prison in England and Wales at any one time approximately one third self-harm. The most common methods used in women's prisons are cutting and scratching, followed by strangulation. Previous studies of self-harm in prisons have mostly focused on prevalence, risk factors and clinical concomitants, with isolated attempts to develop and test theoretical models to aid prediction and intervention with high-risk groups. There has been a very limited focus on understanding the functions or meanings behind this intricate and often misunderstood behaviour. This chapter, using narrative accounts of women, explores this complex area and draws upon the intra-personal and/or inter-personal motivations for self-harming in prison. Attention is also given to research regarding protective factors for self-harm and how these personal or social resources may reduce the impact of negative consequences in the face of stressors in prison.

The pain of maternal imprisonment is the focus of Chapter 5 by Lucy Baldwin, with Mary Elwood and Cassie Brown. Maternal imprisonment is a research area that has garnered interest in the twenty-first century, however much of the focus relates to the impact on the child due to separation by maternal imprisonment. What is less well documented, particularly in the mother's own voice, is the impact prison has on women as mothers, relating to their maternal identity, their self-worth, their maternal role and their journey 'back to good mothering' or 'normality'. Through the narratives of post-prison mothers, the authors explore the pains associated with maternal imprisonment, but significantly also reveal much about their struggle in relation to reintegration into their families once released, and the longer-term impact of having been an imprisoned mother.

Chapters 6 and 7 represent the work conducted by the Inside-Out Prison Exchange Programme. Chapter 6, by Hannah King, Kate O'Brien and Fiona Measham, provides a critical exploration and framework for thinking through the authors' own work with women in prison delivering a prison education programme. Chapter 7 is co-authored with Verity-Fee, Phoenix, Iris and Angel: their writings, prison journeys and voices take centre stage. Through their poetry and creative writing, this chapter provides a platform for their voices and experiences to be heard. Through short reflective biographies that accompany each of their written pieces, together, the authors try to convey a sense of their journey through prison.

References

Ahearne, G. (2016) 'Paying the price: sex workers in prison and the reality of stigma', *Prison Services Journal*, 223: 24–30.

Barry, M. and McIvor, G. (2010) 'Professional decision making and women offenders: containing the chaos?', *Probation Journal*, 57(1): 27–41.

Bartlett, A. (2007) 'Women in prison: concepts, clinical issues and care delivery', *Psychiatry*, 6(11): 444–8.

Brennan, T., Breitenbach, M., Dieterich, W., Salisbury, E. J. and Van Voorhis, P. (2012) 'Women's pathways to serious and habitual crime: a person-centered analysis incorporating gender responsive factors', *Criminal Justice and Behavior*, 39(11): 1481–508.

Brown, M. and Ross, S. (2010) 'Mentoring, social capital and desistance: a study of women released from prison', *Australian and New Zealand Journal of Criminology*, 43(1): 31–50.

Carlen, P. (2010) *A Criminological Imagination: Essays on Justice, Punishment and Discourse*, London: Ashgate.

Carlen, P., Hicks, J., O'Dwyer, J., Christina, D. and Tchaikovsky, C. (1985) *Criminal Women*, Cambridge: Polity Press.

Carlen, P. and Tombs, J. (2006) 'Reconfigurations of penality: the ongoing case of the women's imprisonment and reintegration industries', *Theoretical Criminology*, 10(3): 337–60.

Clarke, R. (2004) *'What works?' for women who offend: a service user's perspective: exploring the synthesis between what women want and what women get.* Research Paper 2004/04, London: The Griffins Society.

Corston, J. (2007) *The Corston Report: a review of women with particular vulnerabilities in the criminal justice system*, London: Home Office.

Covington, S. (2002) *A woman's journey home: challenges for female offenders and their children.* 'From Prison to Home' conference proceedings, Washington, DC: Urban Institute, Justice Policy Center.

Dean, E. (2013) 'A brighter future', *Nursing Standard*, 28(9): 22–3.

Gelsthorpe, L. and Morris, A. (2002) 'Women's imprisonment in England and Wales: a penal paradox', *Criminology and Criminal Justice*, 2(3): 277–301.

Gelsthorpe, L. and Wright, S. (2015) 'The context: women as lawbreakers', in J. Annison and J. Brayford (eds) *Women and Criminal Justice: From the Corston Report to Transforming Rehabilitation*, Bristol: Policy Press, pp 39–58.

Hardwick, N. (2012) *Transcript of the speech given at Issues in Criminal Justice Conference*, 29 February. Sussex: The University of Sussex.

Hedderman, C. (2010) 'Government policy on women offenders: Labour's legacy and the Coalition's challenge', *Punishment & Society*, 12(4): 485–500.

Heidensohn, F. (1968) 'The deviance of women: a critique and an enquiry', *British Journal of Sociology*, 19(2): 160–75.

House of Commons Justice Committee (2013) *Women offenders: after the Corston Report*, London: House of Commons Library.

Hudson, B. (2006). 'Beyond white man's justice: race, gender and justice in late modernity', *Theoretical Criminology*, 10(1): 29–47.

Irish Prison Service Annual Report (2019) *Creating a better environment*, Irish Prison Service. Available at: https://www.irishprisons.ie/wp-content/uploads/documents_pdf/IPS-Annual-Report-2019-Web.pdf [Accessed 4 January 2021].

Light, M., Grant, E. and Hopkins, K. (2013) *Gender differences in substance misuse and mental health amongst prisoners: results from the Surveying Prisoner Crime Reduction (SPCR) longitudinal cohort study of prisoners*, Ministry of Justice Analytical Series, London: Ministry of Justice.

Martin, J., Kautt, P. and Gelsthorpe, L. (2009) 'What works for women? A comparison of community-based general offending programme completion', *British Journal of Criminology*, 49: 879–99.

Maruna, S. (2001) *Making Good*, Washington, DC: American Psychological Association.

Maruna, S. and Roy, K. (2007) 'Amputation or reconstruction? Notes on the concept of "knifing off" and desistance from crime', *Journal of Contemporary Criminal Justice*, 23(1): 104–24.

McIvor, G. and Burman, M. (2011) *Understanding the drivers of female imprisonment in Scotland*, Briefing 02/2011, Glasgow: Scottish Centre for Crime and Justice Research.

McIvor, G., Trotter, C. and Sheehan, R. (2009) 'Women, resettlement and desistance', *Probation Journal*, 56(4): 347–61.

Messina, N. and Grella, C. (2006) 'Childhood trauma and women's health outcomes in a California prison population', *American Journal of Public Health*, 96(10): 1842–48.

Mills, C. W. (1970) *The Sociological Imagination*, Harmondsworth: Penguin.

Ministry of Justice (2018) *Women and the criminal justice system 2017 statistics: a Ministry of Justice publication under Section 95 of the Criminal Justice Act 1991*, London: Ministry of Justice.

NOMS Women and Equalities Group (2012) Judicial engagement: women in the CJS. A Briefing for probation trusts, London: Ministry of Justice.

O'Malley, S. (2018) *Motherhood, Mothering and the Irish Prison System*, Galway: National University of Ireland.

Plugge, E., Douglas, N. and Fitzpatrick, R. (2006) *The Health of Women in Prison Study Findings*, Oxford: University of Oxford.

PRT (Prison Reform Trust) (2011) *Reforming women's justice: final report of the Women's Justice Taskforce*, London: PRT.

PRT (Prison Reform Trust) (2013) *Prison Reform Trust briefing: why focus on reducing women's imprisonment*, London: PRT.

PRT (Prison Reform Trust) (2019) *Prison: the facts: Bromley briefings, summer 2019*, London: PRT.

RR3 (Reducing Reoffending Third Sector Advisory Group) (2012) *A report of the Task and Finish Group: breaking the cycle of women's offending: a system re-design*, London: Clinks.

Seal, L. and O'Neill, M. (2019) *Imaginative Criminology: Of Spaces, Past, Present and Future*, Bristol: Policy Press.

Smart, C. (1978) *Women, Crime and Criminology*, Boston: Routledge & Kegan Paul.

Social Exclusion Task Force (2009) *Short study on women offenders*, London: Cabinet Office.

The Surveying Prisoner Crime Reduction Survey (2014) London: Ministry of Justice.

WIP (Women in Prison) (2012) *Corston Report 5 years on*, London: WIP.

1

Hearing the Voices of Women Involved in Drugs and Crime

Sharon Grace

This chapter focuses on the stories of sixteen women who at the time of their interview were actively engaged in drug recovery in two UK women's prisons. It will explore their journeys into drug use and crime, their experience of addiction and its associated problems and losses. The women's priorities for their recovery and their plans for the future will also be discussed. The chapter begins with an overview of research on women involved in drugs and crime before moving on to focus on the women's own narrative accounts.

Part one: background
Childhood and adult victimisation, trauma, abuse and neglect

The reasons women start using drugs are complex and often centre on coping with the physical and emotional pain caused by abuse or other childhood and adult trauma (Bartlett, 2007; NTA, 2010). Numerous studies report high rates of experiences of abuse among women involved in drugs and crime and directly link these experiences with subsequent substance use and criminal activity (Green et al, 2005; Golder et al, 2014; Kelly et al, 2014). For example, Golder et al (2014) found in their sample of 406 women on probation or parole: 70 per cent reported experiences of physical or sexual childhood abuse; 90 per cent adult interpersonal violence; and 72 per cent non-interpersonal adult violence.

Messina et al (2007) found higher rates of childhood adverse events (CAE) among women in their comparative sample of male and female prisoners – specifically in terms of emotional and physical neglect (40 per cent vs 20 per cent); physical abuse (29 per cent vs 20 per cent); and sexual abuse (39 per cent vs 9 per cent) (see also Grella et al, 2013). Women were also more likely to have experienced more than one of these events, with 23 per cent reporting five or more CAEs before the age of 16 (compared with 13 per cent of men). More generally, women prisoners describe experiencing events such as death or other loss of a loved one (Laux et al, 2008; Few-Demo and Arditti, 2013); little or no parental support; and growing up in families with drug-using parents (Bowles et al, 2012).

Scott et al (2014) suggest that experiences of trauma and abuse act as direct antecedents to factors that precipitate women's involvement in criminal behaviour, such as substance misuse, and that their criminality can therefore be seen as rooted in their life histories (see also Schram et al, 2006). Salisbury and Van Voorhis (2009) argue that childhood victimisation creates pathways into offending through the psychological and behavioural effects it leaves behind, leading to adolescent behaviours such as substance misuse, which in turn act as forerunners to adult criminal activity (Grella et al, 2005).

Mental health and co-morbidity

Belenko and Houser (2012) argue that women's experiences of sexual and physical abuse exacerbate both mental health issues *and* substance misuse problems and that, in comparison with male prisoners, incarcerated women suffer from higher rates of both mental health problems and co-occurring mental health and substance misuse disorders. Butler et al (2011) found higher rates of mental disorder among women (61 per cent vs 39 per cent) in their sample of 1,478 male and female prisoners, as well as significantly higher rates of co-morbidity (46 per cent vs 25 per cent) (see also Lynch et al, 2014). They suggest that these co-occurring disorders increase the risk of involvement with the CJS because they decrease access to effective treatment (see also Colbert et al, 2013). The high rates of PTSD among women involved in drugs and crime suggest that their drug use is frequently associated with coping with their symptoms through self-medication (Green et al, 2005) and thus PTSD can put them at greater risk of developing substance use disorders (Salgado et al, 2007). Grella et al (2013) found a significantly higher rate of PTSD in imprisoned women (40 per cent) compared with women in the general population (12 per cent) (see also Mahmood et al, 2013). Similarly, Grella et al (2013) also found that the use of drugs to cope with that PTSD was significantly higher in imprisoned women (64 per cent vs 6 per cent).

The relationship between mental health disorders and drug use is frequently mutually exacerbating. Co-morbidity puts women at risk of not coping well with prison (Nargiso et al, 2014), being more likely to be involved in prison misconduct or infractions (Houser and Welsh, 2014) and finding readjustment to life outside considerably more challenging – and therefore places this group at greater risk of relapse and reoffending (Johnson et al, 2013). This is compounded by the fact that women with both issues often receive low levels of family support (Mallik-Kane and Visher, 2008) and will have more complex aftercare needs (Johnson, 2014). Blitz (2006) suggests that women offenders with an addiction and/ or mental health disorder understandably struggle to maintain a good level of physiological, emotional and social functioning. Over time they may have come to rely on substances to mask difficult feelings and cope with stressful situations (Buchanan et al, 2011), and frequently perceive themselves as lacking the personal resources to cope with stress or anxiety without substances (Chen, 2009). As a result of these feelings, women involved in drugs and crime often lack the confidence to feel they can make a successful reintegration into their community. Kellet and Willging (2011) suggest this lack of confidence is heightened by the emphasis on individual choice and responsibility placed upon them in prison treatment programmes. They suggest that even if a woman leaves prison feeling empowered by her treatment, with increased self-confidence and optimism about the future (Zurhold et al, 2011), the reality of life on the outside soon undermines that confidence, making women feel that they have failed and are personally to blame for that failure. Relapse back into substance misuse can also be triggered by more general feelings of hurt, loneliness and boredom if women do not receive the right kind of support on release (Essex et al, 2006; Johnson et al, 2013).

Relationships, family and social support

As discussed above, dysfunctional and violent family and intimate relationships often act as catalysts or triggers for substance misuse (Buchanan et al, 2011) and families and/or partners can also undermine women's recovery due their own substance misuse (Bui and Morash, 2010; Kellet and Willging, 2011). Yet many women involved in drugs and crime have little choice but to return to those families or partners on release (O'Brien, 2006; Scott et al, 2014). In addition, the more severe a woman's substance use and criminal involvement, the less supportive and more diminished her social network is likely to be (Staton-Tindall et al, 2007; Salina et al, 2011; Wu et al, 2012; Nargiso et al, 2014), and the more likely that those within her social network will also be substance misusers (Salina et al, 2011). As Kellet and Willging (2011) point out, the option of severing ties with those who are abusive towards them often leaves women with little or no support, or alternatively risks them returning to abusive relationships out of desperation for some support on release from prison. The lack of family support can have a detrimental impact on recovery and desistance from offending (Carmichael et al, 2007), whereas positive pro-social relationships can act as 'buffers' during recovery, providing access to social capital, general support and motivation to avoid drug-using or criminal peers (Wright et al, 2012). While some women may deliberately choose to avoid non-pro-social support and as a result lack social support, others will struggle to (re)establish any support due to the strains placed on those relationships as a result of their past behaviours, and many women involved in drugs and crime recognise the need to make amends for the problems they have caused family members (Bui and Morash, 2010). Clone and DeHart (2014) suggest that social support is more important to women than men and that those who have encouraging and supportive friends are better able to cope with the challenges of re-entry into society, and that supportive families help women both as an emotional source of support and also more practically by helping them re-establish themselves through finding housing and employment opportunities. Zurhold et al (2011) found that women who were successful in their reintegration were more likely to have a non-drug-using partner, whereas those who failed to reintegrate most often had a partner who was a current drug user. However, as Leverentz points out, finding a pro-social spouse is often challenging, especially if women are returning to a criminogenic neighbourhood (Leverentz, 2006; see also Walt et al, 2014). Some of the women in Leverentz's study avoided relationships altogether in order not to repeat past experiences of abusive and drug-related partnerships, whereas others avoided (ex) partners unless they were prepared to support them in their recovery. However, some were able to establish successful relationships with others with a similar past to them and such relationships could provide mutual support in recovery.

Mothers involved in drugs and crime find maintaining and re-establishing relationships with their children to be the greatest challenge while in prison and on release and express considerable distress about their children's welfare (Van Wormer and Kaplan, 2006; McDonald, 2008). They also express anxiety about their ability to be a good caregiver exacerbated by strong feelings of guilt about the impact their drug use and offending has had on their children (Vandermause et al, 2012; Few-Demo and Arditti, 2013). This lack of confidence often results in relinquishing the care of their children to their own mother or other relative (Hanlon et al, 2005). They can also feel profoundly powerless against the risk of their children being taken into state care or becoming embedded in the same cycle of poverty, addiction and offending (Allen et al, 2010). However, their status as a mother is important to them and many are highly motivated to retain or regain custody on release, though most are acutely aware of how difficult this will be (Grella and Greenwell, 2006). Nevertheless, the desire to be a good mother is highly motivating in women's attempts to abstain from drugs (Van Olphen et al, 2009).

Part two: hearing women's voices

The research literature reviewed above provides a comprehensive background to the circumstances and antecedents of women involved in drugs and crime, but most of these studies do not centre on those women's voices. The remainder of this chapter provides detailed accounts of sixteen women's experiences of drug use and crime. It deliberately focuses on their own narratives, and therefore also, and importantly, on their own interpretations of those narratives. Nevertheless, many of their stories resonate strongly with the findings from the research discussed above.

All the women were interviewed face-to-face by the author and were at the time residing in one of two drug recovery wings located in two English women's prisons. It is important to note that they had, at this point in their lives, made the choice to actively engage in a drug recovery programme and thus to live in a community of like-minded women – an environment offering substantial levels of peer support (Grace et al, 2016). As such, their current mind set about their past, present and future life was likely to be influenced by this particular environment, which most saw as considerably more positive than their experience of prison generally (Grace et al, 2016).

History of drug use

All but two of the women had a long history of drug use ranging from 8 to 46 years and with an average of 17 years of use. Most had their main problem with heroin and/or crack cocaine, one had an additional problem with diazepam, another with amphetamines and two described their key current addiction being to alcohol. Several of the women also had a long 'relationship' with methadone – one having been 'stabilised' on it for 15 years before detoxing. Table 1.1 gives a brief overview of the women in terms of age, offending and sentence length.

Vicky's pathway into drug use reflects the historical patterns of drug use over the last half of the twenty-first century:

'I have been on drugs – on and off drugs since the age of 16 which is going on for about 45/46 years. I started off on slimming tablets from the doctor at 13 and it wasn't till I left school at 16 that people said, do you realise what they are? And that was sort of like the start. And within about 18 months of that I'd gone on to injectables, which I stopped in 1982, but then, you know – in those days, back in those days it wasn't heroin as such that you see on the streets now it was more of a pharmaceutical. I would never touch heroin because I thought no you get addicted to that, but I used to take everything like morphine, pethadine, all those. I have spent periods of abstinence; I did seven

Table 1.1: Profile of the women

Interviewee	Age	Sentence	Offence
Vicky[1]	62	4 yrs 5 mths	Allowing premises to be used for supply of Class A drugs
Jodie	42	3 yrs 8 mths	Supply of Class A drugs
Lacey	44	4 yrs 6 mths	Burglary
Becky	35	2 yrs	Burglary
Nicola	34	6.5 mths	Affray and shoplifting (while on licence)
Mary	50	16 mths	Fraud/false imprisonment
Fran	39	On remand	Burglary
Faye	39	On remand	Conspiracy to supply Class A drugs
Samantha	42	14 mths	Shoplifting and dangerous driving
Natalie	27	On recall	Not disclosed
Ruby	31	4 yrs	Robbery
Lucy	35	3 yrs	Burglary (licence recall)
Rosie	19	2 yrs 6 mths	Robbery and GBH
Alice	26	3 yrs	Robbery (licence recall)
Anna	47	5 mths[2]	Shoplifting
Faith	31	4 yrs	Burglary

years back in the mid-80s. But then I started drinking as a substitute I suppose, and then when I started drugs again the alcohol was still there so I actually had two addictions.' (Vicky)

Whereas Ruby's story clearly demonstrates the connection between her drug use and offending behaviour:

'I started on heroin when I was about 14 ... Then it went from heroin to crack cocaine, which I think was my worst one to take. When I was 16, I got an 18-month sentence for two street robberies. I was off my head. I was sniffing solvents and smoking crack with big gangsters from [name of area] in [name of city] and I was only like young ... So I got out and I asked them not to put me back near the area and they did. They put me in [name of prison] and it went again from there. When I was 21 I got another 18-month sentence for pick-pocketing somebody and perverting the course of justice, and I was on ... I wasn't on anything then. I was just taking recreational drugs in the prison and stuff like that. And then I got out ... yeah I was on Methadone but I weren't on drugs.' (Ruby)

This final comment from Ruby illustrates the complex relationship many women had with methadone. Others also experienced addiction to alcohol – often using it as a substitute for other substances:

'Alcohol's my main problem. I was maintained on methadone when I was out there before I came into jail and I was sticking to my methadone programme and not using drugs but I was drinking every day. I got involved with the wrong crowd and because my boyfriend had got sent to jail and I just … cans of Special Brew, strong lager. I would start controlling it and then I was on a non-stop bender for six months before I got locked up myself. I think if I hadn't come to prison I would have ended up dead … heroin and crack … I'd say from being about 16 to 19 when I came in here and got on methadone.' (Alice)

Anna's journey into Class A drug use was through a more recreational route than most of the women, though criminality (in this case that of her husband) was still a clearly related factor:

'Diazepam, heroin, crack cocaine and methadone. I left jail with a habit … Subutex … I started smoking weed when I was 21, I was quite late. And then, like, recreational like speed and Es going out clubbing. And then the big stuff came when I was about … I think I tried it when I was 28 and then I realised I had an addiction around 30 … so all in all, a good … over 20 years I was probably using … I lived with a man who was involved with crime, but because he took it away from the house and just brought money to the house, I ignored it, kind of. So anything I wanted, and I mean anything, I could have. A car, he'd just bring me the money for it; a holiday, we went on holiday in Spain. We lived in [name of city], you know, we had quite an exciting life and it's all been built on excitement.' (Anna)

Vicky, Nicola and Anna all directly associated their offending with their drug use:

'Because my offending was all down to the drug use, all drug related. I thought if there's no drug use there, there's never going to be any offending because I won't be allowing people in my house to deal drugs.' (Vicky)

'I've done six or seven sentences before in my life, through substance misuse.' (Nicola)

'Because take away drugs and drink and I don't commit any …' (Anna)

Reasons for drug use

Having a drug-using and/or criminal partner was a common experience for many of the women and often, like Anna, quoted above, provided the means to access drugs and the encouragement to do so:

> 'I've been using drugs for 22 years. My partner used to sell them years ago and so there was always a free supply of it, that's how I started smoking it.' (Samantha)

> 'I got married when I was 16 to someone very much older than me. He was ten years older than me. He was a drug dealer. I ended up getting pregnant. They took that child away from me because of the domestic violence. He died ten years ago from a heroin overdose.' (Becky)

> 'The partner I have been with for a very very long time, for like 15 years, is a crack addict and that's the only life I known up until like four and a half years ago when I've met someone else … and when I met him [new partner] he was on drugs and he was violent towards me, so I told him I didn't want to be with him anymore and he went and committed a crime, got himself locked up on purpose and was snorting Subutex in the jail, got off the Methadone, and when he come out he's not touched it since. He's been clean for nearly five years now …' (Ruby)

As in Ruby's and Becky's cases above, violence, as well as drug use and criminality, was often present in these relationships. Both Mary and Nicola's progress recovering from drug use was, in their view, undermined by returning to a previous dysfunctional relationship:

> 'For the last like eight years I got into bad relationships and I ended up, I had a bit of a breakdown and ended up borrowing money to supply the people I was with and using bits myself. I got quite suicidal more harm to myself as well, I wanted to do things to myself and it just resulted in me offending. My main drug of choice was crack cocaine but I have used heroin as well … So I'm usually clean and I do stay clean. Like last time I staying clean for 18 months, it's just in certain episodes or things that have happened in my life mainly through men, I've ended up using again do you know what I mean … Because I'd worked on myself the last time I was in prison. I had got out and I'd been doing voluntary work and I had done a lot of positive work on myself. I messed up when my partner got out of jail. I was still working with probation myself at the end of my 12-month licence and he came

back, he had been clean and he came back like a whirlwind and I'd built this little home. I just – I don't know I just basically ... I started messing for a couple of weeks again with drugs.' (Mary)

'I left a violent relationship at Christmas ... because it's not so long since I've left a violent relationship, and he's in [name of town] ... I'd already established that I wanted to be clean and I needed help, and I really wanted to be back on the road to recovery. But I missed out on the actual programme. So I went home and back to a bad relationship, and it all went wrong ... So I knew what it was about. I'd already made my mind up that I was sick of that lifestyle. And I knew by going back to that relationship I had made a terrible mistake ... so I came back bang on with the right attitude, dumped him, came onto [drug recovery wing] and started the programme properly.' (Nicola)

For Nicola, violence had been common throughout her life and was the direct cause of her starting to use drugs in her early teens:

'I've had drug and alcohol problems since I was 13 years old. It started from ... because I was raped when I was ... just before I was 13. And I used it as a way of bunking school and taking substances to escape reality really. When I was 16, I got introduced to heroin and more Class A forms. And then it's like my life kind of spiralled from there. It spiralled from when I was 13 really, looking back. My mum and dad dragged me to rehab kicking and screaming, and I kind of stayed for them years ago. I was never ready for myself, because back then I didn't think much of myself. I thought that I didn't deserve anything more than ... and I kind of, you know, continued to use things as an excuse to carry on. I think I just got so used to the pattern of behaviour, I didn't know how to cope with real life without substances basically.' (Nicola)

Many of the women had experienced multiple traumas and losses throughout their lives which had often precipitated and/or escalated their drug use. For some, their own childhood experiences gave them little chance as children to live secure, safe and healthy lives:

'Well, I've been drinking since I was a little kid anyway ... Nine [years old] ... Just having my mother as my mother ... Yeah she was [a drinker]. She was summat else as well. But I was always looking after her as a kid but, like, every ... even though I was brought up in a certain lifestyle, I guess I was used to it in that routine ... And with my mum, eventually ... and the people that'd be buying things, like cigarettes or beer or food, my mum would be like this in my ear, get them to get me some, you know, that same thing.' (Natalie)

'I started on heroin when I was about 14. I was put into care and I didn't know now't ... well, I knew my mum was a drug addict and stuff like that and a drug dealer, and I was dead against it at school. I even used to write in the school magazine about how it's destroyed my mum and stuff like that. And then I got put into care and I think it just went downhill from there. There was an older girl in there who put me on heroin and put me out prostituting.' (Ruby)

For others, the loss of their own children, through violence, miscarriage and removal into statutory care were triggers for their escalating drug use:

'I got on drugs at the age of 27. That was when my ex- ... I was nine months pregnant. He kicked the baby out of me. The others were taken into temporary foster care because of it. I went home to an empty house and spiralled into drug use. After that it was like a constant merry-go-round, in and out of prison ... Heroin and crack, massive amounts. I was doing up to two grams a day, and at one point I dropped down to five stone weight.' (Lacey)

'Unfortunately though I've had a lot of loss in my life. My mum died. She got ... suspicious circumstances I lost my mum ... And then they [remanded] me to prison for a week, remanded me, and they told me I was pregnant. But by that point I was on 160ml of methadone so ... Anyway everything was alright, everything was going well, and then I got a phone call saying my gran had died and she brought me up. And then I ... I couldn't stop crying and then I noticed I started bleeding. So I went to the hospital and they took me in and they done an examination and they told me the baby's heartbeat had stopped, so I had lost her [grandmother] and my baby.' (Ruby)

'I got married when I was 16 to someone very much older than me. He was ten years older than me. He was a drug dealer. I ended up getting pregnant. They took that child away from me because of the domestic violence ... I lost my son last January to adoption ... I've got six children altogether. Four of them live with my mum, one died, a cot death which sent me off the rails. And yes, one's adopted and four live with my mum and one died. So I've got six ... I've met someone else, now he's the father of my little boy, which we lost last year. It's my own fault, if I had've done more I would have got to keep him, but I wasn't going to contact due to taking drugs, things like that.' (Becky)

Fran, Anna, Faye and Natalie all discussed using drugs to mask pain more generally:

'Now all the time that I'd used drugs, I never had an understanding of it. I knew I used it and I remember one of them [drug worker] saying to me … you know, drugs and drink isn't your problem, you'd be able to put it down if it were, it's your mental health.' (Anna)

'I struggle with my emotional things, bottling things up. I think because I started using at an early age, I didn't know how to properly express my emotions, and stuff like that. So that's one thing that we are working on.' (Fran)

'When I had already stayed clean on the road for about four years anyways, but then when … some personal stuff and everything else happened I just couldn't cope … help myself, had to go back to … The only way I could cope was by using drugs and then obviously that leads to me supplying the drugs and then back to jail … 'Cause you lose all your social skills on drugs, you know what I mean, you shout and scream and you f and blind you sort of … to bring yourself back from that.' (Faye)

'Well, I don't know really. I mean, it's all down to me. Because when I was drinking, I'd drink emotionally and blank it out how I felt. It didn't matter what I was feeling or anything, I'd drink to avoid it.' (Natalie)

Given these stories it is not surprising that many of the women had, or were, experiencing mental health issues. In fact, at least half of the women had or were currently taking some form of medication to help them with their mental health symptoms. However, it is important to note that this level of medicalisation might reflect the ways in which prisons deal with mental health issues more than it does the women's need for such medication (Bartlett et al, 2014). More positively perhaps, some, like Becky and Lacey, had also engaged in counselling while in prison and it was clear that this was the first opportunity they had to discuss the serious trauma they had experienced.

'I have anti-depressants because they evaluated my mood when I came into the prison and they've noticed that I've stabilised since I've been on them yeah.' (Nicola)

'I do take anti-depressant tablets. That got changed in here so I'm a bit of mix because I was on Citalopram and because when I come in

I got methadone you couldn't take Citalopram with methadone so I've been put on Fluoxetine.' (Mary)

'I'm on Sertraline for anti-depression, anti-depressants … and Propananol for anxiety and panic attacks.' (Faye)

'I'm on mirtazapine which are my anti-depressants.' (Faith)

'I'm on anti-depressants. But my worst fear is because I'm finishing a two-year sentence is that I'm not going to handle it when I get out and I still feel depressed so I've had my anti-depressants put up to 300ml … because that's when things go wrong is when I get depressed because all I've known all my life is to block my feelings out is to use.' (Ruby)

'I'm doing CBT[3] now which I think has been a great help because I wasn't aware that I had PTSD but apparently I had.' (Lacey)

'I've got bipolar. I've got a lot of mental health problems … I've been sectioned. I've got bipolar from taking crack, psychosis. I've got a CPN.[4] I've got a drugs counsellor, and I've got a psychiatrist … I get counselling for my … well I've just finished my counselling. I'm just doing it because of the baby that I lost … I've just covered that. I've just done 26 sessions.' (Becky)

It is also clear from these narratives that the women had most frequently turned to drugs as an understandable, if dysfunctional, means to cope with trauma. Over time, as their issues with drugs had worsened, they had also become involved in crime, which was often directly related to their own or their partner's drug use. At this stage in their recovery, most were managing to cope without illicit drugs, though many remained on other medications – predominantly anti-depressants and/or methadone.[5] Many of those who were attempting to reduce their level of medication found doing so in a prison environment, even one aiming to be more therapeutic in its approach, highly challenging as they faced emotions they could no longer mask with substances. The attitudes of officers to these emotional responses exacerbated these challenges:

'None of these [prison officers] have ever done a detox. They don't understand it. Even the drugs workers say they don't fully understand it because they've never done it and it is hard, I mean, there's the hot and cold sweats, there's all your emotions come back, there's your appetite, and it's really hard and for having officers like yapping in your ear and telling you off for the most stupid things, it really gets you down because you've got all these emotions you haven't had for so long.' (Rosie)

'Yeah, because if they [prison officers] don't understand – when the girls are going through detox and that they don't understand the shouting and all the girls' emotions are coming out. All our emotions are out. They're just going to burst into tears and not know what they're crying for and they're going to end up getting warnings, negative comments shouted back at them.' (Alice)

Motivation to stop

The multiple issues that the women had faced throughout their lives were also important in their explanations for wanting to stop taking drugs. They realised that leaving dysfunctional relationships, while repairing those that still mattered, was key to their motivation to recover:

'I was absolutely sick of the drugs … I mean I've got a 16-year-old son whose writing letters to me now saying yes I'm smoking but … I know he wouldn't – I know in my heart of hearts he wouldn't get into trouble but it's just as bad as anything else as far as I'm concerned now. So I'm trying, and he's leaving school in the next five weeks and he's doing my mum's head in. I'll just have to keep speaking to him on visits. Because my daughter did it for a while and she stopped like that and I'm just hoping he'll do the same.' (Jodie)

'I've sorted myself out. I've had enough, I don't want to take drugs anymore. I've lost children through it. I've lost my family through it. I mean, luckily I've got my family back on side.' (Becky)

'And when I came in I don't know what happened. I just woke up and realised I needed to change. Usually when I'm in prison, I'm the one who's either dealing the drugs or … do you know what I mean? Taking drugs, and from that day when I got up and I had lost me Nan. My mum's dead so … because I call my Nan my mum, so I had lost my mum, and I just felt so alone and I knew I had to change … So I said I've come in this jail on my own and I'm going out and I really want to start a family so I got in touch with him [drug worker] and within a week of my asking, in that same week, they had me up here [drug recovery wing].' (Ruby)

'The reason I've been up here so long, is I'm waiting to go on the mother and baby unit … when I come back it hit me really hard and

I thought, do you know, I need to do something drastic, because if I don't my life's never going to change.' (Lucy)

Many of the women did not see methadone as the answer to their problems and were keen to give it up before being released, particularly Lacey, who was concerned that taking methadone might bring her into contact with other drug users once released:

'When I got out in 2011 … I wasn't touching drugs. Big mistake was, I was still on methadone, 180mls. Now I think that's just swapping one drug for another. That's my opinion, you know? It might help in a few cases but I don't think people should be kept on it after the six months because that's just licencing old behaviour … And I also found, if you go out and you've stopped like Methadone and that, you're bumping into the same old people and it's the same old associates. And I don't think it really matters about the area … if you want to find them you will.' (Lacey)

'I was still on methadone when I came on the house. I detoxed after about two months. My decision, they don't push it, you know I mean there's people on the programme obviously you've seen them all go this morning that still feel quite comfortable on the methadone. I didn't, I got it into my head you know well if I'm doing this programme I don't want to be on methadone. Because to me that's part and parcel of, you know the behaviours surrounding going queuing up for meds and things like that.' (Vicky)

Being in recovery

Most of the women defined themselves as being in recovery – some even saw themselves as fully recovered. However, most were aware of the precarious nature of this status – with a realistic understanding that they might always be at risk of relapse.

'I'll be in recovery for the rest of my life … Definitely because, you know, I don't know what's around the corner do I? It would only take me to use once and that would be it. I can't lapse, its relapse for me. It's all or nothing with me and it always has been. So yes, I will always be in recovery. I know I will. I can honestly say I won't touch drugs again, I really won't unless they are prescribed to me by a doctor … I will be in recovery for the rest of my life, but where I am now, that's how I feel that I won't use again and I am worth more than I granted myself before.' (Jodie)

'Yeah ... are you ever recovered? I'll always be in recovery I have to be. I have to be aware. I've got a choice now. The physical has gone, I'm not addicted to anything. I know that there's people that can help me with my mental, I don't have to sit within my own thoughts, I can express them. So recovery for me, I'll always be in recovery. I've done where I've hammered the recovery groups and I've gone, and I've gone and I've gone and I've relapsed ...' (Anna)

'You'll always be in recovery, do you know what I mean, you're never a fully recovered drug addict, as far as I'm concerned anyway, because there's always, whether it's ten years down the line, ten months, there's going to be struggles you know.' (Faith)

'To me once an addict always an addict – you've got an addictive natures; once an alcoholic, always an alcoholic. I mean I've heard people say on this course, one girl she's gone home with it .... I've got no drug use. I've no cravings. Therefore why did you use originally? So we've all got them to some degree, and we've all got like .... it's all about changing your behaviour really and your goal process. It's... it's all very well to sit round and be negative and, oh well. Life is shit at the moment. There's nothing I can do about it. But it's thinking constructively and thinking like how you make the negative into a positive, and what are the pros and cons of you going back on drugs?' (Lacey)

When asked what recovery meant to them, most of the women thought that this would mean a drug-free lifestyle and the associated benefits of no longer having drugs (including methadone) as their main priority:

'Yeah ... Hopefully I'll be recovered. Not taking methadone or anything like that, because I see that as just like a substitute basically. Just not to have to think about, oh, I need to go there first. My brother lives in [name of town] and he always invites me down, but I'd say I can't because my chemist is open on a Saturday ... Just not to be focused around that yeah ... it would be just nice not to have to do that on a daily basis.' (Fran)

'In recovery definitely. That I'm drug free and I've no intention of using drugs. I'm on methadone but it's medication to ease me back into the community. So I just – I use it as a crutch is that what the saying is? As a crutch ... just to stabilise myself and get myself back in the community. Once I move from supported housing into my own accommodation then I'll detox off that as well.' (Samantha)

Many of the women were actively making plans for their release. Faith was aware that she needed to keep occupied once back in the community and would continue to need support:

'And now I want to move forward … whether it's voluntary work or not, I need something to keep me occupied while I'm out there, and agencies to work with me. Because I'll still need that support, even though I've got … my partner, there, I'll still need that support when I get out, from different agencies and that.' (Faith)

Anna was uncertain about what was best for her once released and was fearful of the challenges that therapy would present to her:

'I don't know yet, for what I'm really feeling … And I can get a bit of anxiety around it, because I'm not sure yet which way I'm going to go, whether I go into long term therapy or access in the community, I have decided yet … Or do I go into full therapy and break me down, and have a look at certain issues that I don't like looking at. I'm not sure yet. I'm not sure. It scares me, the therapy one … and plus, because I was full-on with recovery in the community and I relapsed, will it be too much for me? Should I just stick to my family, my children? I don't know, but I have to do what's best for me. My head tells me therapy.' (Anna)

Establishing their own home was a clear priority for several of the women. Avoiding hostels was also a priority – particularly for women who had had negative experiences of them in the past:

'I'm going to get into supported housing. I'm trying to link up with some voluntary work as well to keep me occupied. I want my own place … Yeah, I've never had my own place before. They've always put me in hostels or bed and breakfasts and it just doesn't work for me. That's where I seem to mess up because other people in there are doing it.' (Samantha)

'But I'm frightened of going out into hostels and all because I've been there and I know the situations. I've got a lot of – I was homeless and I've got a lot of psychological trauma.' (Mary)

'Well … my personal officer, is trying to sort something out because every time I've been released they've either released me to a bail hostel, that's why I breached because I didn't like it there, or any other time I've just been released with nowhere to go. I have got a place where I can live, my boyfriend's, but I want my own place.' (Alice)

For Ruby, home was associated with independence and the chance to start a family:

> 'I want to start a family but I want to get a job first, which I've got support out there anyway ... And for me it makes me more depressed because I start thinking about a home and stuff like that and because I'm constantly like locked in here I need that little bit of freedom back to get me used to going home and stuff outside, my own independence, because in here really you haven't got your own independence.' (Ruby)

For Alice and Faith, having supportive, pro-social partners was key to their stability once released:

> 'My boyfriend just got out of prison yesterday and he's not even had one – I thought he'd have a drink, he's not an alcoholic like me. I thought of course he'll have a drink, he's just got out, and he's not even had a drink. He went, I'm staying off it for you. I was well surprised.' (Alice)

> 'I'm lucky that I've got a partner that doesn't use. He brings my little boy up, bless him. He's had to quit work after 26 years, to bring my little lad up while I'm in here. He's moved areas, we've moved thirty miles away from where I used to live. So it's a case of a fresh start, do you know what I mean, a new town, fresh start. And he's standing by me 100 per cent so ... because not everybody's got somebody out there ... and if they have, there's a lot of people who have got partners or friends who they're going out to that are using. I'm lucky. I'm lucky for him to stand by me really because, like I say, he doesn't drink, he doesn't use drugs. Do you know, he's never been in trouble? I don't even think he's ever even had a parking ticket, to be honest with you. God know why he puts up with me, I really don't know.' (Faith)

Others were reconnecting with their families which they saw as very positive, though not always straightforward, as family members had their own struggles:

> 'I mean [name of daughter] is amazing she's like a mother in this relationship, she really is.' (Jodie)

> 'I speak to my daughter on the phone now. My mum's got more hope in me. I just want to get out and just be a normal mum to my children ... I had two chances to come on here, and I had a lot going on with

my son. He's 16. He's just started taking MCAT. He said he had been sexually abused by my cousin, so I had all that going on.' (Becky)

'I have had a lot of support from my son because he accessed [drug service] rehab in the [name of town] and he's been five years clean now. So I thought myself I should have done it first not him telling me and that's given me that incentive. And the relationship between us now is so much better.' (Vicky)

'I was going to relocate here but I've got a brother who's dying. He's got Hodgkins Lymphoma and he's in a coma and that at the moment. I've buried five members from jail and I really don't want to go down that path again. They've now got him in a coma and they've done a bone marrow transplant as well. He will eventually die of it but I'm just hoping that I'll be out in time.' (Lacey)

Conclusion

It is clear from the literature that the link between drug use and female criminality is very strong (Covington, 2002). Indeed, globally, more women are incarcerated for drug offences than for any other crime (Moloney and Moller, 2009). Drug use among women offenders is exceptionally high – higher than among male offenders – and is often the key driver in their offending (Light et al, 2013). Moreover, women are more likely than men to report needing help with their drug use on entry to prison (Light et al, 2013). The reasons behind women's drug use are more complex than that of men (NTA, 2010), particularly in terms of the reasons they start using drugs which is often to cope with physical and emotional pain caused by abuse or other childhood and adult trauma (Bartlett, 2007).

The central aim of this chapter was to give space for the voices of women involved in drugs and crime to be heard. Their stories chime with research evidence more broadly in that it is clear that trauma, abuse and neglect, as both children and adults, were all too common an experience in their lives. Such experiences often led to substance use which offered a way to cope with psychological pain, but which also led these women to criminal activity. What is equally evident from their stories are the women's impressive levels of resilience and their hopes for the future. As the women themselves identified very clearly, those hopes rested upon staying clean, making a home, getting work and reuniting with family and pro-social partners. However, the risk is that, without effective support on release, the progress women make in prison is undermined by the structural and personal barriers they will face on the outside (Grace, 2017). There is a real danger in embedding a sense of empowerment within women through prison-based recovery programmes, which tend to place a strong emphasis on personal responsibility for change, if long-term holistic aftercare is not available on release (Grace, 2017). Without such aftercare, we risk setting women involved in drugs and crime up to fail. More fundamentally, it is important to question the degree to which a custodial sentence was truly necessary for any of these women; to ask whether the damage done to their already precarious lives through their incarceration was too great a price to pay; and to argue whether instead a community sentence, with holistic, trauma-informed support, would be a far better way to support their recovery from both crime and drugs.

Notes

[1] All names are pseudonyms.
[2] Anna was given a 12-week suspended sentence that she breached, receiving 12 weeks in custody plus 8 weeks for the breach.
[3] Cognitive Behavioural Therapy.
[4] Community Psychiatric Nurse.
[5] One of the DRWs insisted on the women detoxing prior to coming onto the recovery programme. The other allowed the individual woman to reduce at her own pace and she could remain on methadone throughout the programme should that be her choice.

References

Allen, S., Flaherty, C. and Ely, C. (2010) 'Throwaway moms: maternal incarceration and the criminalisation of female poverty', *Affilia: Journal of Women and Social Work*, 25(2): 160–72.

Bartlett, A. (2007) 'Women in prison: concepts, clinical issues and care delivery', *Psychiatry*, 6(11): 444–8.

Bartlett, A., Dholakia, N., England, R., Hales, H., van Horn, E., McGeorge, T., Moss, B., Ovaisi, S., Tukmachi, E. and Patel, S. (2014) 'Prison prescribing practice: practitioners' perspectives on why prison is different', *International Journal of Clinical Practice*, 68(4): 413–17.

Belenko, S. and Houser, J. (2012) 'Gender differences in prison-based drug treatment participation', *International Journal of Offender Therapy and Comparative Criminology*, 56(5): 790–810.

Blitz, C. (2006) 'Predictors of stable employment among female inmates in New Jersey', *Journal of Offender Rehabilitation*, 43(1): 1–22.

Bowles, M., DeHart, D. and Reid Webb, J. (2012) 'Family influences on female offenders' substance use: the role of adverse childhood events among incarcerated women', *Journal of Family Violence*, 27(7): 681–86.

Buchanan, M., Murphy, K., Smith Martin, M., Korchinski, M., Buxton, J., Granger-Brown, A., Hanson, D., Hislop, G., MacCauley, A. and Elwood Martin, R. (2011) 'Understanding incarcerated women's perspectives on substance use: catalysts, reasons for use, consequences, and desire for change', *Journal of Offender Rehabilitation*, 50(2): 81–100.

Bui, H. and Morash, M. (2010) 'The impact of network relationships, prison experiences, and internal transformation on women's success after prison release', *Journal of Offender Rehabilitation*, 49(1): 1–22.

Butler, T., Indig, D., Allnut, S. and Mamoon, H. (2011) 'Co-occurring mental illness and substance use disorder among Australian prisoners', *Drug and Alcohol Review*, 30(2): 188–94.

Carmichael, S., Gover, A., Koons-Witt, B. and Inabnit, M. (2007) 'The successful completion of probation and parole among female offenders', *Women and Criminal Justice*, 17(1): 75–97.

Chen, G. (2009) 'Gender differences in crime, drug addiction, abstinence, personality characteristics and negative emotions', *Journal of Psychoactive Drugs*, 41(3): 255–66.

Clone, S. and DeHart, D. (2014) 'Social support networks of incarcerated women: types of support, sources of support, and implications for re-entry', *Journal of Offender Rehabilitation*, 53(7): 503–21.

Colbert, A., Sekula, K., Zoucha, R. and Cohen, S (2013) 'Health care needs of women immediately post-incarceration: a mixed method study', *Public Health Nursing*, 30(5): 409–19.

Covington, S. (2002) *A woman's journey home: challenges for female offenders and their children*, 'From Prison to Home' conference proceedings. Available at: http://www.urban.org/UploadedPDF/410630_FemaleOffenders.pdf [Accessed 22 April 2021].

Essex, E., Petras, D. and Massat, C. (2006) 'Predictors of loneliness among court-involved and substance abusing mothers', *Women and Criminal Justice*, 17(2–3): 63–74.

Few-Demo, A. and Arditti, J. (2013) 'Relational vulnerabilities of incarcerated and re-entry mothers: therapeutic implications', *International Journal of Offender Therapy and Comparative Criminology*, 58(11): 1297–320.

Golder, S., Hall, M., Engstrom, M., Higgins, G. and Logan T. (2014) 'Correlates of recent drug use among victimised women on probation and parole', *Psychology of Addictive Behaviours*, 28(4): 1105–16.

Grace, S. (2017) 'Effective interventions for drug using women offenders: a narrative literature review', *Journal of Substance Misuse*, 22(6): 664–71.

Grace, S., Page, G., Lloyd, C., Templeton, L., Kougali, Z., McKeganey, N., Leibling, A., Roberts, P. and Russell, C. (2016) 'Establishing a "Corstonian" continuous care pathway for drug using female prisoners: linking Drug Recovery Wings and Women's Community Services', *Criminology and Criminal Justice*, 16(5): 602–21.

Green, B., Miranda, J., Daroowalla, A. and Siddique, J. (2005) 'Trauma exposure, mental health functioning, and program needs of women in jail', *Crime and Delinquency*, 51(1): 133–51.

Grella, C. and Greenwell, L. (2006) 'Correlates of parental status and attitudes toward parenting among substance-abusing women offenders', *The Prison Journal*, 86(1): 89–113.

Grella, C., Lovinger, K. and Warda, U. (2013) 'Relationships among trauma exposure, familial characteristics, and PTSD: a case-control study of women in prison and the general population', *Women and Criminal Justice*, 23(1): 63–79.

Grella, C., Stein, J. and Greenwell, L. (2005) 'Associations among childhood trauma, adolescent problem behaviors, and adverse adult outcomes in substance-abusing women offenders', *Psychology of Addictive Behaviours*, 19(1): 43–53.

Hanlon, T., O'Grady, E. and Bennett-Sears, T. (2005) 'Incarcerated drug-abusing mothers: their characteristics and vulnerability', *The American Journal of Drug and Alcohol Abuse*, 31(1): 59–77.

Houser, K. and Welsh, W. (2014) 'Examining the association between co-occurring disorders and seriousness of misconduct by female prison inmates', *Criminal Justice and Behavior*, 41(5): 650–66.

Johnson, I. (2014) 'Women parolees' perceptions of parole experiences and parole officers', *American Journal of Criminal Justice*, 40(4): 785–810.

Johnson, J., Schonbrun, J., Nargiso, C., Kuo, R., Shefner, R., Williams, C. and Zlotnick, C. (2013) '"I know if I drink I won't feel anything": substance use relapse among depressed women leaving prison', *International Journal of Prisoner Health*, 9(4): 169–86.

Kellet, N. and Willging, C. (2011) 'Pedagogy of individual choice and female inmate re-entry in the US Southwest', *International Journal of Law and Psychiatry*, 34(4): 256–63.

Kelly, P., Cheng, A.-L., Spencer-Carver, E. and Ramaswamy, M. (2014) 'A syndemic model of women incarcerated in community jails', *Public Health Nursing*, 31(2): 118–25.

Laux, J., Dupney, P., Moe, J., Cox, J., Lambert, E., Ventura, L., Williamson, C. and Benjamin, B. (2008) 'The substance abuse counseling needs of women in the criminal justice system: a needs assessment approach', *Journal of Addictions and Offender Counseling*, 29(1): 36–48.

Leverentz, A. (2006) 'The love of a good man? Romantic relationships as a source of support or hindrance for female ex-offenders', *Journal of Research in Crime and Delinquency*, 43(4): 459–88.

Light, M., Grant, E. and Hopkins, K. (2013) *Gender differences in substance misuse and mental health amongst prisoners: results from the Surveying Prisoner Crime Reduction (SPCR) longitudinal cohort study of prisoners*, Ministry of Justice Analytical Series, London: Ministry of Justice.

Lynch, S., DeHart, D., Belknap, J., Green, B., Dass-Brailsford, P., Johnson, K. and Whalley, E. (2014) 'A multi-site study of prevalence of serious mental illness, PTSD, and substance use disorders of women in jail', *Psychiatric Services*, 65(5): 670–74.

Mahmood, S., Vaughn, M., Mancini, M. and Fu, Q. (2013) 'Gender disparity in utilization rates of substance abuse services among female ex-offenders: a population-based analysis', *The American Journal of Drug and Alcohol Abuse*, 39(5): 332–9.

Mallik-Kane, K. and Visher, C. (2008) Health and prisoner re-entry: how physical, mental and substance abuse conditions shape the process of reintegration, Washington DC: Urban Institute Justice Policy Center.

McDonald, C. (2008) 'Gender-responsive treatment and the need to examine female inmates' lives in prison and prior to prison', *Corrections Compendium*, 33(6): 7–30.

Messina, N., Grella, C., Burdon, W. and Prendergast, M. (2007) 'Childhood adverse events and current traumatic distress: a comparison of men and women drug dependent prisoners', *Criminal Justice and Behaviour*, 34(11): 1385–401.

Moloney, K. P. and Moller, L. F. (2009) 'Good practice for mental health programming for women in prison: reframing the parameters', *Public Health*, 123(6): 431–3.

Nargiso, J., Kuo, C., Zlotnick, C. and Johnson, J. (2014) 'Social support networks characteristics of incarcerated women with co-occurring major depressive and substance use disorders', *Journal of Psychoactive Drugs*, 46(2): 93–105.

NTA (National Treatment Agency) (2010) *Women in drug treatment: what the latest figures reveal*, London: NTA.

O'Brien, P. (2006) 'Maximising success for drug-affected women after release from prison', *Women and Criminal Justice*, 17(2–3): 95–113.

Salgado, D., Quinlan, K. and Zlotnick, C. (2007) 'The relationship of lifetime polysubstance dependence to trauma exposure, symptomatology, and psychosocial functioning in incarcerated women with comorbid PTSD and substance use disorder', *Journal of Trauma and Dissociation*, 8(2): 9–26.

Salina, D., Lesondak, L., Razzano, L. and Parenti, B. (2011) 'Addressing unmet needs in incarcerated women with co-occurring disorders', *Journal of Social Service Research*, 37(4): 365–78.

Salisbury, E. and Van Voorhis, P. (2009) 'A quantitative investigation of women probationers' paths to incarceration', *Criminal Justice and Behaviour*, 36(6): 541–66.

Schram, P., Koons-Witt, B., Williams, F. and McShane, M. (2006) 'Supervision strategies and approaches for female parolees: examining the link between unmet needs and parolee outcome', *Crime and Delinquency*, 52(3): 450–71.

Scott, C., Dennis, M. and Lurigio, A. (2014) 'Women's participation in a jail-based treatment program in a large urban setting: a process evaluation', *Criminal Justice Research Review*, 15(4): 73–80.

Staton-Tindall, M., Royse, D. and Leukefeld, C. (2007) 'Substance use criminality, and social support: an exploratory analysis with incarcerated women', *The American Journal of Drug and Alcohol Abuse*, 33(2): 237–43.

Vandermause, R., Severtsen, B. and Roll, J. (2012) 'Re-creating a vision of motherhood: therapeutic drug court and the narrative', *Qualitative Social Work*, 12(5): 620–36.

Van Olphen, J., Eliason, M., Freudenberg, N. and Barnes, M. (2009) 'Nowhere to go: How stigma limits the options of female drug users after release from jail', *Substance Abuse Treatment, Prevention and Policy*, 4(10): 1–10.

Van Wormer, K. and Kaplan, L. (2006) 'Results of a national survey of wardens in women's prisons: the case for gender specific treatment', *Women and Therapy*, 29(1–2): 133–51.

Walt, L., Hunter, B., Salina, D. and Jason, L. (2014) 'Romance, recovery and community re-entry for criminal justice-involved women: conceptualizing and measuring intimate relationship factors and power', *Journal of Gender Studies*, 23(4): 409–21.

Wright, E., DeHart, D., Koons-Witt, B. and Crittenden, C. (2012) '"Buffers" against crime? Exploring the roles and limitations of positive relationships among women in prison', *Punishment in Society*, 15(1): 71–95.

Wu, E., El-Bassel, N., Gilbert, L., Hess, L., Lee H-N. and Rowell, T. (2012) 'Prior incarceration and barriers to receipt of services among entrants to alternative to incarceration programs: a gender-based disparity', *Journal of Urban Health: Bulletin of the New York Academy of Medicine*, 89(2): 384–95.

Zurhold, H., Moskalewicz, J., Sanclemente, C., Schmied, G., Shewan, D. and Verthein, U. (2011) 'What affects reintegration of female drug users after prison release? Results of a European follow-up study', *Journal of Offender Rehabilitation*, 50(2): 49–65.

2

Knifing Off? The Inadequacies of Desistance Frameworks for Women in the Criminal Justice System in Ireland

Vicky Seaman and Orla Lynch

Research on crime and offending has traditionally drawn on men's experiences when theorising on causes, motivations and outcomes for individuals who engage in criminal behaviour. Women have rarely featured in this space, and when they do, oftentimes they are essentialised and deterministic frameworks dominate. In spite of the absence of women's voices from this research area, there is an underlying assumption that theories on crime and offending are gender neutral, in that the theories that exists are assumed to have relevance for both men and women. Recent research in this area challenges these assumptions and shows that women's pathways into crime and motivations for offending differ from those of men (Daly, 1992; Chesney-Lind, 1997; Salisbury and Van Voorhis, 2009). In addition, this research shows that women's experiences of desistance are also not easily mapped onto existing theoretical frameworks.

For example, recent reports have documented that women who encounter the Irish criminal justice system (CJS) have complex traumatic developmental histories compounded in adulthood by mental health problems, addiction, domestic violence, homelessness and challenging family and interpersonal relationships (IPRT, 2013; McHugh, 2013). This mirrors the findings of the Corston report (Corston, 2007) that focused exclusively on women in prison in the UK and found significant divergence in the experience of men and women, primarily in relation to interpersonal relationships, social expectations and gender norms:

> First, domestic circumstances and problems such as domestic violence, child-care issues, being a single-parent; second, personal circumstances such as mental illness, low self-esteem, eating disorders, substance misuse; and third, socio-economic factors such as poverty, isolation and unemployment. When women are experiencing a combination of factors from each of these three types of vulnerabilities, it is likely to lead to a crisis point that ultimately results in prison. (Corston, 2007: 2)

While Corston (2007) attests to the complexity that is inherent in the experiences of women who come into contact with criminal justice systems, the notion of vulnerability mentioned is somewhat problematic, and it is important that it is not intertwined with causality or individual attribution; ultimately, the issue of agency cannot be ignored. While we know that a range of issues are often prominent in the lives of women within any CJS, rather than focusing on causality, the concept of equifinality is more useful: a recognition that there are multiple pathways into and out of offending for women.

However, the issues of causality and vulnerability are ongoing discussions in the literature on crime, offending and victimhood, and particularly in the case of women involved in crime, though gender has long been a factor (albeit neglected) in criminological research. Masculinity was taken as the *default*, and most early theories of crime omitted women (Heidensohn, 1968; Bertrand, 1969) and those that did examine women and crime, such as Lombroso, Thomas and Pollack, took a biological determinist or positivist view (Heidensohn, 1996; Smart, 1977). Carlen (1985) points out that these early theories are 'at their most benign to be faintly comical; at their most malignant to be blatantly sexist' (Carlen et al, 1985: 1). Within criminological research, early accounts of victimology treated women in a similar fashion; women were merely the object of crime, and victim blaming, victim culpability and victim precipitation were commonplace in the literature (Walklate, 2007; Davies et al, 2017). From this work came the notion of the ideal victim (Christie, 1986) – a young or elderly *innocent* female harmed by a stranger. This ideal victim became the apex of a hierarchy of victimhood – a true victim – one with no culpability, nor a risky lifestyle, nor a blemished past. This caricature of victimhood has dominated our understanding of offenders and victims to this day (Davies et al, 2017) and shaped how we think about women and crime. Given that those who commit crimes are more likely to be the victims of crime, the notion of the ideal victim does little to explain the experience of women who encounter the CJS but serves only to vilify those women who do not fit the caricature.

This chapter is concerned with addressing how we might come to know about women involved with the CJS, in particular through accessing how women think about, experience and approach the process of desistance, but also how the theorising on the process of desistance discounts women's experiences, silences women's voices and fails to capture the complexity of the journey outside of gender norms. This chapter draws on the experiences of women who have encountered the CJS in Ireland and considers how key concepts central to desistance theory are not fit for purpose based on these women's life histories.

Social roles and gendered crime

While women generally commit less crime than men, they can, and do, commit all types of crimes albeit in smaller numbers (Heidensohn, 1987; Gelsthorpe, 2007). According to the official statistics available for the Republic of Ireland regarding offence type and gender, in 2018 14 per cent (1,005) of the 8,071 committals to prison were female (Irish Prison Service, 2018). These statistics show that while women are present as offenders for each category of crime, their numbers are far fewer. Of the 34 committals to prison for homicide offences in Ireland in 2018 only three were female, and of the 465 committals for other violent crimes (threats to murder, assaults etc), 8 per cent were female (Irish Prison Service, 2018). Of the 939 prison committals in 2018 for theft and related offences, 213 were female (23 per cent) representing 39 per cent of all female committals to prison in Ireland for 2018 (Irish Prison Service, 2018). In comparison, 17 per cent of the 4,269 male committals to Irish prisons in 2018 were for theft and related offences. These statistics reflect Heidensohn's (2010) point that women are most often associated with property crimes, commit a wide variety of crimes but in smaller numbers than men and commit a lesser rate of the more serious crimes in general (Walklate, 2004).

In attempting to understand the issues underlying involvement in *types* of offending, early research by Smart (1977) pointed to the expectation that aggressiveness and ambition is encouraged among boys whereas girls are more closely supervised and encouraged to be passive and domesticated. In addition, Smart noted the expectation for women to be non-violent or play a secondary role to men in any norm-violating activities (Smart, 1977). Building on Smart's work, Messerschmidt (1997: 68) points out that 'violence becomes incomprehensible in an analysis that concentrates exclusively on sex differences', and that crimes deemed to be role-inappropriate for women are traditionally avoided in criminology theories, or are 'deviantized as inappropriate at best, "masculine" at worst'. Messerschmidt (1997: 68) suggests that criminology does not have 'the theoretical language capable of representing violence by women' except to view it as totally abnormal; the view of violence by women is based on the view of male violence as 'macho, tough, aggressive'. Importantly, both Smart and Messerschmit are stating that any difference in behaviour is explained by different opportunities, the trajectory of socialisation between the sexes and issues of social control and reference solely to innate characteristics is problematic (Heidensohn, 1987).

Apart from not having the language to represent women's experiences, approaches to women and crime do not adequately capture the pressure of social and gender norms; the pressure to be a 'well-behaved woman' and of shame and guilt when a woman violates any moral standards is significant (Smart, 1977; Heidensohn, 1996; Chesney-Lind, 2006). This has long been recognised by feminist authors and Bertrand (1969) points out that societal reactions to women who engage in criminal activity depend not on the crime but on the social values violated or jeopardised by the illegal behaviour. She notes that the response to such violations is influenced by how far a woman strays from her socially ascribed role. For example, in the 1990s the US media reported with voyeuristic enthusiasm on 'bad girls' and the perceived increase in girls and women committing violent crimes (Chesney-Lind, 2006). This media trend was a backlash against the feminist movement seeking to show that increased female emancipation leads to girls behaving badly (Chesney-Lind, 2006). Similarly, media reporting in Ireland on female perpetrated crime has been found to skew in favour of the more sensational crimes and the language used in headlines and articles about female offenders is highly charged and emotive (Quinlan, 2011; Black, 2015). This approach led Chesney-Lind (2006) to reflect on a masculinisation framework that ignores gender and assumes that women and men are motivated in the same ways to commit crimes. She sets out a simple dichotomy of good femininity and bad femininity – violating these accepted standards leads to a rejection of true womanhood and thus demonisation (Chesney-Lind, 2006).

Underpinning this masculinisation is the notion that femaleness carries a certain stigma and has a devalued status (Schur, 1984). Because women commit fewer crimes, the crimes they do commit are somewhat of a curiosity seen as doubly deviant: they have not only broken the law but more importantly they have broken social rules by operating outside of their expected conventional roles (Heidensohn, 1987). This has an impact on how women are treated in the CJS as they are judged not just on their crime but also on how far from the feminine ideal they have strayed (Chesney-Lind, 2006; Heidensohn, 1987).

Adherence to traditional family roles can similarly impact the outcome for women in court proceedings (Heidensohn, 1987; Gelsthorpe, 2007). Research has shown that if a woman is seen to be a 'bad mother' then the punishment ordered by the court is more severe than if she could show she was a responsible carer for both herself and her family members (Heidensohn, 1987, 2006). Complicating matters further, in Ireland women are often held on remand for a charge that is unlikely to receive a custodial sentence (IPRT, 2013). This overuse of remand and short sentencing for females is partly due to a lack of viable alternatives for women (IPRT, 2013), but it has also been suggested that it is due to an attitude of patriarchal protectionism. A 2019 report published by the UN working group on the issue of discrimination against women in law and practice found that the institutions involved in decisions leading to the confinement of women (criminal, medical and psychiatric) are often dominated by men and the concerns particular to females are underrepresented, resulting in 'gender discrimination and overreliance on gender stereotypes' (United Nations Human Rights Council, 2019: 6). Oftentimes women are stereotyped as weak, vulnerable and in need of protection (United Nations Human Rights Council, 2019).

Walklate (2004) writes about gender in the court system, how psychiatry and the legal system interact and how this interaction differs for men and women. She asserts that studies of psychiatric court reports for men and women reveal that the accounts are written in remarkably different ways. For example, men are assumed to have agency while women are not; men are seen to deliberately plan their behaviour, while women are seen to be unintentional or irrational in their behaviours (Walklate, 2004). It appears that a woman intentionally committing a crime is more feared than the crime itself. The assumption tends towards a mental health (or some other intrinsic disfunction) explanation, rather than anything that might be a challenge to our social and gender expectations of women. However, despite the different manner in which women are treated in the CJS, that is not to say that women and men who engage in criminality do so from the same place; life histories, experiences and opportunities need to be understood to understand women's journey into crime.

Pathways: intersection of victimisation, mental illness, substance misuse and crime

In one of the first comprehensive comparative studies on the life-histories of male and female offenders, Daly (1992) examined the trajectories of 40 men and 40 women who faced similar charges. Her aim was to understand the participants as individuals with a biography that was relevant to their experiences (Daly, 1992). She wanted to describe the women's criminal actions in the context of their often 'desperate and difficult' lives (Daly, 1992: 21) rather than in comparison with the male standard so dominant in criminological literature of the time.

For the women in Daly's study, there were five general pathways that emerged:

- *Harmed and harming women* – abused or neglected as children, acts out violently, low coping skills, psychological problems, uses drugs/ alcohol to cope.

- *Battered women* – abuse typically starts when the woman is older, violence from an intimate partner. Although many of the women in Daly's (1992) study had been in violent relationships, it is specified that there was a group of women for whom domestic violence was the only issue that led them to be before the court.
- *Street women* – kicked out of or ran away from abusive homes as children, engaged in petty crime, used/sold drugs and got involved in prostitution to survive life on the streets.
- *Drug connected women* – got addicted to drugs and/or involved in the sale of drugs through their relationships, either with an intimate partner or a family member.
- *Other/Economically motivated* – motivated to engage in criminal behaviour because of economic circumstances of poverty or greed, and do not have abuse histories, drug and alcohol issues nor histories of violent behaviour.

(Daly, 1992; Wattanaporn and Holtfreter, 2014)

While abuse and victimisation are strong themes in any analysis of women's pathways into crime, there is not a direct nor a causal relationship between abuse and offending, though it is one of many risk factors. Salisbury and Van Voorhis (2009) found three dominant pathways to imprisonment in their study of women probationers: (i) childhood victimisation associated with a historical and current mental illness and substance misuse issues; (ii) relational pathway focusing on dysfunctional adult intimate relationships, intimate partner violence, self-efficacy, mental illness and substance misuse issues; (iii) social and human capital focusing on relationship dysfunction, low education, poor employment history, availability of family supports and self-efficacy (Salisbury and Van Voorhis, 2009).

Importantly, of the studies that focus on pathways to criminal behaviour, while there are a number of delineated routes outlined, the interconnectedness of these routes, and the often chaotic nature of life experiences, particularly around victimization, mental health issues, substance abuse and criminal behaviour cannot be underestimated (DeHart, 2008; Salisbury and Van Voorhis, 2009; Lynch et al, 2012a, 2012b, 2017).

For example, Lynch et al (2012a) looked at pathways into criminal behaviour for women with and without serious mental illness and found that women with serious mental illness were more likely to have been victimised and had higher rates offending than the women without mental health issues. Delving deeper, they found that childhood trauma was a major predictor of adult victimisation and of mental illness. While childhood and adulthood victimisation are not on their own significant predictors of offending, they heighten the risk for developing mental health issues which in turn heightens the risk of there being an offending history (Lynch et al, 2012a).

Tellingly, the same study found that the women involved did not have adequate treatments available to them to address their mental health and trauma related issues (Lynch et al, 2012a).

Furthermore, the international literature points to evidence that there is a higher incidence of mental illness among women in prison than men (Gehring, 2018). A 2005 study of the prevalence of mental illness in the Irish prison population found that 41 per cent of women in prison, both those remanded and sentenced, had a diagnosed mental illness. In comparison, only 16 per cent of all male committals, remanded and sentenced, had a diagnosed mental illness. The rate among sentenced prisoners was higher at 60 per cent for women and 27 per cent for men serving (Kennedy et al, 2005). Moreover, it was found that most prisoners with a mental illness also had drug and alcohol issues (Kennedy et al, 2005).

Understanding the life-histories of women who engage in crime is essential in understanding the process by which women move toward and away from offending and related behaviours, though ultimately the complexity of experiences for women who encounter the CJS cannot be captured in current approaches to desistance. For most of these women, offending is a part of an intricate pattern of behaving that is influenced by personal history, poverty, social experiences, interpersonal relationships, neglect, abuse and addiction.

Poverty, gender and social responsibilities

Almost universally, the impact of poverty is felt most severely by women and children (Holtfreter et al, 2004). EU statistics measuring the rate of risk of poverty and social exclusion found the risk for women to be 23.3 per cent in comparison to 21.6 per cent for men, with the primary cause for this disparity being that single parent households are more likely headed by women, followed by inadequate family support benefits and also a lack of affordable childcare (Ec.europa.eu, 2019). Forty-seven per cent of single parents were found to be at risk of poverty and social exclusion in 2017 (Ec.europa.eu, 2019).

Among women who encounter the CJS, poverty is an acute issue and research over the past 30 years has demonstrated that most of these women are mothers who are economically marginalised (Heidensohn, 1987; Carlen, 1988; Daly, 1992; Holtfreter et al, 2004). Reinforcing the academic findings, data from both the UK's 2007 Corston Report and the Irish Penal Reform Trust's 2013 report found that a high proportion of women in prison in the UK and Ireland are mothers and come from economically disadvantaged backgrounds (Corston, 2007; IPRT, 2013). Though there are no current statistics detailing the number of mothers in the Irish prison system, in the UK one fifth of women in prison were found to be single mothers prior to imprisonment (Prison Reform Trust, 2019).

Early research on this topic emphasised that women offenders mostly commit property crimes, and Heidensohn (1987) inferred that these behaviours were primarily economically motivated. Carlen's more nuanced study of women in prison in Scotland found that survival, coercive control and financial vulnerability lead some of the women towards addiction, crime and prostitution (Heidensohn, 1987). Carlen (1988) explored the relationship between class, economic marginalisation and crime for women and quotes a still relevant excerpt from Cecil Bishop's 1931 book *Women and Crime*:

> So deplorable is the state of affairs in most slum districts that many men, and probably more women, turn criminal for no better reason than they can no longer endure the conditions in which the chance of birth has cast their lot ... People who live in a hell on earth cannot be expected to endure indefinitely without protest. (Bishop, 1931: 32)

Carlen used the term 'sod-it syndrome' to describe the attitude of some of her research participants who saw property crime (for example, shoplifting or cheque fraud) as a solution to any financial problems they were having (Carlen, 1988). While this one-dimensional approach to understanding offending does not capture the complexity of women and offending behaviours, recognising poverty as a provocation to criminality serves to shift the debate on crime and offending from the presumed innate characteristics of the perpetrator to the structural conditions of city living, gender inequality and neglect. In doing so, survival and existence become concepts relevant for understanding offending.

Importantly, poverty is not merely income poverty, and differences in how men and women experience poverty are highly relevant. Fukuda-Parr (1999: 100) points out that 'poverty can be defined as the denial of the opportunities and choices most basic to human life – the opportunity to lead a long, healthy, and creative life, and to enjoy a decent standard of living, freedom, dignity, self-esteem, and respect from others'. For women, this often translates into a financial dependence on partners and time poverty owing to their caring responsibilities and participation in substantial (unpaid) domestic work (United Nations Human Rights Council, 2019). Both tasks leave less time available to engage in paid employment thus ultimately leading to income poverty (Pressman, 2003).

Economic and social inequalities linked with the CJS can result in people being caught in a trap of poverty and crime (United Nations Human Rights Council, 2019). For example, in Ireland the 1947 Vagrancy Act prohibiting begging was replaced in 2011 by the Criminal Justice (Public Order) Act which criminalises begging that is deemed to obstruct, harass or intimidate (IPRT, 2012). Although this is a slight improvement to the 1947 act, arresting, convicting and fining or imprisoning a person for begging does not solve the deeper structural issues that lead to the need for begging in the first place. For many women, engaging in criminal activities for economic gain is often their only available opportunity to provide for themselves and their families (United Nations Human Rights Council, 2019). By criminalising vulnerable individuals in this way, the Irish Human Rights Commission has stated that the Irish state is abdicating its responsibility to protect its citizens: rather than dealing with begging via health and social services, they allow the CJS address the issue (IPRT, 2012).

Desistance: a gendered process

Desistance from criminal behaviour is defined in literature as 'the long-term abstinence from crime among individuals who had previously engaged in persistent patterns of criminal offending' (Maruna, 2001: 26). Theories of desistance have developed over the years to recognise that the development of a pro-social identity (Maruna, 2001) and cognitive transformations supported by an openness to change, 'hooks for change' and the construction of a new identity are key to sustaining long-term desistance (Giordano et al, 2002; Paternoster and Bushway, 2009). McNeill (2016) pointed to the need to consider the role of communities in the process of desistance. He uses the term 'tertiary desistance' to emphasise that, for those who had been in prison, a sense of acceptance by and belonging to their community is central to sustained and stable desistance. Graham and McNeill (2017) further develop this and posit that tertiary desistance should lead to a point where the individual is no longer defined by their criminal history or by their desistance from crime.

A key concept in desistance is the notion of 'knifing off', a term originally coined in the work of Sampson and Laub (2003) in their longitudinal study of juvenile offenders; in its most basic form it refers to knifing the present off from the past (Maruna and Roy, 2007). Using the military and reform schools as examples of institutions catalytic to knifing off, Laub and Sampson say that 'knifing off' offenders from their usual environments along with the offer of a 'new script' for their future is key to the desistance process (Laub and Sampson, 2001: 49).

The literature on desistance, as in other areas of criminology, uses the 'male standard' as the yardstick to describe and attribute the process of desisting from crime to various structural and individual factors (Giordano et al, 2002; Heidensohn, 2010; Rodermond et al, 2016). Such literature is largely not applicable to women, and while there are a limited number of good quality studies on women who encounter the CJS in Ireland, the majority of research in this area comes from the UK, mainland Europe and the USA and are not always transposable to the Irish context. This is due in part to the fact that the profile of offending is different in different regions, variances in social and cultural norms, the natures of social welfare systems, the nature of the CJS, the supports in place for women in the community and other issues such as the role of criminal organisations, street culture and so on.

Attending specifically to female desistance, a meta-analysis by Rodermond et al (2016) examined both quantitative and qualitative studies of female desistance and asked if male-based desistance theories could also be applied to females. The quantitative studies show that factors such as positive outcomes in romantic relationships, motherhood, employment, education, financial security, stable mental health and reduction in drug/alcohol use were associated with reduced criminal behaviour and total desistance from crime. The qualitative studies found similar associations while also revealing a more nuanced story as to how these factors impacted and interact with each other to give both positive and negative outcomes.

Motherhood

Motherhood is one of the factors where the narrative analysis reveals much more than is shown by quantitative data. While having children is often presented as evidence of a way to promote pro-social bonds between and within families, it can also be a major source of stress (Giordano et al, 2002; Bachman et al, 2016; Curcio et al, 2018), especially when combined with other existing stressors such as financial strain or a lack of social and structural supports. In the case of motherhood and its role in desistance, it is necessary to note that while for women becoming a parent has the potential to lead to a reduction in offending, it only does so when other stressors and demands are low (Rodermond et al, 2016).

For women with children or other caring responsibilities, accessing the necessary supports can be difficult because, as is often pointed out, 'there are no creches at an AA meeting.' For single parents this is a difficult process in itself, but with additional stressors such as addiction, trauma and poverty, gaining access to the supports needed might not be an option. For example, addiction treatment centres can mean long-term separation from children who may have to go into state care, losing housing – inevitably leading to concerns about getting the children back post-treatment – and the potential of homelessness. The complexity of what motherhood means in terms of life impact is not captured in desistance theory.

Furthermore, research by Giordano et al (2002) looks at offenders whose offending behaviour started young and continued into adulthood, finding that having children did not have as direct an effect on these research participants. In this study, the influence of motherhood on desistance was a factor that could only be understood when other issues were considered: the type of offense, the longevity of offending, family history, peer networks and so on. Giordano et al (2002) discovered, for example, that for those labelled as serious offenders motherhood itself was not sufficient to reduce their offending behaviours.

Bachman et al's (2016) research on the effect of motherhood on desistance noted that several studies used community-based samples of older teens and women in their early twenties who had committed minor offenses, had not been in prison and in many cases had not even been arrested. Such research does not represent the life-course of a woman in her thirties or forties with multiple convictions and prison sentences behind her, along with other complex issues. This may be because the latter cohort are more difficult to access for research purposes, though it is also a result of assumptions about women and patterns of offending, as well as the visibility of some women who have engaged with the CJS.

Relationships

Another significant element of approaches to desistance is the role of social bond theory. This framework points to how family connections, marriage and employment serve as a means of increasing the likelihood of having positive interactions and relationships with individuals who are not involved in offending. This theory advocates that engaging in situations and with people who do not promote offending have the capacity to change a person's view on the consequences of crime, thus leading to desistance (Bushway et al, 2001). However, as Cambridge (2019) points out, for people with addictions and a history of imprisonment, access to supportive positive relationships is often limited.

For male desisters, marriage to a woman who is not criminally involved is one factor to which they often attribute their success (Leverentz, 2006). For women who have a history of criminal convictions, the situation is more complex as they are more likely than men with a history of criminal convictions to be in a relationship with a partner who is also criminally involved (Giordano et al, 2002; Leverentz, 2006; Rodermond et al, 2016). The likelihood of the woman offending was found to increase if the partner was criminally active and decrease if they were not (Leverentz, 2006; Rodermond et al, 2016).

For women who are criminally involved, it is not the act of the romantic relationship alone that influences change: a cognitive transformation is relevant, particularly how the women see their own choices and behaviours as well as their own sense of self worth. The influence of a relationship on a woman's desistance efforts is supported if there is already an openness to change and the potential for a shift to occur in how she sees herself (Giordano et al, 2002; Rodermond et al, 2016). Giordano et al (2002) found that some of their respondents stayed in unhappy marriages because they wanted to have the respectability of being a married woman and for their children to have a father; for other women, being single was their preferred option as they had a history of bad relationships with antisocial partners (Giordano et al, 2002). The impact of social expectations, financial worries and cultural norms need to be an integral part of how we think about the impact of relationships and desistance. Current simplistic approaches whereby milestones (for example, relationships and marriage) are assumed to bring about personal change are unrealistic, especially in the case of women.

Desistance, employment and social responsibilities

Reflecting on social bond theory, platonic and professional friendships that allow the development of pro-social bonds by increasing an individual's self-worth and modelling pro-social behaviours and responsibilities can positively impact a woman's efforts to make changes in her life (Abrams and Tam, 2018). While employment is often thought to be a key opportunity for women to build positive social bonds, it is not just the attachment to the job that will bring about this change, but what the relationships developed during employment mean to the person (McNeill and Weaver, 2007). However, as might be expected, the opportunities for women with a criminal record to gain access to situations where they can build positive social bonds are limited by caring responsibilities, shame, stigma, the influence of family, friends or romantic partners and marginalisation. Many people who have multiple criminal convictions or have spent time in prison are limited in their access to a non-criminal world (IPRT, 2012), thus limiting the likelihood that new relationships will have a positive influence on their offending behaviours.

Employment for women who are involved in the CJS does not have a clear benefit in terms of their ability to desist from offending behaviour. This is largely due to the intersection between structural conditions, such as the type and precarity of work available to unskilled women workers and the needs of women in terms of their caring responsibilities, personal investment and satisfaction in their role. Rodermond et al (2016) found that studies varied as to whether employment was positively related to desistance for women or not. Several studies point to the fact that many women were in minimum wage positions that did not provide enough financial security or job satisfaction to inspire the women or support their desistance effort.

In addition to the nature of employment available to women, the issue of social stigma was a significant barrier to employment. For example, a study on education programmes in prison by Case and Fasenfest (2004) found that, for women, there was a significant lack of self-esteem and an embarrassment around their personal history and 'criminal record' that led to an unwillingness or inability to effectively engage in job seeking. According to Case and Fasenfest (2004: 38), this outcome is not seen to the same degree among male inmates: as a result, they suggested that tailored programmes that included life-skills education, as well as pre- and post-release psychological support for women to help them navigate their 'new social ground', would be useful. Curcio et al (2018: 195) also found that female offenders had a greater challenge obtaining 'human, social and state capital' than their male counterparts and that, by developing these types of capital, female offenders have better desistance and redemption outcomes. Recognising this issue, Maguire and Raynor (2006), McNeill and Weaver (2010) and McNeill et al (2012) have all pointed to the need to support the development of skills (capital) and emphasise that desistance interventions should focus on this personal development, but also present realistic opportunities to use these skills (social capital).

Maruna and Roy (2007) say that 'knifing off opportunities' that could lead to a reduction of criminal behaviour has potential to explain the desistance process. Referencing Caspi and Moffitt (1993), they describe knifing off as the elimination of old options, but suggest the term 'structural restrictions on criminal opportunities' as an alternative to the rather brutal 'knifing off' metaphor (Maruna and Roy, 2007: 109).

Leverentz (2010) looks at the concept of people breaking away from their criminal lifestyle by avoiding 'people, places and things', a phrase commonly used by those involved in twelve-step programmes such as Alcoholics Anonymous and Narcotics Anonymous (Leverentz, 2010). The idea here is that if you avoid the people you once used drugs or alcohol with, the places you frequented and things, for example, drug paraphernalia, that could trigger you to have a craving or fall into old behaviours, you have a better chance of success in your recovery from addiction. However, for many women who have criminal convictions and a history of substance use, their neighbourhoods, family members, spouses and friends are often heavily intertwined with their drug use and criminality (Tracy et al, 2010). Facing structural limitations and without sufficient human or financial resources to remove themselves from their neighbourhood, women simply do not have the luxury of reinventing their whole lives to avoid certain people, places and things. Instead, they make the best effort they can to address some of the issues that have directed their lives thus far, and this is an individualised complex process.

Considering this research gap in relation to 'knifing off', the question appears to be: can women knife off their past in the same way that men do, or are they bound by different social expectations and responsibilities? The term 'knifing off' suggests it is definitive, black and white, you do or you don't, but the women in the research discussed in the next section demonstrate that the gender-based complexity of interpersonal relationships, structural limitations around motherhood and other responsibilities and limited employment options means that knifing off does not reflect any of the processes described in their life trajectory.

Hearing women's voices: a content analysis of the interviews

This article is based on interviews (n=6) conducted with women who encountered the CJS. The women were recruited by posters displayed in a service for people who have spent time in prison and in a hostel for women. Ethics permission was given for this study by SREC, the Social Research Ethics Committee of University College Cork, Ireland. Interviews were carried out in a private room in both services by one of the authors, a Support Worker with 20 years' experience in the field. None of the participants were clients of the interviewer. Interviews lasted between 1 and 1.5 hours and were recorded on a digital recording device. As per SREC regulations, interviews were immediately transcribed and anonymised and the digital file was deleted.

The participants are all residents in the south of Ireland, all but one spent time in prison and they range in age from mid-20s to early 60s. All participants described problematic a relationship with drugs and/or alcohol and all described experiencing abuse both as children and in adulthood.

The transcripts are analysed in a line-by-line fashion, taking a modified grounded approach (Charmaz, 2006). While issues of desistance and particularly knifing off were relevant to the analysis, the authors sought to ensure that the voices of the participants directly informed the themes that emerged from the data. The key themes that emerged are discussed below.

Results and discussion

The women in this study carry a heavy burden. They carry a personal shame associated with their convictions and time in prison, but they also carry the shame of their families for their violation of the social norms of being a woman, a mother and a daughter. They also bear the guilt of how their time in prison has impacted their families, especially when the burden of their children falls on extended family. The emotional toll for women who have been in prison adds to the difficulties they encounter in trying to establish a life after their sentence: there is a cost to them personally in managing these emotions, but there is also a significant cost in terms of what they owe to others, a debt that will overshadow their recovery.

Danielle spent time in prison and lived at a women's hostel following her prison sentence. She talked about her post-prison addiction and recovery challenges while also dealing with some complex emotions following her sentence:

Figure 2.1: Key themes from grounded analysis

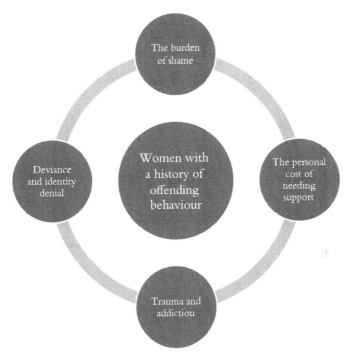

'The biggest thing for me emotionally when I came out of prison would have been trying to deal with the impact of being in prison, how it affected my family, the guilt, the shame, y'know you're struggling with all these emotions and y'know you just have to work very very hard on yourself.' (Danielle)

Reinventing your whole life is no small task. Eliminating old options and putting structural limitations on criminal opportunities is a huge step. For Danielle, this means avoiding the centre of the city where she lives to avoid old associates and triggers. Avoiding your city centre can make life difficult; it can limit your options for supports, employment and access to services.

'You really have to reinvent your whole life, you really have to change all areas of your life from the people you used to know, avoiding places that y'know I would have gone to, avoiding the city centre.' (Danielle)

Moving to another city is not currently a viable option for Danielle, who is in receipt of a social welfare payment and the Housing Assistance Payment. In Ireland, eligibility for these payments is dependent on you applying in the area where you normally reside. This makes moving to another city or county very difficult as she would have to prove a local family connection or valid reason for her move such as a college place or employment.

Danielle talked about forming deep friendships in prison and in the hostel in order to survive life in both institutions; this poses a dilemma for her after her release. When she runs into these friends, while simultaneously trying to cut ties with people who are active drug or alcohol users and people she used to commit offences with, she struggles with balancing her need to stay removed from these triggers but also not wanting to offend the women. Here she describes one particular incident:

> 'I was in a petrol station the other day ... and a girl who is now on the streets ... approached me for money in the shop and I was embarrassed because she looked very dishevelled and y'know the other people in the shop were kind of looking at me then, and I just felt embarrassed and I felt ashamed. Things like that can really set me back because it reminds me of where I was.' (Danielle)

Limiting your opportunities and relationships in order to support recovery from addiction can lead to isolation if there is not an alternative set of opportunities available to make new friends; this, in tangent with the *obligation* women feel to existing friends and family whom they have to rely on, is paralysing. Danielle attends recovery groups which offers a network of support, but again tries to do so while avoiding the city centre where she is most likely to bump into old associates.

A study by Tracy et al (2010) on network relationships of women in substance abuse treatment talks about the dual role of support in women's lives, some positive and some harmful. For example, having a family member take care of children can facilitate access to supports, but can also give the space to enable the person the time and space to use drugs or alcohol; an offer of a place a stay could be a safe place to get back on their feet, or could be a place to use drugs or alcohol. Furthermore, the need to rely on family means the opportunity to avoid some problematic behaviours is unrealistic and toxic relationship dynamics that are problematic for the women are unavoidable. Cutting themselves off from these family members or friends could mean cutting off the only form of support they feel they have despite the negative factors.

The women interviewed in this study routinely discussed fractured relationships with their families, in particular with their parents. Some had been rejected by their families, others had cut off contact with their families of origin as they realised these relationships were toxic to their efforts to move forward with a non-criminal lifestyle. Barbara spoke about her mother's influence over her life and offending behaviour. She talked about being taught to shoplift as a child and the normalisation of such behaviour and how she internalised a belief that she was a criminal. When asked if anyone had tried to help her as a child, she said:

'there was no helping me. I was uncivilized like, I was just doing what I was doing, that was it like ... I was built to do what I done like.' (Barbara)

For Barbara, separating her life from her mother's life is a challenge. As a single mother herself without much support, she often needs her mother to help with childcare. She describes situations where an argument with her mother will lead to amplified feelings of anger, which for Barbara can lead to poor decision making and the potential for relapse on alcohol or tablets; Barbara knows she is very likely to offend while under the influence. Many of her convictions are as a result of situations like this where her coping skills are tested.

'she could say one word and that's it me gone off on it for the night and I just ... I don't have the tools to exit her out of me I just have the tools to keep her away, I don't have the tools for her words to go away.' (Barbara)

While Barbara can put physical distance between herself and her mother, the impact of the difficulties in their relationship remains a constant influence in her life.

All but one of the women in this study spoke about experiencing domestic violence from partners or a parent, some as a witness, others as the direct victim. Abbie's now ex-husband was violent towards her, and she talked about feeling trapped and isolated in that situation. Abbie struggled with alcohol addiction – a problem she says was made worse as she drank to cope with the violence in her marriage. Abbie talked about her husband forcing her into psychiatric units to address her drinking:

'When you're under the influence of alcohol or any substance you completely lose your power. Nobody listens to you. I remember begging a doctor in the house ... and saying look please, I don't want to go in ... and he didn't listen to me, just listened to my husband, signed the form that was it, I was signed in.' (Abbie)

She managed to stop drinking, though she talks here about how she did not actually get a chance to work on the issues behind her drinking as she was focused on surviving within the family and being a mother:

'It was motivated purely because I wouldn't have been accepted in the family if I was drinking, and I wanted my children, I love my, I loved my kids and I got a long stretch, but I never had the freedom to sort anything out about myself.' (Abbie)

In Abbie's case, as for many women in relationships dominated by violence, her husband's criminal behaviour went unpunished, and her victimhood unrecognised. Abbie's attempts to escape the violence in her marriage resulted in her first arrest as she was driving under the influence to escape a violent beating. Here she describes her interaction with the arresting officers:

'They have no regard for anybody who is any way disempowered, no regard. Like back then I wasn't heard, back then I wasn't, not only was I not heard but I was disrespected even more. I was already coming from a vulnerable place, but I was disrespected even more. It was horrendous.' (Abbie)

Abbie removed herself from this harmful relationship, but this brought other complications, homelessness, further convictions and wider family tensions while also dealing with the impact of the trauma she experienced in her marriage.

Maruna and Roy (2007) discuss whether knifing off happens to people, or if they make it happen for themselves – external structures vs personal agency – using examples of prison, the military and marriage. In this study, joining the military was not an option mentioned by any of the women interviewed, and the only mentions of marriage were in a negative context.

A prison sentence does indeed knife the person off from their life on the outside but does so at huge cost. It also introduces the women to a network of people who may still be criminally active, making it more difficult to take the path of desistance from crime. In Claire's case, she was also cut off from her newly-found recovery supports in the community and here she describes her dilemma towards the end of her prison sentence:

'I was torn, I was torn as to what road I wanted to take, I knew I was coming to the end of my sentence, ... I had contacts built up in prison that if I had wanted to go back into that world, I had a plan around that yet at the same time I had contacts in recovery where I had a plan around that.' (Claire)

Claire returned to treatment on release from prison and continued her addiction recovery journey. It is evident that she had an openness to change and valued the opportunities presented to her, but here she describes this very challenging psychological process:

'Physically I started to kind of get better everything was good, but spiritually I felt very damaged, very fucked, very black like inside.' (Claire)

She talks about the isolation, the detachment and the lack of opportunity or motivation to engage in a meaningful life. Prison, rather than as is sometimes conveyed as an opportunity for change, was a barrier to reintegration, she was left behind and things had moved on without her:

'I was here and life was over there and I just couldn't fucking connect, I just couldn't, I couldn't jump in ... I wanted the life I had back, but everything had moved on. I came out and ... people changed, people had moved on, I had changed you know, and life as I knew it wasn't there ... I think I was just spiritually deflated and emotionally shut down.' (Claire)

For those with children these challenges are further amplified, and their support needs are often greater than what is available to them from within their family and social network. Baldwin (2018: 49) says 'there are few ideals that elicit more emotion and arguably more judgement than that of mother and child'. Adding criminal convictions, a history of addiction, mental health difficulties, poverty, trauma, social worker involvement in the family, criminalised family members, unstable tenancies or homelessness and the weight of society's judgement and personal feelings of 'failure as a mother', these emotions grow and feed off each other.

Becoming a mother can be a joyful experience for someone who wants to start a family and is confident about doing so, but an unexpected pregnancy for a woman who is criminally active, addicted to drugs and without supports can be a highly stressful and negative experience (Kreager et al, 2010). In the literature, some studies show that becoming a mother generally leads to a reduction in crime or total cessation in crime (Rodermond et al, 2016), however research has also found that mothers who reoffend following a period of cessation report that feeling overwhelmed and stressed by motherhood is a factor in their return to offending (Rodermond et al, 2016). Motherhood is challenging regardless of circumstances. For mothers who are in and out of prison, struggling with addiction or addiction recovery, housing instability, domestic violence and mental health difficulties while negotiating their motherhood role with child protection services or family members who are helping out with childcare, being a mother can be a significant source of stress.

Esther has six children and describes her constant struggle with homelessness, addiction and motherhood.

'I was struggling with my addictions ... struggling around housing. Some of my kids were in the HSE[1] and stuff ... I would have ended up pregnant again .... I did a journey of that I suppose you know, mother baby units and then back to hostels again. I was doing parenting courses, treatment centres again and in and out of treatments and stuff trying to get clean.' (Esther)

Esther lived with uncertainty. Decisions pertaining to her life and the life of her children were made by others, agents of social control, both formal and informal – while most likely taken with the best intentions, her sense of personal agency was depleted. Despite all the supports available to Esther she felt that she had used up their resources and was beyond help.

'I felt like I outran all them places, outdid them kind of thing.' (Esther)

Esther talks about a shift in her thinking after the birth of her youngest child. Esther could foresee the outcomes for her and her child if she continued to use drugs and offend.

'After my other baby em ... I really thought like if I go back using after this child and she goes back into the system I knew deep down I'd end up back on the streets.' (Esther)

The complexity of Esther's case lay not only in her current situation with her children, her housing needs and her offending, but in her history of trauma, abuse and victimisation. She realised that the only way forward was to address this, and not addressing it would ultimately lead to her own destruction.

'I knew I'd end up dead because I hadn't dealt with the trauma when I left Cork, I boxed that off. ... I was always dealing with my addictions, never dealing with the trauma part. So there was always that in the back of my head and I just ... I knew if I didn't get that sorted, I would've had a nervous breakdown, I would have either killed myself or killed someone.' (Esther)

Esther was ultimately able to connect the current difficulties in her life to anticipated future difficulties (Paternoster and Bushway, 2009), thus taking the first steps towards recovery. However, the barriers to success are significant and personal growth and development are but one element of a lifelong process away from crime, chaos and addiction. To develop this initial step and maintain their commitment, the person must be able to credibly imagine a new possible non-offending self (Paternoster and Bushway, 2009), but the reality of being allowed to become this new self – to not face a process of identity denial – is a significant hurdle. Bachman et al (2016) say that once people start to imagine their new identity and begin connecting with pro-social activities and people, establishing positive relationships with family members, children and romantic partners, this can serve as a catalyst to their desistance from crime. This all sounds wonderful, but the opportunity to engage in these activities and establish positive relationships are not always readily available to women who feel outside the margins of society, who are seen as deviant both in their identity and their behaviour and are dealing with the impact of trauma.

Conclusion

Research on crime and offending predominately focuses on the experience of male offenders, and frameworks describing these experiences have long been assumed to apply to women. While over the past 50 years there have been some prominent voices drawing attention to this issue, none perhaps more so than Carlen (1985, 1988) when it comes to knowing about and thinking about women who are engaged with criminal justice systems, we are still theoretically bereft.

This small study aims to add to the growing body of work that exists to attest to women's experiences in the CJS and challenge the male-dominated norms that have informed the field of criminology. This work shows that women's experiences of desistance are not easily mapped onto existing theoretical frameworks, women's experiences are not comparable to men's both theoretically and experientially and, importantly, women's voices are key to overcoming these issues.

This work took a modified grounded approach (Charmaz, 2006) with a view to allowing the participants' voices to emerge from the data and directly inform the analysis and conclusions. Despite the small sample size, a wealth of information has emerged that speaks to women's experience of desistence, not least the issues of motherhood, the complexity of interpersonal relationships for women, the social sanctions experienced by women, the notion of double deviance and the lack of opportunity in the community for women after prison. While early accounts of desistance (for men) focused on the journey that the individuals themselves experience around identify shift, hooks for change, developing positive support networks and so on (Maruna, 2001), later accounts move to considering the important role of society in assisting with this journey (McNeill, 2016). For women in this study, the dynamics are inverted: the role of relationships, identity denial, the possibility of developing new support networks, marriage and peer networks dominate as they try to forge out a *new* life and desist from offending. For women, the space for personal growth and development, identity shift and seizing hooks for change are luxuries that are often not afforded to them;

women are bound by their social responsibilities, hindered by gender roles and norms and shunned by society as they try to change.

For women, achieving disistance reflects their life experiences, opportunities and limitations. Opportunities are limited for women in the workplace, childcare responsibilities weigh heavily on their lives and society judges harshly. Women cannot merely walk away from negative personal relationships; family ties are not easily severed and new opportunities are stymied by the perception of double deviance that is applied only to women. Women in the CJS are often labelled as complex, but perhaps we should consider that our ways of thinking about offending do not account for the complexity of women's lives. Work on women's desistance should start here and move outwards to provide a rich and accurate picture of the journey women who desist must travel.

Note

[1]   Health Service Executive, the Irish government body that oversees the child and family agency – Tusla (www.tusla.ie). In this case, the person is indicating that her children are in the care system.

References

Abrams, L. and Tam, C. (2018) 'Gender differences in desistance from crime: how do social bonds operate among formerly incarcerated emerging adults?', *Journal of Adolescent Research*, 33(1): 34–57.

Bachman, R., Kerrison, E., Paternoster, R., Smith, L. and O'Connell, D. (2016) 'The complex relationship between motherhood and desistance', *Women & Criminal Justice*, 26(3): 212–31.

Baldwin, L. (2018) 'Motherhood disrupted: reflections of post-prison mothers', *Emotion, Space and Society*, 26: 49–56.

Bertrand, M. (1969) Self-image and delinquency: a contribution to the study of female criminality and woman's image', *Acta Criminologica*, 2(1): 71–144.

Black, L. (2015) 'The representation of offending women in the Irish press', *Irish Probation Journal*, 12: 160–78.

Bushway, S., Piquero, A., Broidy, L., Cauffman, E. and Mazerolle, P. (2001) 'An empirical framework for studying desistance as a process', *Criminology*, 39(2): 491–516.

Cambridge, G. (2019) ' "Seeking peace of mind" – understanding desistance as a journey into recovery and out of chaos', PhD thesis, Cork: University College Cork.

Carlen, P. (1988) *Women, Crime and Poverty*, Milton Keynes: Open University Press.

Carlen, P., Christina, D., Hicks, J., O'Dwyer, J. and Tchaikovsky, C. (1985) *Criminal Women*, Cambridge: Polity Press.

Case, P. and Fasenfest, D. (2004) 'Expectations for opportunities following prison education: a discussion of race and gender', *Journal of Correctional Education*, 55(1): 24–39.

Caspi, A. and Moffitt, T. E. (1993) 'When do individual differences matter? A paradoxical theory of personality coherence', *Psychological Inquiry*, 4(4): 247–71.

Charmaz, K. (2006) *Constructing Grounded Theory*, London: SAGE.

Chesney-Lind, M. (1997) *The Female Offender. Girls, Women and Crime*, Thousand Oaks: SAGE.

Chesney-Lind, M. (2006) 'Patriarchy, crime, and justice', *Feminist Criminology*, 1(1): 6–26.

Christie, N. (1986) 'The ideal victim', in E. Fattah (ed.) *From Crime Policy to Victim Policy*, London: Palgrave Macmillan, pp 17–30.

Corston, J. (2007) *The Corston Report: a review of women with particular vulnerabilities in the criminal justice system*, London: Home Office.

Curcio, G., Pattavina, A. and Fisher, W. (2018) 'Gender differences on the road to redemption', *Feminist Criminology*, 13(2): 182–204.

Daly, K. (1992) 'Women's pathways to felony court: feminist theories of lawbreaking and problems of representation', *Southern California Review of Law and Women's Studies*, 2: 11–52.

Davies, P., Francis, P. and Greer, C. (eds) (2017) *Victims, Crime and Society*, London: SAGE.

DeHart, D. (2008) 'Pathways to prison', *Violence Against Women*, 14(12): 1362–81.

Ec.europa.eu (2019) 'Europe 2020 indicators – poverty and social exclusion'. [online] Available at: https://ec.europa.eu/eurostat/statisticsexplained/index.php?title=Europe_2020_indicators_-_poverty_and_social_exclusion&oldid=214512 [Accessed 17 March 2020].

Fukuda-Parr, S. (1999) 'What does feminization of poverty mean? It isn't just lack of income', *Feminist Economics*, 5(2): 99–103.

Gehring, K. (2018) 'A direct test of pathways theory', *Feminist Criminology*, 13(2): 115–37.

Gelsthorpe, L. (2007) 'Sentencing and gender', in R. Sheehan, G. McIvor and C. Trotter (eds) *What Works with Women Offenders*, Cullompton: Willan Publishing, pp 40–60.

Gelsthorpe, L. (2010) 'Women, crime and control', *Criminology & Criminal Justice*, 10(4): 375–86.

Giordano, P., Cernkovich, S. and Rudolph, J. (2002) 'Gender, crime, and desistance: toward a theory of cognitive transformation', *American Journal of Sociology*, 107(4): 990–1064.

Graham, H. and McNeill, F. (2017) 'Desistance: envisioning futures', in: P. Carlen and L. Ayres França (eds) *Alternative Criminologies*, London: Routledge, pp 433–51.

Heidensohn, F. (1968) 'The deviance of women: a critique and an enquiry', *The British Journal of Sociology*, 19(2): 160–75.

Heidensohn, F. (1987) 'Women and crime: questions for criminology', in: P. Carlen and A. Worrall (eds) *Gender, Crime and Justice*, Buckingham: Open University Press, pp 16–27.

Heidensohn, F. (1996). *Women and Crime* (2nd edn), New York: Palgrave Macmillan.

Heidensohn, F. (2006) 'New perspectives and established views', in: F. Heidensohn (ed.) *Gender and Justice. New Concepts and Approaches,* Cullompton: Willan Publishing, pp 1–10.

Heidensohn, F. (2010) 'The deviance of women: a critique and an enquiry', *The British Journal of Sociology*, 61: 111–26.

Holtfreter, K., Reisig, M. and Morash, M. (2004) 'Poverty, state capital and recidivism among women offenders', *Criminology and Public Policy*, 3(2): 185–208.

IPRT (Irish Penal Reform Trust) (2012) *The vicious circle of social exclusion and crime: Ireland's disproportionate punishment of the poor*, Shifting Focus, Dublin: Irish Penal Reform Trust.

IPRT (Irish Penal Reform Trust) (2013) *Women in the criminal justice system. Towards a non-custodial approach*, Dublin: Irish Penal Reform Trust.

Irish Prison Service (2018) *Annual report 2018*, Longford: Irish Prison Service.

Kennedy, H., Monks, S., Curtin, K., Wright, B., Linehan, S., Duffy, D., Teljeur, C. and Kelly, A. (2005) *Mental illness in Irish prisons: psychiatric morbidity in sentenced, remanded and newly committed prisoners*, Dublin: National Forensic Mental Health Service.

Kreager, D., Matsueda, R. and Erosheva, E. (2010) 'Motherhood and criminal desistance in disadvantaged neighborhoods', *Criminology*, 48(1): 221–58.

Laub, J. and Sampson, R. (2001) 'Understanding desistance from crime', *Crime and Justice*, 28: 1–69.

Leverentz, A. (2006) 'The love of a good man? Romantic relationships as a source of support or hindrance for female ex-offenders', *Journal of Research in Crime and Delinquency*, 43(4): 459–88.

Leverentz, A. (2010) 'People, places, and things: how female ex-prisoners negotiate their neighborhood context', *Journal of Contemporary Ethnography*, 39(6): 646–81.

Lynch, S., DeHart, D., Belknap, J. and Green, B. (2012a). *Women's pathways to jail: the roles and intersections of serious mental illness and trauma*, Washington DC: US Department of Justice, Bureau of Justice Assistance.

Lynch, S., DeHart, D., Belknap, J., Green, B., Dass-Brailsford, P., Johnson, K. and Wong, M. (2017) 'An examination of the associations among victimization, mental health, and offending in women', *Criminal Justice and Behavior*, 44(6): 796–814.

Lynch, S., Fritch, A. and Heath, N. (2012b) 'Looking beneath the surface', *Feminist Criminology*, 7(4): 381–400.

Maguire, M. and Raynor, P. (2006) 'How the resettlement of prisoners promotes desistance from crime', *Criminology & Criminal Justice*, 6(1): 19–38.

Maruna, S. (2001) *Making Good*, Washington, DC: American Psychological Association.

Maruna, S. and Roy, K. (2007) 'Amputation or reconstruction? Notes on the concept of "knifing off" and desistance from crime', *Journal of Contemporary Criminal Justice*, 23(1): 104–24.

McHugh, R. (2013) *Tracking the needs and service provision for women ex-prisoners*, Dublin: Association for Criminal Justice Research and Development.

McNeill, F., Farrell, S., Lightowler, C. and Maruna, S. (2012) *How and why people stop offending: discovering desistance*, Glasgow: The Institute for Research and Innovation in Social Services.

McNeill, F. (2016) 'Desistance and criminal justice in Scotland', in: H. Croall, G. Mooney and M. Munro (eds) *Crime, Justice and Society in Scotland*, London: Routledge, pp 200–15.

McNeill, F. and Weaver, B. (2007) *Giving up crime: directions for policy*, Glasgow: SCCJR.

McNeill, F. and Weaver, B. (2010) *Changing lives? Desistance research and offender management*, Glasgow: SCCJR.

Messerschmidt, J. (2004) *Flesh and Blood*, Lanham, MD: Rowman & Littlefield Publishers.

Paternoster, R. and Bushway, S. (2009) 'Desistance and the "feared self": toward an identity theory of criminal desistance', *Journal of Criminal Law and Criminology*, 99(4): 1103–56.

Pressman, S. (2003) 'Feminist explanations for the feminization of poverty', *Journal of Economic Issues*, 37(2): 353–61.

Prison Reform Trust (2019) 'Why focus on reducing women's imprisonment?', [online] Available at: http://www.prisonreformtrust.org.uk/Portals/0/Why%20Women%20England%20and%20Wales.pdf [Accessed 17 March 2020].

Quinlan, C. (2011) *INSIDE: Ireland's Women's Prisons Past and Present*, Dublin: Irish Academic Press.

Rodermond, E., Kruttschnitt, C., Slotboom, A. and Bijleveld, C. (2016) 'Female desistance: a review of the literature', *European Journal of Criminology*, 13(1): 3–28.

Salisbury, E. and Van Voorhis, P. (2009) 'Gendered pathways: a quantitative investigation of women probationer's paths to incarceration', *Criminal Justice and Behavior*, 36(6): 541–66.

Sampson, R. and Laub, J. (2003) 'Life course desisters? Trajectories of crime among delinquent boys followed to age 70', *Criminology*, 41(3): 555–92.

Schur, E. (1984) *Labeling Women Deviant*, New York: Random House.

Smart, C. (1977) *Women, Crime and Criminology*, Abingdon: Routledge & Kegan Paul Ltd.

Tracy, E., Munson, M., Peterson, L. and Floersch, J. (2010) 'Social support: a mixed blessing for women in substance abuse treatment', *Journal of Social Work Practice in the Addictions*, 10(3): 257–82.

United Nations Human Rights Council (2019) *Women deprived of liberty. Report of the Working Group on the issue of discrimination against women in law and practice*, United Nations Human Rights Council.

Walklate, S. (2004) *Gender, Crime & Criminal Justice*, Cullompton: Willan Publishing.

Walklate, S. (2007) *Handbook of Victims and Victimology*, London: Willan.

Wattanaporn, K. and Holtfreter, K. (2014) 'The impact of feminist pathways research on gender-responsive policy and practice', *Feminist Criminology*, 9(3): 191–207.

3

Sex Work, Criminalisation and Stigma: Towards a Feminist Criminological Imagination

Maggie O'Neill and Alison Jobe

Selling or swapping sex for economic need was a theme in the lives of the women Carlen interviewed. It was often taken for granted as an 'expectation' and a form of survival. There are no official records on the number of women in prison who have sold sex (Ahearne, 2016) and indeed no official records on the numbers of women selling sex more generally in society. In this chapter, we draw upon interviews with women from one participatory research project we conducted in the UK. We explore their life trajectories and find that their narratives are 'vivid chronicles of the times' in which they live, including experiences of the criminal justice system (CJS) and leaving prison (Carlen et al, 1985). We argue that women's narratives can point to future possible trajectories and modes of doing justice with women, working against the grain of what Hudson (2006) calls 'white man's justice'. The participatory research that underpins this chapter is, for us, an example of biographical research as 'criminological imagination' (Carlen, 2010) that enables us 'to grasp history and biography and the relations between the two within society' (Mills, 2000). In *Criminal Women* (1985: 162), the prison regime is described as being based around the will to 'discipline, infantalize, feminize, medicalize and domesticate' and in the final part of the chapter we reflect on the extent to which this relates to women who sell sex and their experiences of the CJS.

In what follows, we outline what we mean by a criminological imagination and we present women's stories of selling or swapping sex as told to us and/or to their peers. These stories give a rich understanding of women's experiences of selling sex and give an insight into how the criminal justice landscape continues to frame women's experiences. Stories *about* women who sell sex are typically one dimensional. Women who sell sex are often represented in law, policy and practice as deviant, criminal or as victims who lack agency. Motivations to, and experiences of, selling sex are frequently misunderstood and misrepresented in policy and research. Only through women's stories, in their own words, can we challenge the 'myths, metaphors and misogyny' (Carlen et al, 1985: 13) that still, 36 years later, work to frame and dictate sex working women's experiences.

Feminist criminological imagination

What do we mean by the criminological imagination? Carlen (2010) has articulated the 'criminological imagination' by exploring the imaginary promise of criminal justice, asking 'what is crime and what is justice?' while simultaneously seeking to both analyse and pave the way for the future of the discipline. Her work has predominantly focused on women in the CJS and women in prison, and *Criminal Women* tells the stories of four women, in their own words, mediated through Carlen's feminist analytic lens, to critique and challenge the 'myths, metaphors and misogyny' that impact 'female lawbreakers and women prisoners' including 'class-riven and still deeply sexist society' (Carlen et al, 1985: 13).

The criminological landscape in which *Criminal Women* was written focused largely on men. Maureen Cain (1990) argued that feminist criminologists should start by addressing how gender differences are constructed and maintained. There was, at that time, an assumption that criminological theories would apply to women (but in practice most do not) and, in challenging the institutionalised patriarchy within criminology, policy and practice, sociologists such as Pat Carlen (1988) and Sandra Walklate (1998) made female defendants and victims visible. Indeed, for Carlen, women who commit crime should be given a privileged audience when they speak of their reasons for breaking the law (Carlen, 1992).

A key limitation of this early work is that it tends not to include the experiences of women of colour. As research evidences, Black women are more likely to receive harsher sentencing and experience greater levels of sexual abuse in prisons (Davis, 2001). In 'Beyond white man's justice', Barbara Hudson (2006) also articulates the need for women to be given a privileged audience, to be able to speak from their experience and subject positions, in their own words; the 'outsider' must be able to put their claims in their own terms and not have to accommodate to the dominant modes of legal or political discourse. Being able to tell our story in our own words is vital to reach inter-subjective understanding. Hudson demonstrates that the constructions of law and 'the liberal philosophies on which Western law is based, reveal the closures of law and, therefore, the limits of justice that can be expected by marginalised Others' (2006: 31). She points out that it has been more difficult for women, and in particular women of colour, to gain rights relating to the body than to gain access to property rights or rights in the public sphere. She evidences the 'dithering over definitions of "racial" crimes' and 'differences in sentencing attributable to the race/ethnicity of victims' that combine to evidence 'the entrenched whiteness of criminal law' (2006: 32).

Female criminality has been explained historically through problematic reductive, positivist, biological and psychological approaches (Cain, 1990; Carlen et al, 1985, 1992, Chesney-Lind, 1992; Heidensohn, 1985; Gelsthorpe, 1990; Walklate, 1998). Sociological theories were slightly more critical and take into account gender as a construct, especially those influenced by emerging feminist scholars who shifted the focus to issues of control, power and the marginalisation of women (Smart, 1977, 1990). Criminology as a discipline was initially dominated by men, with a focus on male deviance and crime. Early feminists attempted to link criminology to the wider sphere of women's oppression and in Carlen's work a clear focus on female agency and subjectivity is at the heart of a feminist criminological imagination.

The importance of subjective experiences captured through first-person narratives is that they are more personal, providing detail hard to gain otherwise; give an insight into thoughts, feelings, lived experiences; and potentially enable an explanation and understanding of 'why' things happen. They help us to access the structural, cultural and material realities of women's lives and their choices and agency. Women's agency is, of course, often constrained by social conditions not of their own making.

Finally, subjective experiences, as told in Carlen's *Criminal Women* and in the research we share below, is an example of a criminological imagination, illuminating the relationship between biography, history and society that trouble more simplistic, positivist theories of crime and women's offending. Biographical or narrative criminology helps us to understand lives as lived in the context of 'discriminatory and exploitative class and gender relations' (Carlen et al, 1985: 9).

The importance of subjective experiences and autobiographical accounts
Criminal Women:

> Tells the stories of four women who, in attempting to become women of their own making, become embroiled with the criminal justice and penal systems to such an extent that today, as non-criminals and non-prisoners, they are still subject to the misogynous mythology which

inseminates stereotypes of female law breakers and women prisoners. (Carlen et al, 1985: 1)

Criminal Women (Carlen et al, 1985) was written, in part, to critique mainstream criminological theory of the era that categorised women who break the law as having a fixed identity. A key point is that 'the essential criminal woman does not exist' (Carlen et al, 1985: 10) and Carlen evidences this by inviting women to tell their own stories, their biographies, in their own words. Woven into each story or narrative, Carlen highlights the intersecting oppressions and analyses multiple forms of oppression and marginalisation in the women's subjective experiences.

Adapting Carlen's key phrasing, that there is no typical criminal woman, academic research *with* or *by* sex workers tells us that there is no such thing as a typical sex worker. In contrast, women selling sex have been categorised in law, public policy and media discourses as 'culpable offenders' or 'innocent victims'. Accounts of selling sex inform us that the realities of sex work are much more diverse, complex and contradictory than these categories suggest. In this chapter, through participatory research *with* and *by* women selling sex, we explore the diversity and complexity of the lived experience of sex work.

We all lead 'storied lives' (O'Neill et al, 2014). Telling stories is a basic cultural competence and helps us to make sense of our pasts but also our present and future (Fischer, 2011). A 'biographical or narrative turn' took place in sociology around the late 1970s and early 1980s, associated with the (re)emergence of 'micro social theories' (Nurse and O'Neill, 2018).

For Carlen:

> autobiographical accounts demonstrate in fine detail how, under certain material and ideological conditions, either law breaking and/or other forms of deviant protest may indeed comprise rational and coherent responses to women's awareness of the social disabilities imposed upon them by discriminatory and exploitative class and gender relations. (Carlen et al, 1985: 8–9)

The four women in Carlen's book often transgress conventional gender roles and, like their male counterparts, crime is a way of achieving money and independence. A central claim is that doing crime can be understood as a 'rational and coherent response' to women's awareness of unequal and exploitative conditions and relations. Women's lives are complex and understanding lived lives must enable a more reflexive understanding of women's experiences. Themes include early experiences of incarceration, including time at approved school; relationships with men figure centrally, connected to patriarchal structures and processes; and sexual violence and rape. At the beginning of Christina's story she tells us 'in my father's house we went on tippy toes' (Carlen et al, 1985: 59); she was later placed under court protection at the age of 14, was in an approved school at 15, running away was a common occurrence, at 18 she experienced solitary confinement, she sold sex as a teenager, was a shoplifter, cat burglar and pimp. In and out of prison, a major turning point for her was her encounter with the prison psychiatrist, Dr P. The narrative reflects upon her inner world, the periods of crisis and making her way out of prison on her own and in her own time.

Biographical and participatory methods in criminology

In the introduction to this chapter, we stated that women's narratives can point to future possible trajectories and modes of doing justice with women. One method for achieving this is by combining biographical research and participatory research. We argue that participatory research (including participatory arts) offers a counter hegemonic way of doing research that can place women's experiences and voices centre stage. At the same time, it can challenge exclusionary discourses and practices in research, and facilitate a space for women to tell their stories, in their own time, with empathic witnessing. In the participatory and biographical research we discuss below we also used the walking interview as a biographical method to understand the women's relationship to place, their embodied experience and how this connects to understanding (Seal and O'Neill, 2019, O'Neill and Roberts, 2019).

A key proponent of Participatory Action Research (PAR) is Orlando Fals Borda (1988) who suggests that the interrelationship between academic knowledge and people's wisdom is at the heart of PAR and can give rise to the 'critical recovery of history' that in turn might foster mutual recognition, trust and appreciation, thus shifting the subject–object tension (researcher/offender) towards a subject–subject relation (woman/woman). Better understanding and knowledge of women's lives and lived experiences is a key result of participatory and biographical research because of the approach which serves to foster inclusion, participation, valuing women's voices and interventions in policy and practice.

Ethical principles and challenges of PAR

We stress here the importance of conducting research ethically and note that participatory research has its challenges and critics. When working with marginalised groups, it is very important to be aware of the power relations between the teller of a story and the listener, and in particular the interpretation of cultural norms by both teller and listener (Andrews et al, 2008).

The research we discuss in this chapter strives to provide an evidence base to inform service provision and knowledge, policy and practice and to help improve the lives and needs of women (over 18 years) who sell or exchange sex. The ethical principles underpinning this research are also the core values of PAR: (1) inclusion: community co-researchers were included in the research in design/execution and delivery; (2) participation: peer led discussion/debate on all aspects of the process and 'what works' was central to the project, while regular team meetings and participatory training sessions were integral to the process; (3) valuing all voices: with peer researchers, we were able to include women and voices that were harder to reach by university researchers; and (4) community driven outcomes: we were all committed to social change that was of importance to and indeed driven by the communities taking part in the research.

There are clear risks and challenges to be aware of with participatory research and Cooke and Kothari (2001: 15) have named 'participation as the new tyranny to show that concepts reduced to buzz words can flip transformative practice into serving the interests of the powerful and maintain the status quo'. Participation takes time – it cannot simply be a short-term project – but the pressure to find funding for research is often predicated on developing new projects rather than developing old or current ones, and researchers on increasingly short-term contracts counter the need for time and a longer durée experience. The pressure and acceleration of academic life usually brings compressed time, lack of time for developing more relational research and a pressure to have 'impact' in research excellence terms. This is often without the necessary time to build relationships and build upon previous knowledge, experience and expertise.

This research is built upon a long history of relationships with sex worker support agencies in the region, as well as the authors' involvement in research, training and the development of a regional forum in collaboration with voluntary and statutory sector agencies (see www.neswf.co.uk).

Sex work and sex working

Historically, the 'prostitute' has been constructed in criminal justice frameworks as a female deviant and a law breaker. The policing of sex work has focused on and worked to criminalise women selling sex in public spaces. At the same time, female street sex workers have also disproportionally been the victims of serious and violent crime (Sanders et al, 2017 [2009]). This historical focus on public ('on street') female sex work has shaped contemporary understandings of the selling of sex and criminal justice policy or practice (O'Neill, 2001, 2010; Phoenix, 2009).

It is evident from a growing body of research that sex work exchanges involve a range of genders, sexualities, relationships, embodiments and practices (Smith and Laing, 2012; Laing et al, 2015). However, despite the move towards gender neutral language in recent legislation (for example, Policing and Crime Act, 2009) on prostitution and in police guidance (see NPCC, 2015), the focus of much law, policy and practice in the UK remains focused on women selling sex in heterosexual exchanges.

Current academic research also tells us that the selling of sex takes place in a range of social spaces, including public spaces ('on street'), private spaces ('off street') and increasingly through online platforms (Sanders et al, 2018). Despite this diversity, criminal justice agencies in the UK remain focused on the selling of sex in public spaces. The complexity of the lived experience of people selling sex has been neglected by the CJS – the focus remains on 'protecting communities' rather than the sex workers themselves, managing public space by promoting zero tolerance to 'on street' sex work and the regulation of 'off street' working (Phoenix, 1999, 2009; Scoular and O'Neill, 2007; O'Neill, 2010).

While the selling of sex is not illegal in England and Wales, many of the activities surrounding 'prostitution' are criminalised. Offences include soliciting or loitering in a public place to sell sex and 'brothel keeping'. The latter prevents two or more sex workers working together from one address for safety without breaking the law. Current law and legislation focuses on reducing the demand and supply of sexual services. Measures introduced in the Policing and Crime Act 2009 were influenced by a Home Office consultation in which all commercial sex was constructed as violence against women and girls ('Paying the Price'; Home Office, 2004). Through 'Paying the Price', activists lobbied for female sex workers to be understood as victims of violence and for a welfare approach to so-called desistance from selling sex. Notably absent from these consultations about sex work was a diversity of the voices and experiences of those selling sex themselves.

Scoular and O'Neill (2007) have described the outcome of this consultation as a form of 'enforced welfarism'. The current law works to fix the identity of women as the 'prostitute-victim'; a partial subject to be responsibilised to exit sex work, with limited agency or voice, excluded from certain forms of citizenship, and whose only socially acceptable 'moral' option is to exit sex work or be labelled as deviant or criminal (Scoular and O'Neill, 2007). On the current law, Carline and Scoular (2014) argue that:

> any attempt to address what may be harmful in prostitution is ultimately and inevitably distorted by a neo-abolitionist approach to sex work which universalizes a gendered paradigm, simplifies the causes of inequality and relies upon the criminal law to reduce the demand and supply of commercial sex, creating more harm as it does. (Carline and Scoular, 2014: 610)

Through the continued criminalisation of the selling of sex, we see the continued construction of women who sell sex as the morally deviant 'other'. Hence, 'deviant identities' become the basis of law reform rather than addressing structural and social factors that facilitate entry routes into sex work (O'Neill, 2010).

Much of the current criminal justice legislation and practice on the selling of sex is socially harmful in practice to those who sell sex. In this chapter, we argue that contemporary criminal justice frameworks on selling sex in England and Wales are engaged in 'crime' construction through public moral argument and social censure. The history of sex work is told through the lens of the social censure of sex work and sex workers. Evidence strongly suggests that violence against sex workers is endemic; the prevention of violence against women and men who sell sex is more likely to be achieved by the discontinuation of laws that criminalise sex work and sex workers. Further criminalisation of sex work or those who sell sex is not a viable solution to violence prevention (Sanders and Campbell, 2007; O'Neill and Jobe, 2016; Scoular, 2016; Sanders et al, 2018).

Through female sex workers' interviews with their peers, we examine the impact of current laws and regulation on their lives. Through the accounts of women selling sex in public spaces ('on street'), 'off street' and online, we explore how lives, experiences and identities are shaped by criminal law, policy and practice. In this analysis we found that the processes of criminalisation (sex workers as 'offenders') and victimisation (sex workers as 'victims') work to reinforce sex work stigma through processes of labelling, humiliation and circuits of exclusion (Rose, 2000).

Hidden stories: peer research with female sex workers

The research 'Peer talk: hidden stories' sought to provide an evidence base to inform service provision, knowledge, policy and practice in one region of the UK.[1] We set out with the following research aims:

1. What are the lived experiences and needs of women selling sex both on and off street, including their use and experience of services?
2. What are the experiences of key stakeholders providing services to sex workers?
3. What are the key issues highlighted by both sex workers and stakeholders?
4. To produce targeted information for local service providers, policymakers and key regulators in the region.

To contribute to research, academic and policy debates, we used a participatory peer-driven methodology that would enable us to build the research capacity of academic and practitioner partners for the longer term in the region. Key aims were to make a difference to women's lives and to move beyond what Hudson calls 'white man's justice', using a feminist criminological imagination (Carlen et al, 1985, 2010).

In this chapter, we focus on the first of these research questions: what are the lived experiences and needs of women selling sex both on and off street, including their use and experience of services? Women's accounts of selling sex highlight the diversity and complexity of lived experience and move beyond monolithic representations *of* women who sex work. Through this, we hope in this chapter to challenge current criminal justice frameworks, where both 'crime' and 'victimhood' are constructed through public moral argument and social censure. While research questions 2–4 were addressed in the original research (see O'Neill et al, 2017), they are not the focus of this chapter.

Twelve women completed participatory research training workshops with us. This included five current or former sex workers, five project workers and two project volunteers. At the first training session, we used creative methods to create a safe space for women to think about the research in

Figure 3.1: Creative methods to promote dialogue and imagination

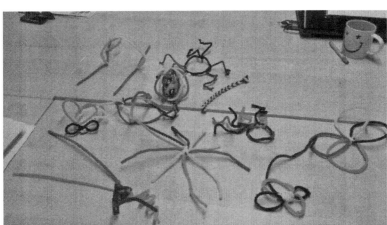

Images of the sculptures made by the women to show how they felt about being part of the research project.

a less intimidating way. Through creative methods, we invited women to explore how they felt about the research and to express what was important to them about participating in the project.

Throughout this creative exercise, community co-researchers communicated that it was important to develop partnership working, build bridges and work together with stakeholders to address the issues that they experienced. We discussed experiences of stigma, humiliation, violence and feeling trapped, as well as aspirations and hopes for the future. Working together, developing partnerships and being valued as a person was of central importance and meaning to the women.

The participant information sheet, consent form, topic guide and questionnaire were developed in collaboration with the community co-researchers and project workers. Community co-researchers then undertook nine interviews with escorts selling sex from flats and online; 17 interviews with women selling sex 'on street', or who had until recently worked selling sex. Twenty-one interviews were also undertaken with stakeholders.

In the next section we give an overview of some key themes from 26 peer-to-peer interviews and then present two women's accounts in depth.

Why sell sex?

'On street' sex workers described a range of contributing factors that led to their initial involvement in selling sex on the street. Some women were influenced by peers or described coercion by romantic partners. Drug addiction was a common feature of reasons for initially engaging in selling sex. Economic and social factors such as poverty, benefit sanctions, homelessness and police clampdowns on begging were also influencing factors.

As with the women's accounts in Carlen (1985), under certain conditions 'law breaking' and 'deviance' is a logical response to lived experiences and sexual and social inequalities. Women's accounts should be understood in the context of regional deprivation, government policies of austerity and cuts to social housing and welfare, the feminisation of poverty and lack of employment or training opportunities for women in the region.

In the first three accounts of *Criminal Women* (1985), there is evidence that 'crime' and activities labelled as deviant can be engaged in for success. Many of the 'off street' sex workers who participated in our study describe engaging in sex work to meet economic aspirations. Reflecting the aspirations of much of neo-liberal consumer society, 'off street' sex workers highlighted the economic benefits of sex working. They described sex work enabling them to buy a home and provide for their families, and that they were able to buy luxuries such as cars or holidays. Women also valued the flexibility of the work: being able to choose working hours; the job fitting in around childcare; and the job allowing a good work/life balance. Here, Caro describes her reasons for selling sex:[2]

'It is my choice, gives me independence, money, (I) can get on the property ladder, a car, can help family with the bills, and have the more luxury life afforded by money. I've been able to save to a certain extent ... Before I worked in retail and couldn't have afforded the life I have now unless I had a rich partner – this work gives me independence.' (Caro)

Encounters with criminal justice agencies

In this section, we explore participants' accounts of their interactions with criminal justice agencies. These experiences are framed by the current regulatory frameworks governing the selling of sex in England and Wales. Most women were aware of the laws on sex work, and this framed their sex working. Betsy describes becoming aware of the law after being cautioned for soliciting. When asked if she knew the laws on sex work, Betsy said:

'Not at first, but I soon realised – I actually got arrested for it but I just got a caution.' (Betsy)

Fifteen of women who described selling sex 'on street' said they had criminal convictions. The majority of the women's convictions were for acquisitive crime: shoplifting, theft, burglary, robbery, fraud and deception. Some were for 'violence' (two participants mentioned actual bodily harm, another stated grievous bodily harm), criminal damage, affray, drug offences, obstructing a police officer and soliciting and prostitution.

Most of the women selling sex 'on street' had had contact with the police in relation to their sex working and responses were mixed. Women described their encounters with officers from the 'vice' team who take a 'welfare-based' approach. They also had contact with routine patrol officers.

One woman who had an Anti-Social Behaviour Order for soliciting felt that she was targeted by police. She said: 'the police used to target me, one of the conditions was to not sit on my own doorstep!'

In another peer interview, Sian said:

'Police could be more supportive of working girls, they made me feel low and degraded. A bloke picked me up, would not pay me and tried to rape me. I got dumped in the middle of nowhere. The police would not help – they said "we're not a taxi service".' (Sian)

Women selling sex from private flats ('off street') or online describe fewer encounters with the police than women selling sex 'on street'. This is likely connected to the continued focus of policing on the management of selling of sex in public spaces. Women selling sex 'off street' described keeping their sex working secret, including from close family and friends. Katy said: 'It's like leading a secret life'. This maintenance of secrecy had implications where women were victims of violence, as the next section describes.

Reporting violence

The policing of sex work has seen an apparent shift, from categorising women selling sex on street as 'offenders' to viewing women selling sex principally as 'victims' within a 'welfarist approach'. The National Policing Sex Work Guidance sets out strategic key principles for policing as follows:

> Sex workers should not be approached as offenders per se but people who may become victims of crime for whom police services have a responsibility to protect ... The majority of sex workers are not committing any criminal offences but police have a role in their protection against any forms of violence exploitation and coercion. (NPCC, 2015: 6)

In our research, some women's accounts of contacting the police about violence contrast with this. 'On street' sex workers described multiple experiences of violence – when they reported this violence to the police, police responses were mixed. Working with other organisations to report an incident appeared to make a difference. In the following example, Fran described being attacked by a client and her experience of reporting this to the police:

> 'I thought they weren't going to believe me but [agency name] helped me through it. Some [police are] ok, some judge coz of prostitution.' (Fran)

In contrast, Rowena describes her experience with the police following being raped by a client. Her first negative experience with reporting to the police meant that she didn't report two subsequent rapes:

> 'I've been raped three times by clients, in the past because [the first time] I was raped, I contacted the police who took me to that place past [name of town] police station [SARC], did all the DNA gathering and as soon as they found out I was a working girl the police actually said the jury will laugh at you and the judge will tear you apart if this goes to court. Which made me obviously not pursue the charges. Because it's just ridiculous they just treat you like you're scum the police ...

because of the lack of support I got and I was belittled and made to feel stupid so I didn't report the other two.' (Rowena)

The continued criminalisation of sex work, and the stigma of selling sex, frames women's experiences of, or ability to, seek justice via the police or courts. Maisie was subject to an Anti-Social Behaviour Order and felt unable to contact the police over fears she would be arrested. She said: 'I daren't tell the police because of my ASBO, I'm scared I'll get arrested.'

In an ideal world, the women from our research wanted a police response to sex work that made their job safer. They stressed the need to be believed, that offences against them should be taken seriously and that an increase in prosecutions would help send a strong message that the police were taking crimes against them seriously. Specifically, they wanted to be protected by the law instead of targeted as criminals and they wanted to be listened to.

Women selling sex 'off street' described incidences of violence from clients and feeling uncomfortable to approach the police for help if they needed it. Sam describes a client hitting her and her hitting him back. Sam also describes feeling unsafe while on an 'out-call' and later finding out the client concerned had physically attacked other escorts previously. Pam describes a client who pushed her physical boundaries during 'rough sex' and Laura also describes encountering some aggressive clients.

Many of the interviewees were concerned about being exposed as an escort and the impact that speaking to the police might have on keeping their sex work secret from family and friends:

'It's such a secret world. I feel like I can't go to the police. I would ring my friend or ring the agency I'm working for and ask them what to do to or ask for help because it's so suppressed and demonised. It's really bad because at a time when you need help you feel like you can't ring somebody so then it's like I'm dobbing myself in so where do I go for help?' (Caro)

Impact of criminalisation and sex work stigma

Nine women selling sex 'off street' describe earning relatively large sums of money from their work as escorts. In practice, however, there were barriers to achieving the economic aspirations described earlier in the chapter due to the criminalisation and stigma of sex working.

Women describe difficulties in saving money they earn from working as an escort: as the money earned is cash in hand, it is difficult to put into the bank and pay tax on the money earned. Other women describe not being able to share money with family due to family not knowing that they sold sex and a fear that there would be questions about where the money had come from. Most women working 'off street' kept their sex working secret and hidden from their family and friends.

One woman described the precarious nature of sex work, the difficult choices women have to make to manage their earnings and the stigma associated with earning money from sex working. She talked about wanting to pay taxes but, because of the stigma associated with sex work, she believed she was at risk of possible blackmail by a third party. She said 'If you don't do this, I will tell, it makes you vulnerable, you are in a vulnerable position legally'.

Another woman told us about a friend who was the victim of a robbery. £3,000 was taken from her house and, because she was an escort, she felt she would not be taken seriously by the police.

'The compounded restrictions make your life irregular cos you do not feel like a normal person, you are not recognised as a business women and you are unable to access normal things people access, you can't spend more than 3k in cash otherwise the money laundering act comes into play. So many restrictions on having cash, you are forced into spending it so a lot of it gets wasted. Some women are generous with money and other people capitalise and so it does end up becoming a darker existence than it needs to be.' (Harriet)

Stigma and moral censure also impact on a woman's decision to access and be open with sexual health agencies.

'I went to a walk in [health centre] and as soon as I said I was a sex worker – I got passed from pillar to post. They made it so complicated. I got told you need counselling. I got told "you need help- you're not right" … It took 3 weeks for me just to get a full screening done because they would not drop it that I needed to go on these courses to clear my head and see what I was doing was wrong. And at first when I went in I didn't think I was doing anything wrong but after 2 weeks of someone telling you are doing something wrong you start to believe it.' (Jess)

Prison

In the interviews women talk mostly about the barriers they experience on leaving prison, the lack of support and access to housing and the need to help transition from prison back into communities. Five of the women working on street had been sentenced to prison, as well as one of the off street workers. It is clear from both interviews with sex workers and interviews with stakeholders that support on leaving prison is a major issue, reinforcing the fact that the aims of both the Women in Prison manifesto (Carlen et al, 1985) and the Corston Report (2007) have not been met. Women working on street recommended more support around housing on release from prison.

In the interviews, one woman talks about the humiliation of going to prison and being separated from her children because of an offence linked to drug dealing, an offence related to her relationship with her abusive ex-partner. Five participants described gaps in their drug use due to a prison sentence:

'I lost my family, work, I've been in prison, and people change their opinions of me.' (Erin)

These women wanted greater access to mental health and drug use support for women in prison and greater support into accommodation on leaving prison. These recommendations were reinforced in the stakeholder interviews. One stakeholder said that 'bricks and mortar' were not the problem, there was housing available, but rather how to give women the best start in independent living is currently lacking, even more so for women leaving prison who are not supported into accommodation.

Women's stories: walking and talking with Kath and Nina

In this section we include two women's stories, Kath and Nina. We begin with Kath who was involved in selling sex 'on street' when we met her. One way of understanding the geography of street sex work and how the spaces of street sex work might impact on the lives of women selling sex is to map the relevant spaces and places and walk with sex workers living and working there (O'Neill et al, 2017; O'Neill and Roberts, 2019; Sanders-McDonagh and Peyrefitte, 2018). In our research we were also interested in gaining an understanding of where services providing support to women are located and how women experienced these services. Kath created a map of the spaces and places that are important in her everyday life, including the services she used and where she worked. We asked Kath to talk us through an everyday route she might take from home or from a local sex worker support agency. We then walked with Kath along her route map.

From walking with Kath, we got a sense of the area being small. Everyone knows everyone. In such a small geographical area, being seen with researchers might be a problem. Kath began to get uneasy as we walked further along the route and seemed worried that she might be taken to be a 'snitch'. Along the walk Kath told us how she got to know about the sex work support organisation, and how she began selling sex.

Kath's story

Kath was a trainee manager at a food outlet and moved in with her boyfriend. Her relationship broke down and meanwhile her Mum had downsized and there was no possibility of moving back home. Kath tried to get support from the local authority housing department and was told that, because she had a job, she had to pay for her bed and breakfast. Kath was told she would only get support if she was unemployed. Meanwhile, her Mum gave her some space to stay until she got herself sorted. Kath then gave her job up in order to get support with accommodation and was placed in a local hostel.

At the hostel, Kath made friends with a woman who was working selling sex and, as Kath had no money, she saw this as a way of making some. During a peer interview, Kath said:

'I had to quit my job, housing benefit said they couldn't put me in a hostel if I was working and I was only working part time so I couldn't afford a flat on my own so I quit my job where they put me was in the middle of people who were using drugs so I ended up having a worser [sic] habit, I ended up working on the streets … I ended up starting (selling sex) because I'd been put in a hostel and I had to quit my job so because I quit my job I couldn't get any dole money. So the council told me to quit my job but the dole wouldn't give me any money so there was a girl working in my building so I worked with her, started going out with her to get money for food and things. Main reason was drugs really, and money for food and stuff. (And) Rent.'

Kath's involvement in selling sex was impacted by changes in the benefit rules and the circumstances surrounding her placement in hostel accommodation. She describes the impact of being homeless and placed in a hostel with people using drugs as the reason she 'ended up working and with a drug habit'.

At the time of the interview, Kath had no partner. She has two children: she had the first when she was 16 and only sees one of her children. Kath has lived in supported housing for eight months with four other women. Kath has used drugs since she was 17 and went into rehab at 23 – after this, she 'was clean for two years'. Kath uses 'crack, cocaine and benzos'.

Kath has worked for three years in sex work, starting at the age of 26. Kath describes drugs, food and rent as instrumental in her sex working. Money is crucial – the least she has charged for sexual services is £20 and the most is £200. The main problem she describes facing is that clients 'do not want to pay or want to pay a lower price'. A good client, she describes, is someone who 'pays, doesn't talk and is fast'. A bad client 'does not pay, negotiates the price, wants extras for free and won't let you go when you have had enough'. Kath doesn't always use condoms, if the clients are regular or if she 'thinks they are alright'.

Kath speaks about the violence and abuse she has encountered when selling sex and the precautions she takes to protect herself:

'Always get verbal abuse. Been punched, punched in the head, grabbed and robbed. Didn't report it [to the police] – didn't see the point.'

'I feel safe knowing there are cameras on the street … [in relation to precautions] I've carried blades in my sock, took needles out with me in my bag, always have phone with me to dial 999 … I have an alarm, like a rape alarm.'

Kath indicates in her interview that she has little faith in the police. She says:

'Police just made me feel worthless … as soon as you say to the police that you're a working girl and it was a punter they don't they won't even look into it they just like. And that works both ways as well, like if I'd been attacked or raped off a punter or if a girl attacks or robs them, either way the police just won't touch it, don't want to get involved.'

However, Kath does describe one positive experience with the police where they helped her when a client refused to pay:

'I did a service for someone and he wouldn't pay me so I phoned the police and they took me home and then they took the man round all his friends and family to get me the money and they made him get out of the van and walk over and give me the money because he admitted to it. So … they were nice in that one.'

Kath is accessing drug treatment support, has 'cut my using right down' and is accessing methadone support. However, she sometimes misses her appointments if she ends up working all night and needs to sleep during the day. Kath says she has told her drugs worker she sells sex but 'could not talk about the ins and outs especially because he is male'. She says she might feel happier with a female worker and that she is sometimes scared to go (because of anxiety) to the drugs service and would like it if they could come to her at the hostel.

Kath had suggestions regarding how sex work could be safer. She would like more information about the law:

'what you are allowed to do and what you are not. If there was a place I could go and it was monitored … like a certain area to work in and more police checks in the area to check the girls are alright.'

Kath told us she was keen to exit sex work and to continue with her education. Here Kath describes the difficulty of exiting sex work when living and working in a small area that clients regularly frequent:

'Sometimes I'd get phone calls off punters so that would trigger me off to go back working, or I'd relapse and end up having to go back out to work.'

Kath told us about her aspirations for the future:

'[I'll be] hopefully in my own home, drug free and not working.'

Kath wants to train as a counsellor and gain qualifications in counselling.

At the launch event for the project, Kath spoke about her experiences of being involved in the research as a community researcher, that she had exited sex work and had begun her counselling training with the support of a local support agency.

Nina's story

This is Nina's story, who in a peer interview described selling sex from private 'off street' flats. Nina says that she didn't finish her education and left school at 15. She said she 'would go back if she wanted to do anything'. Nina is a single parent, is divorced and her family lives nearby.

She describes herself as 'a bit of recluse, due to circumstances'. She 'has not found people she trusts' and has a small number of friends.

Nina lives in private rented accommodation and her landlord is not aware of her work. She had experienced homeless as a teenager: 'my Mam threw me out numerous times, have never been homeless since then'.

Nina describes her marriage as a 'ten-year roller coaster ride'; it was a 'stormy relationship'. She went to prison for 18 months because of her involvement in her husband selling drugs. The marriage was violent, he was involved in gangs and when she went to prison, she lost her house. She describes feeling very bad for her children, but her mam looked after them during this time:

'I went to prison while we were married. I got 18 months for drugs. He was going round taxing people and he was in a gang and no one could do anything about it and I was roped into it. It was my wake up call. The hardest thing was my kids and I compensated by giving them stuff.'

Nina sought support for anxiety and depression from her GP, but she felt she needed more help, so she self-referred herself to a mental health charity.

'Instead of being on tablets anti-depressants they talk and it helps you to get to the root. Then you can put back into it. I volunteered in self-help groups.'

It was important to Nina that she 'put back in' the work supporting other people and groups, given the support she had received.

Nina has had 'no involvement with probation and social services' and she has not had a problem with health services, although she does go to a sexual health service out of area to avoid being seen, very keenly feeling the stigma related to sex work. It is a big issue for her. Nina says she is 'not honest about my job and don't disclose, I would feel judged'. When visiting health services, for example, 'I make things up, I prepare a script as to what I will say, I pretend my boyfriend has been sleeping about. You have to lie I cannot be open with services about sex work.'

Nina says that she:

'would like to be able to be open at sexual health services and not feel like I am judged. I go out of town, as people might know me locally. I have a GP but would not ask them for an STD check. It's the stigma that comes with it and people just don't understand.'

'I work off street, it is the best way to work and I keep home and work separate. I work incalls, between 9 and 7 men come to me in a flat I use. I have done outcalls but prefer incalls. I did an outcall and the family came round and I was stuck in the house hiding upstairs.'

In relation to violence, Nina says, 'nothing bad has happened to me. If you work later than seven the risks increase'. Nina describes working 'on and off for 2 years' following a conversation with a woman, selling skin products, about debt problems:

'She said she had sold sex and she gave me a number and I rang up and then panicked and backed out and then another month I had to and they sent someone out to interview me and take some photos. I didn't sleep all weekend. First day, first three clients I was fine. I liked being in control and having the money. My kids needed money. In my head I didn't know what it was going to be like, I imagined it was going to be awful and it wasn't, and I am actually quite good. I have a plan I should be able to have a comfortable old age.'

Nina describes typical clients as being different ages: young, middle age and older 'business men, taxi drivers, manual workers, middle management'.

'They tell me loads, build relationships it isn't just about sex. A bad client is a needy client. I like to see my regulars, it's not always about the sex. They say I look forward to coming to see you once per week – share the pressures, offload, if kids are going off the rails.'

Nina describes feeling safe at work, working within set times and:

'in my own environment, they are coming into my space. I have the confidence to say, if they are out of order, I feel put them back in their place. I feel that I adapt to different personalities I am good at managing "incidents". If I was assaulted I wouldn't ring the police. I deal with my own stuff.'

Nina understands the law but would like to know more. 'I would like more information about the way the law works'.

Nina described her hopes for the future:

'I would like some holiday lets, I want to buy 2 apartments and do as holiday lets and then get more. So when I am a bit older. This is my pension. Once they are up and running, I will just do the change overs. This is my business plan.'

Conclusion

The sale of sex is associated in law and the public imagination with moral deviance. Regulation takes place through enforcement of laws and, in the process, a particular ideology is reproduced and sex workers are excluded in many ways from access to social justice. Exclusionary discourses of victimhood and rehabilitation, rooted in deviancy and a social censure model of regulating sex work structured by capitalism, commodification, sexuality and sexual relations, are instrumental in limiting women's access to social justice.

Through peer interviews with women who sell or have sold sex, we have explored their life trajectories using participatory methods, and find that their narratives are indeed 'vivid chronicles of the times' in which they live (Carlen et al, 1985). Such narratives are evidence that the law and constructions of 'crime' and 'victimhood' have social consequences.

None of the women interviewed who worked 'off street' had contacted the police in relation to a violent client, and the majority stated they wouldn't feel comfortable approaching the police for help if they needed it, out of embarrassment at being identified and questioned about their work. Women described the precarious nature of sex work and the difficult choices women have to make to manage their earnings, as well as the stigma associated with earning money from sex working.

All but one of the women who worked 'on street' had previously been homeless and spoke about the 'horrible' experience they had being homeless and the impact it had on them. Drug addiction was also a common feature for many. Violence was a common experience on street – many women had experienced high levels of violence including rape, assault and robbery. Overwhelmingly, the women described feeling judged by support services, especially the police and Social Services but other services too, in a way that impacted upon them accessing healthcare and other support.

These accounts lead us to ask the question: should the selling of sex feature in criminal law at all? Women's accounts suggest that the issues to be addressed are poverty, availability of work, the benefits system, homelessness, equal access to healthcare and stigma and violence against those who sell sex. This and other research reinforces time and time again that regulating sex work through criminal justice processes has a profoundly dangerous impact on sex workers' lives. Lowman's (2000) enduring argument is that long-term criminalisation of sex workers plays a key role in the continuum of violence committed against them, in what he describes as 'deadly inertia'.

A key recommendation from the research was to address the safety of sex workers as a priority (O'Neill et al, 2017). The research recommended that local strategies were needed to improve routes to reporting violence for sex workers and the development of a regional strategy to action this. Peer researchers and the women they interviewed suggested that non-judgemental support from local services was imperative, including support on release from prison. Local service providers participated in dissemination events that focused on thinking through how recommendations could be actioned and how local service provision could be improved. The research also built upon and developed existing relationships with local service providers via a regional forum. The participatory process is ongoing.

Finally, as Carlen et al argued in 1985, women's accounts of their own lives can work to challenge the deeply-embedded sexual and social inequalities in society; inequalities that are evident in the criminal law construction of criminality, deviance and victimhood that currently govern the selling of sex in England and Wales. Conducting participatory research with sex workers is important to seek transformative change, challenge inequalities and promote social justice. Participatory research methodologies, including visual and biographical work, can serve not only to raise awareness and challenge stereotypes and hegemonic practices, but to produce critical texts and images that may mobilise change. In this chapter, we hope to have reinforced the importance of biographical/autobiographical research pioneered by Carlen et al (1985). Moreover, we have demonstrated that doing research in participatory ways can create a better understanding of their experiences of the CJS, inform and improve service provision and challenge outdated norms of 'justice' by promoting feminist analysis and praxis as a feminist criminological imagination.

Notes

[1] This research was authored by Maggie O'Neill, Alison Jobe, Colleen Bilton, Kelly Stockdale, Kath, Hannah and community co-researchers.
[2] The names used here are pseudonyms.

References

Ahearne, G. (2016) 'Paying the price: sex workers in prison and the reality of stigma', *Prison Services Journal*, 223: 24–30.

Andrews, M., Squire C. and Tamboukou, M. (2008) *Doing Narrative Research*, London: Sage.

Cain, M. (1990) 'Towards transgression: new directions in feminist criminology', *International Journal of the Sociology of Law*, 18(1): 1–18.

Carlen, P. (1992) 'Criminal women and criminal justice', in Muncie, J. McLaughlin, E. and Langan, M. (eds) *Criminological Perspectives: A Reader*, London: Sage, pp 475–83.

Carlen, P. (2010) *A Criminological Imagination. Essays on Justice, Punishment, Discourse*, London: Taylor & Francis.

Carlen, P., Hicks, J., O 'Dwyer, J., Christina, D. and Tchaikovsky, C. (1985) *Criminal Women*, Cambridge: Polity.

Carline, A. and Scoular, J. (2014) 'Saving fallen women now? Critical perspectives on engagement and support orders and their policy of forced welfarism', *Social Policy & Society*, 14(1): 103–12.

Chesney-Lind, M. (1992) *The Female Offender: Girls, Women and Crime*, London: Sage.

Cooke, B. and Kothari, U. (2001) *Participation: The New Tyranny?*, London: Zed Books.

Corston, J. (2007) *The Corston Report: a review of women with particular vulnerabilities in the criminal justice system*, London: Home Office.

Davis, A. (2003) *Are Prisons Obsolete?*, New York: Seven Stories Press.

Fals Borda, O. (1983) *Knowledge and People's Power: Lessons with Peasants in Nicaragua, Mexico and Colombia*, New York: New Horizons Press.

Fischer, W. (2011) *Biographical reconstruction as applied knowledge or professional competence?* Paper presented at the mid-term conference of the Biographical Perspectives on European Societies, Research Network 03 of the European Sociological Association, Nuremberg, Germany.

Gelsthorpe, L. (1990) *Feminist Perspectives in Criminology*, London: Oxford University Press.

Heidensohn, F. (1985) *Women and Crime*, London: Macmillan.

Home Office (2004) 'Paying the Price: a consultation paper on prostitution', Available at: http://news.bbc.co.uk/nol/shared/bsp/hi/pdfs/16_07_04_paying.pdf [Accessed 22 September 2021].

Hudson, B. (2006) 'Beyond white man's justice: race, gender and justice in late modernity', *Theoretical Criminology*, 10(1): 29–47.

Laing, M., Pitcher, K. and Smith, N. (eds) (2015) *Queer Sex Work*, London: Taylor & Francis.

Lowman, J. (2000) 'Violence and the outlaw status of (street) prostitution in Canada', *Violence Against Women*, 6(9): 987–1011.

Mills, C. W. (2000) *The Sociological Imagination*, Oxford: Oxford University Press.

NPCC (The National Police Chiefs' Council) (2015) National policing sex work guidance. Available at: https://library.college.police.uk/docs/appref/Sex-Work-and-Prostitution-Guidance-Jan-2019.pdf [Accessed 1 November 2021].

Nurse, L. and O'Neill, M. (2018) 'Biographical research in the UK: profiles and perspectives', in H. Lutz, M. Schiebel, E. Tuider (eds) Wiesbaden: Springer VS. https://doi.org/10.1007/978-3-658-21831-7_59

O'Neill, M. (2001) *Prostitution and Feminism: Towards a Politics of Feeling*, Cambridge: Polity Press.

O'Neill, M. (2010) 'Cultural criminology and sex work: resisting regulation through radical democracy and participatory action research (PAR)', *Journal of Law and Society*, 37(1): 210–32.

O'Neill, M. and Jobe, A. (2016) 'Policy briefing: adult sex work, law and policy: new horizons in the 21st century', *Discover Society*, Issue 39 (December).

O'Neill, M., Jobe, A., Bilton, C., Stockdale, K., Kath, Hannah and community co-researchers (2017) *Peer talk: hidden stories. A participatory research project with women who sell or swap sex in Teesside*, Stockton-on-Tees: A Way Out. Available at: http://dro.dur.ac.uk/22993/1/22993.pdf

O'Neill, M., Roberts, B. and Sparkes, A. C. (eds) (2014) *Advances in Biographical Methods: Creative Applications*, London: Routledge.

O'Neill, M. and Roberts, B. (2019) *Walking Methods: Research on the Move*, London: Routledge.

Phoenix, J. (1999) *Making Sense of Prostitution*, London: Macmillan.

Phoenix, J. (2009) *Regulating Sex for Sale: Prostitution, Policy Reform in the UK*, Bristol: Policy Press.

Policing and Crime Act (2009) Available at: https://www.legislation.gov.uk/ukpga/2009/26/pdfs/ukpga_20090026_en.pdf [Accessed 20 September 2021].

Rose, N. (2000) 'Government and control', *The British Journal of Criminology*, 40(2): 321–39, Available at: http://www.jstor.org/stable/23638480 [Accessed 22 September 2021].

Sanders, T. and Campbell, R. (2007) 'Designing our vulnerability, building in respect: violence, safety and sex work policy', *The British Journal of Sociology*, 58(1): 1–19.

Sanders, T., O'Neill, M. and Pitcher, J. (2017 [2009]) *Prostitution: Sex Work, Policy and Politics*, London: Sage.

Sanders, T., Scoular, J., Campbell, R., Pitcher, R. and Cunningham, S. (2018) *Internet Sex Work: Beyond the Gaze*, London: Palgrave Macmillan.

Sanders-McDonagh, E. and Peyrefitte, M. (2018) 'Immoral geographies and Soho's sex shops: exploring spaces of sexual diversity in London', *Gender, Place and Culture*, 25(3): 351–67.

Scoular, J. (2016) *The Subject of Prostitution: Sex Work, Law and Social Theory*, London: Routledge.

Scoular, J. and O'Neill, M. (2007) 'Regulating prostitution: social inclusion, responsibilization and the politics of politics of prostitution reform', *British Journal of Criminology*, 47(5): 764–78.

Seal, L. and O'Neill, M. (2019) *Imaginative Criminology – Of Spaces Past, Present and Future*, Bristol: Policy Press.

Smart, C. (1977) *Women Crime and Criminology*, London: Routledge.

Smart, C. (1990) 'Feminist approaches to criminology', in: L. Gelsthorpe and, A. Morris (eds) *Feminist perspectives in criminology*, Milton Keynes: Open University Press, pp 70–84.

Smith, N. and Laing, M. (2012) 'Introduction: working outside the (hetero) norm? lesbian, gay, bisexual, transgender and queer (LGBTQ) sex work', *Sexualities*, 15(5/6): 517–20.

Walklate, S. (1998) *Understanding Criminology*, Buckingham: Open University Press.

4

Criminal Women in Prison Who Self-harm: What Can We Learn from Their Experiences?

Tammi Walker

In England and Wales, women in prison make up a minority of the total custodial population yet acts of self-harm are around five times more common among incarcerated women. Policymakers have introduced suicide prevention programmes in prisons (HM Prison Service, 2001) and, while there has been a multiagency effort to improve how acts of self-harm are documented across prisons, the accounts of *why* women in prison self-harm is yet to be fully addressed. This chapter will explore the motivations associated with self-harm for imprisoned women and what we can learn from their experiences. Drawing on the voices of women, the chapter will provide insight into the *intra-personal* and/or *inter-personal* motivations for self-harming in prison. The chapter will finish with a reflection of what has stayed the same and what has changed since Carlen et al's (1985) original book in relation to self-harm.

Background

Self-harm is a challenge for the criminal justice system (CJS) due to its associations with physical injury, psychology co-morbidity and increased lifetime suicide risk (Hawton et al, 2013). The conceptualisation and definition of what has been characterised as 'self-harm' remains problematic. A number of different terms and definitions are used in research, policy and practice spheres. Terms such as 'attempted suicide', 'self-injury', 'deliberate self-injury', 'self-mutilation', 'suicidal gesture', 'abortive suicide', 'self-inflicted violence' and 'para-suicide' are used interchangeably. Walker and Towl (2016) note how issues of confusion continue to remain by the use of multiple definitions. It is clear, though, that individuals may self-harm either with or without any intention to kill themselves. The differing terminology used in literature can lead to difficulties in making comparisons across studies (Walker and Towl, 2016).

Her Majesty's Prison and Probation Service (HMPPS) (as stated in PSI 64/2011) defines self-harm as 'any act where a prisoner deliberately harms themselves irrespective of the method, intent or severity of any injury' (HM Prison Service, 2001). This can include self-harm by cutting, scratching, head-banging, punching a wall, self-poisoning, fire setting, suffocation, swallowing and/or insertion of objects and wound aggravation. This definition focuses on the behaviour itself rather than on what the individual intended to achieve by engaging in it. When attempting to gather accurate statistics on self-harm, in both prison and community samples, the methods have been criticised due to difficulties in identifying and classifying what behaviours are 'self-harming and when self-harm is different from a suicide attempt' (Powis, 2002). Further, the motivations for engaging in self-harming behaviours are very complex, and individuals who have no experience of self-harm may find it an intensely confusing behaviour (Walker and Towl, 2016).

Self-harm and imprisoned women

There are 12 prisons in England and Wales run by HMPPS which imprison women. Two of the twelve operate as 'open' prisons: Askham Grange near York and East Sutton Park in Kent. Women make up around 5 per cent of the overall prison population in the United Kingdom (Prison Reform Trust, 2018), and over the last two decades there has been a marked increase in the number of imprisoned women. The number of women imprisoned more than doubled between 1995 and 2010, from 1,979 to 4,236, and has since remained at around 4,000 (Women in Prison, 2019).

Some critics have referred to this as the 'new punitiveness', which has played a role in an increased number of incidents of self-harm and self-inflicted deaths in prisons by virtue of such increases in overall prisoner numbers (Towl and Walker, 2015). Such changes are more than structural, they are cultural too. Not only are there more women in prison, but they are more likely to be viewed largely in terms of their convictions than to be viewed in a more rounded way as citizens with a range of aspects and needs. This is all part of the 'new punitiveness' (Towl and Walker, 2015). Historically, one challenge has been to ensure that services for women are not simply modelled on those for the gender-based majority but rather take account of sometimes differing gender-based needs.

Data provided by the Ministry of Justice demonstrated in 2019 that women in prison had significantly higher documented rates of self-harm than men – 2,244 incidents per 1,000 women versus 467 per 1,000 men (Ministry of Justice, 2019). Despite women making up a minority of the total custodial population, the prevalence of self-harm has been estimated to be five times higher in female prison estates. Studies of self-harm in prison populations are limited, and until 1997 the focus for reporting self-harm incidents in the prison population was on 'attempted suicide', despite prisoner intent being frequently unknown (Ministry of Justice, 2013). Some incidents were more likely to be fatal than others, but the point at which a self-harm incident became an attempted suicide was unclear. From 1997, all self-harm incidents had to be reported, and this led to an increase in reported incidents in the prison population. However, the Ministry of Justice have now omitted self-harm statistics before 2004 from publications because they were considerably underreported compared with current standards.

Since 2004, prisons in England and Wales have used the Assessment, Care in Custody and Teamwork (ACCT) procedure. This process was intended to be a prisoner-centered, proactive, flexible care-planning arrangement that promotes the intensive case management of high-risk individuals (HM Prison Service, 2001). Over the years, the ACCT scheme has been subject to a number of evaluations (Rickford and Edgar, 2005; Humber et al, 2011; Harris, 2015). Logan and Taylor (2019) argue that, in general, the ACCT procedure appears to be a useful way of managing the risk of self-harm and suicide. However, the implementation of the ACCT procedure is not thought to be complete in all cases (not everyone at risk is on an ACCT, and the majority of people who commit suicide are not subject to any interventions for at-risk prisoners) or effective enough in some (Rickford and Edgar, 2005; Marzano et al, 2011; Pratt, 2016).

Methods of self-harm are heterogeneous. Hawton et al (2013) found in their analysis of prisons in England and Wales between 2004 and 2009 that the most common methods of self-harm for both sexes are cutting and scratching; for imprisoned women, the next most frequent method used is self-strangulation. Other methods of self-harm include impact injury, wound aggravation, ligature, suffocation and biting. The use of ligature has been an area of concern across the wider prison estate among in-prison suicides due to its associated high rate of lethality and availability of ligature points within prison design (Marzano et al, 2016).

A suggested reason for why women in prison are thought to be particularly at risk of self-harm is because many of them are vulnerable and disempowered *before* they were imprisoned; it has been proposed that being in custody compounds this vulnerability and disempowers women further (McKenzie et al, 2003; Harris, 2015; Logan and Taylor, 2019). The majority of women in prison have extensive traumatic victimisation histories, including childhood abuse, intimate partner violence and violence from non–intimates and carers (Walker and Towl, 2016). Women in prison are far more likely to have experienced sexual and domestic violence than the general female population: evidence indicates that between 50 per cent and 80 per cent of imprisoned women have experienced domestic and/or sexual abuse (Corston, 2007; Walker and Towl, 2016). Moreover, the rates of women in prison with sexual victimisation histories far exceed those of women in the general community (Walker and Towl, 2016). Imprisoned women often describe episodes of *poly-victimisation* (multiple trauma) throughout their life, including chronic and severe abuse. Many women in prison are therefore victims as well as perpetrators.

Logan and Taylor (2019) illustrate that women entering prison are more likely than men to be separated from those for whom they have a primary caregiving role (for example, their children), resulting in their dependents being put into care and future contact being jeopardised (for example, Corston, 2007). Remand status, substance withdrawal, prior incarceration, single cell accommodation, poor social support and negative experiences of imprisonment (for example, bullying) have been found to be particularly relevant risk factors for women (see Marzano et al, 2011; Walker and Towl, 2016). Long-term vulnerabilities are often cited as primary reasons for self-harming, whereas prison-related variables (such as transfers, or fear of bullying or violence) are commonly described as proximal or triggering factors.

There is limited research to contextualise factors underpinning the disproportionate rate of self-harm among female prisoners. Kenning et al (2010) found that imprisoned women described incidents of self-harm as impulsive and unstoppable acts related to intense feelings of anger, hurt and frustration, over which they had little or no control. Marzano et al (2010) described the association between the role of psychiatric co-morbidity, namely depressive disorder, and past episodes of near-lethal self-harm. Such research is significant as it addresses near-lethal self-harm as a distinct entity, delineating these acts from what would be historically generalised as attempted suicide or parasuicide (McHugh and Towl, 1997). Further, large-scale research is necessary to contextualise the role of suicidal thoughts as precursors to self-harm in this area (Kidger et al, 2019). Additionally, an understanding of motivations and context preceding acts of self-harm among this group is important in the delivery of effective interventions.

The Women Offenders Repeat Self-Harm Intervention Pilot II (WORSHIP II) attempted to understand these acts of self-harm (Walker et al, 2017). This study will now be discussed and will then be followed by an exploration of the research that has been undertaken to highlight the *intra-personal* and/or *inter-personal* motivations for self-harming by women in prison.

Women Offenders Repeat Self-Harm Intervention Pilot II (WORSHIP II)

WORSHIP II was a pilot randomised control trial conducted in three closed female prisons in England and Wales between 2012 and 2015 (Abel et al, 2015). The study was piloting the use of Psychodynamic Interpersonal Therapy (PIT) as a potential therapeutic intervention for reducing repetitive self-harm. Female prisoners (*n 113*) included in the study were randomised into two groups and offered four to eight PIT sessions or four sessions of active control (AC) over 20 months, involving emotionally neutral activities in which talk about emotive topics and self-harm were specifically avoided. Of the 113 women in prison who took part in the WORSHIP II, 108 (95 per cent) had completed ≥50 per cent of the structured interview in association with a trial investigator. The interview detailed patterns, methods, functions, triggers and the intended lethality of self-harm that women in prison engage in across prison and community settings. Content drew upon the Deliberate Self-Harm Inventory by Gratz (2001), a literature review, and included open questions so descriptions of self-harm were recorded in the participants' own words. Qualitative data, such as accounts of participants describing the functions of self-harm and the triggers and emotions that lead to it, were analysed using a thematic analysis framework (Braun and Clarke, 2006). Before attention is given to the motivations behinds the acts of self-harm by imprisoned women, this chapter will provide information about the sample in this part of the WORSHIP II study (Walker et al, 2021).

The average age of women in the WORSHIP II sample was 29, 92 per cent self-identified as white, 61 per cent were single and 58 per cent received visits from family or friends at the time of the study. Over half had children and, at the time of the interview, over half had been sentenced. A high number of women experienced domestic violence, had past contact with mental health services, past experiences of sexual abuse as a child and substance dependence (Abel et al, 2015).

When discussing their accounts of self-harm, most women (99 per cent) reported self-harming both while in and out of prison. The first episode of out-of-prison self-harm started at a mean age of 14 years, whereas the age at which the first episode occurred while in prison was 26 years. The women voiced the types of self-harm they had previously undertaken across both environments – references to cutting and sharp trauma were the most frequently recorded categories across both settings.

On recent acts of self-harm occurring over the past month, 74 per cent reported cutting and 22 per cent attempted ligature. Many women undertook self-harm while on their own in prison and medical attention was sought in only 59 per cent of cases; however, this was mostly limited to superficial wound cleansing rather than injury requiring hospitalisation

(Abel et al, 2015). Attention will now be given to work that has explored the psychological functions of self-harm by women in prison, both within the WORSHIP II study and other research.

Psychological functions of self-harm

Though occurrences of self-harm for women in prison may appear similar in nature, the act of self-harm may serve an array of distinct purposes and functions for the individual (Jeglic et al, 2005; Walker et al, 2021). When discussing the psychological functions of self-harm, this may be seen as the result of *intrapersonal* and/or *interpersonal* reinforcement that can be characterised as being either positively or negatively reinforcing (Nock and Prinstein, 2004). However, it must be noted that self-harming behaviour may serve a number of different functions at any given time (Suyemoto, 1998; Walker and Towl, 2016). Thus, a range of unmet needs may be met through an act of self-harm.

Intrapersonal functions

Intrapersonal functions refer to the role that emotions play within each of us on an individual level. When this has been explored across a variety of community settings with women who have not offended, it has been found that those who engage in self-harming behaviours often voice that the main function it serves is to relieve feelings of *unwanted emotions* and to gain emotional control (Briere and Gil, 1998; Nock and Prinstein, 2004). In particular, the feeling of anger has been found to precipitate self-harm (Herpertz et al, 1997; Brown et al, 2002).

With regard to the limited research that has been undertaken within criminal justice contexts, the findings reveal an emotional regulatory function of self-harm for imprisoned women. Negative emotions have been often found to precipitate self-harm, in particular, anger or aggression in custodial settings; 72 per cent of self-harming women and adolescent girls in prison presented with anger within 24 hours prior to their self-harm incident (Snow, 2002). Further work has examined the antecedents of self-harm compared with suicide attempts, and it was concluded that negative feelings such as anger might trigger self-harm, whereas life stressors preceded suicide attempts (Snow, 2002; Miller and Fritzon, 2007). Imprisoned women and adolescent girls have also stated that anger is an emotion they feel prior to engaging in self-harm (Chapman and Dixon-Gordon, 2007).

In the WORSHIP II study, women were asked: 'What emotions do you manage by self-harming?' Common emotions identified by the women were anger, sadness and frustration. Emotions also played a vital role for imprisoned women when discussing the functions ('What does self-harm do for you?') and often described self-harm as a means of providing release or relief from emotions such as anger, frustration and stress. These emotions were often thinking about or disclosing their high levels of trauma, past experiences of domestic violence, childhood sexual abuse and adult sexual abuse. Other qualitative studies with women prisoners supports the notion that self-harming helps them to attain positive emotional relief (Kenning et al, 2010). Forensic learning-disabled service users also described relief from unwelcome emotions as the primary reason for self-harm (Duperouzel and Fish, 2010).

For women in custody, self-punishment as a function of self-harm has also been reported. Out of a sample of 50 imprisoned women and adolescent girls, 15 suggested that self-harm was a way of self-punishing (Miller and Fritzon, 2007). Lastly, shame is another emotion linked to self-harm. In a sample of 89 imprisoned women and adolescent girls who engaged in self-harm, over half identified shame as being a precipitating element (Milligan and Andrews, 2005). It would seem that many commentators maintain that the increased rate of self-harm among imprisoned women acts as a means of emotional regulation, but it is less clear *why* self-harm is used rather than another technique or strategy to escape aversive feelings. Attention also needs to be given to the interpersonal features of self-harm for imprisoned women.

Interpersonal functions

Interpersonal functions involve individual motives that aim at influencing the external environment. In the past, self-harm within criminal justice settings has been pejoratively referred to as 'manipulative'. It has been argued that self-harm functions to attract attention, have an impact on the environment or achieve some other goal that could be considered as manipulative (Dear et al, 2000). Numerous studies support this view (Pattison and Kahan, 1983; Franklin, 1988; DeHart et al, 2009), however, these studies used non-traditional means for operationalizing 'manipulative' motives, such as if participants noted any reason for self-harm other than suicide (Franklin, 1988). From the limited work that has been undertaken with women in prison, it may be argued that, despite this methodological issue, there may well be some value to the concept that imprisoned women use self-harm for more interpersonal, relational and communicative functions, compared with individuals in the community. However, this does not serve to legitimate the use of pejorative nomenclature such as the attribution that an individual is 'manipulative'.

In an early study conducted with 81 imprisoned women and adolescent girls, emotional relief and escape were the most common reasons for self-harm, however, 'manipulation' was recorded as the third most common reason for a recent incident of self-harm (Dear et al, 2000). Readers may wish to consider whether this reflects more on the women and adolescent girls themselves or the staff writing such records. More indirectly, in a later study sample of 50 forensic mental health women service users, 26 per cent were categorized as having made threats and 28 per cent expressed a desire to transfer to another facility or another related environmental change just prior to their incident of self-harm, suggesting some communicative intent (Miller and Fritzon, 2007).

Imprisoned women in the WORSHIP II study discussed the triggers to their recent self-harm and expressed that conflict with others (for example, due to arguments or being falsely accused) were the most common cause (Walker et al, 2021):

'To blank out memories and get rid of frustration and anger I get from officers treating me like I'm a piece of sXXX. I want to remain polite and not get any negative IEPS [Incentives and Earned Privileges Scheme] in prison but it's hard when you're not respectful, so I got back to my room and self-harm, so I don't explode in front of them.' (02105)

This was followed by intrusive voices, thoughts and feelings provoking self-harm that was, at times, described as a result of command hallucinations:

'Recently, self-harm has turned into suicide attempts because I'm struggling with hearing negative voices.' (03079)

'Release of pressure caused by voices.' (01083)

Participants also voiced that issues to do with children, in relation to memories, custody and distance, were key triggers to self-harm:

'Kids – maybe going to lose them, they won't talk to me.' (01020)

'Worrying about children. No birthday card off children … realising I've lost the kids.' (01041)

It would seem from these studies that rows, difficulties in relationships, problems of communication, mental health and issues to do with children are common antecedents of self-harm for women in prison.

Lastly, when discussing their recent episode of self-harm, women in the WORSHIP II study were asked: 'At the time of your self-harm, what final outcome did you most intend and expect?' The response was recorded in their own words. Cumulatively, non-suicidal references made up 79 per cent of all thematically coded responses. However, references to suicide ('To kill myself', 'To take my own life', 'Wanted to die') were the most coded single response (20 per cent). Self-harming as a means of feeling better, providing emotional release and to facilitate a sense of mental escapism were also expressed. Several quotations detailing more violent methods of self-harm, such as the use of ligature and strangulation, were expressed in association with suicidal intent:

> 'When I ligature, I expect to die. When I cut myself it feels good, it releases my tension but then I feel bad later because I've got scars.' (03084)

> 'Fire – I wanted to kill myself. Others [self-harm] was just a release of stress and panicking and being alone.' (01031)

What can we learn from imprisoned women's experiences?

The WORSHIP II study is the largest study to date examining imprisoned women's experiences of self-harm. It explored the patterns, methods, functions, triggers and intended lethality of self-harm in female English prisons (Walker et al, 2021). Notably, the majority of women in the study described a significant history of trauma, with over two-thirds having experienced violent relationships or been sexually abused as children and as adults. Most women had engaged in self-harm both in and out of prison. First episodes of self-harm often occurred during adolescence; this parallels studies of self-harm in the community setting. When discussing recent episodes of self-harm in prison over the past month, cutting to the upper limb and ligaturing/self-strangulation were the commonest methods and these acts often occurred when women were alone in their cell.

When women were asked about what triggered their acts of self-harm, participants reported that conflict with others (for example, arguments or being falsely accused) was the most common precipitant, followed by difficulties coping with intrusive voices and concerns related to being separated from their children, that is, thinking about their children, worrying they were losing them including custody of their children and distance from family. Reports from women that their self-harming functioned as a means of providing release, or relief, from negative emotions were frequent. These results contribute to a growing evidence base that suggests self-harm acts as a means of regulating troubling emotions among incarcerated women (Jeglic et al, 2005; Dixon-Gordon et al, 2012).

The women were asked what their intention and expected outcome was at the time they engaged in their most recent episode of self-harm. Expected outcomes were heterogeneous. Responses referenced a strong sense of hopelessness, often stemming from past traumatic events; this has been demonstrated in previous studies of incarcerated women who attempted near-lethal self-harm (Marzano et al, 2011). This is likely to be influenced by the multiple sources of trauma that the large majority of women who took part in the study had experienced in their lives.

Reflections on *Criminal Women* (1985) and imprisoned women who self-harm

The experiences of imprisoned women today are not dissimilar from those who were in custody when Pat Carlen published *Criminal Women* (1985). Reflecting on 1985, women in prison were more likely to be imprisoned for non-violent crimes and to be given shorter sentences. Many had already suffered poverty and deprivation, experienced institutional care and become addicted to drugs and alcohol. Imprisoning women at this time, as today, served to remove the few remaining ties that connected them to society (family relationships, home, job), and made them less able to cope both in prison and on release.

In *Criminal Women*, the theme of self-harm is discussed in the last autobiographical story in the quartet, that of Josie O'Dwyer. The account presented by Josie is one of deprivation, violence and courage, all essential to survival in a women's prison. By voicing her 'private pain to inform a public issue', she explains the systems of abuse and exploitation existing within women's prisons, in particular Holloway and Styal Prison (Carlen et al, 1985: 181). She documents the fear and intimidation of Borstal: the 'smashing up'; 'winding up' of prisoners culminating in self-harm; the 'setting up' of prisoners resulting in violence and injury to other prisoners; the major intrusiveness of the regime; the exploitation of private prisoner information; the denial of having an identity; and the recourse to psychiatric intervention (Carlen et al, 1985: 142). Josie sets out the consequences for failing to survive death, institutionalisation, self-harm, insanity. She recounts her survival strategies, how she learnt to influence the limits of the system; she was the 'Momma' of her wing. The sharing of the pain among imprisoned women is discussed.

In her discussion, Josie describes that 'cutting and other forms of self-harm are common responses to the pains and tensions, to the emotional and the sexual deprivations experienced by women and girls in prison' and how many women 'turn it on themselves' (Carlen et al, 1985: 170). Josie is clear that she has never self-harmed herself as she 'could hit back', but is adamant that the emotions that causes her to 'smash up' are the same for the women who 'cut themselves'. The account ends with how the women cope with emotional deprivation: 'You learned to block it all off and then it became a knot inside you, a wound that gets worse, a wound that doesn't heal' (Carlen et al, 1985: 178–9). The account of Josie in *Criminal Women* (1985) and the 'pains of imprisonment' (Sykes, 1958) are in many ways no different to the experiences of the women in the WORSHIP II study and the other research cited in this chapter.

It does need to be recognised, however, that there have been some improvements in the Prison Service's strategy for England and Wales for preventing self-harm and suicide. For example, the use of the ACCT procedure for preventing and managing the risk of self-harm and suicide in custodial settings, the increase in specialist screening and support now available to new admissions to prison from their often stressful reception into the establishment, prisoners being doubled up to reduce isolation and minimise the opportunity to harm themselves and women being imprisoned close to home with the potential for meaningful social support (Walker and Towl, 2016). The provision of health care in the prison system has changed over the last three decades. There are now in-reach teams in every prison establishment in England (Royal College of Nursing, 2010). These teams were intended to act as community mental health teams that operate outside the prison system, incorporating within them the outreach and crisis resolution functions of the specialist teams that were developed across the United Kingdom with the publication of the National Service Framework for Mental Health (Department of Health, 1999).

Since the early 1990s, there has been the establishment of peer support schemes, one of the first by the Samaritans (the 'Listener Scheme') which involves volunteers visiting prisons to select, train and support prisoners who become known as 'listeners' (Walker and Towl, 2016). They work within the same structure as Samaritans by providing confidential, non-judgemental, emotional support. Any prisoner can volunteer to become a listener to support their peers who are in distress, but they are required to undergo a comprehensive training process. Trained listeners are supported by the local Samaritans branch who regularly visit to support, debrief and provide ongoing training to the (Samaritans, 2011). Now, nearly every prison in England and Wales has the scheme.

Prisons for women: incorporating trauma-informed care and practice

The changes that have been implemented since the 1980s have brought some improvements, however, women imprisoned in English and Welsh prisons continue to self-harm at extraordinary rates. Their human misery behind bars is still prevalent in 2021.

It is argued that this is because the prison regime continues to focus on identifying risk factors for self-harm (Livingston, 1997), and early research studies were based on mental health models that were mainly concerned with only describing self-harm rather than understanding it (Liebling, 1993). The role of mental health problems and individual characteristics were overemphasised in these studies at the expense of other factors such as childhood and adult trauma, adequacy of social networks and levels of self-esteem. We cannot change the individual characteristics of women at the time of entry to prison – that is, individual characteristics and experiences and environmental risk factors, which include the prison-setting influences. However, at the time of reception into prison a comprehensive plan could be developed for each imprisoned woman which takes into account the environment and has a focus on *her story.*

As we have seen earlier in the chapter, the experience of trauma is far from uncommon for many imprisoned women. In 2016, a general population survey in 24 countries assessed the exposure to 29 traumatic event types and of the nearly 69,000 adults (over 70 per cent) reported a traumatic event, with 30.5 per cent stating they were exposed to four or more types (Benjet et al, 2016). The prevalence of Post-Traumatic Stress Disorder (PTSD) in prison populations is not reliably known, despite several reports by authors that state PTSD is a major health problem in prisoners because of the high rates of exposure to physical, sexual and emotional violence over their lifetime (Battle et al, 2003; Wolff and Shi, 2012). In 2018, Baranyi et al (2018) undertook a systematic review and meta-analysis to estimate prevalence rates of PTSD in prison populations worldwide. Original studies in which prevalence rates of PTSD in unselected samples of incarcerated people were reported were systematically searched between 1980 and June 2017, and 36 publications were included in the final meta-analysis. The authors conclude that there is evidence for a significant sex difference in prevalence rates. PTSD in female prisoners is approximately three times more frequent than in male prisoners.

With this knowledge about imprisoned women and PTSD, Stathopoulos (2012) published a paper that examined different approaches to address women's victimisation histories in custodial settings. Although Stathopoulos was concerned with sexual abuse, and she focused mainly on Australian prisons, two of the frameworks highlighted appear to be promising interventions to deal with the poly-victimisation histories of women in prison. The first framework involves prisons approaching the care of imprisoned women from a *trauma-informed care and practice framework.* Being 'trauma informed' means having knowledge of the role that victimisation has played in the life of the survivor and using this understanding 'to design service systems that accommodate the vulnerabilities of trauma survivors and allow services to be delivered in a way that will facilitate consumer participation in treatment' (Harris and Fallot, 2001: 4). This framework is very different to *trauma-specific services* that are specifically designed to treat symptoms related to sexual or physical abuse or other trauma.

Trauma-informed services provide all aspects of provision though a 'trauma lens' (Guarino et al, 2009), not just those directly addressing the impacts of trauma. Harris and Fallot (2001) state that the focus is to generate an organisation that understands the woman's past history and current experiences of abuse from a holistic perspective; they view her symptoms in the context of her life and her traumatic experiences. Professionals must recognise that victimisation is often more than just a single event. It may include different types of trauma, repeated traumas and/or multiple events that threaten a woman's worldview (Harris and Fallot, 2001). When a woman is imprisoned, their memories and feelings about their experiences of poly-victimisation may resurface or trigger new ones and this has the potential to result in overwhelming feelings of guilt and shame. Stathopoulos (2012) maintains that the principles of trauma-informed care include:

- understanding trauma and its impacts;
- promoting safety;
- ensuring cultural competence;
- supporting control, choice and autonomy;
- sharing power and governance;
- integrating care;
- promoting the knowledge that healing happens in relationships; and
- the idea that recovery is possible.

Trauma-informed care and practice within the prison system has a small empirical evidence base. Evidence from trauma-informed correctional services in the USA suggests that this approach is working to reduce some of the key issues impacting the safety of women (Bradley, 2017). For example, in Massachusetts, findings have demonstrated that self-harm has reduced by 15 per cent, prisoner–staff assaults have fallen by 62 per cent and prisoner–prisoner assaults have decreased by 54 per cent (Covington, 2015). Correspondingly, the same trial found that suicide attempts had fallen by 60 per cent and prisoner fights had fallen by 46 per cent. This suggests a considerable improvement in safety for both staff and prisoner.

With regard to the UK, an example of prisons becoming trauma informed occurred in the English female prison estate in 2015 and was pioneered and funded by the charity One Small Thing. This charity was created by Lady Edwina Grosvenor (a prison philanthropist) when she was disappointed with the lack of progress in the women's estate. Partnering with Dr Stephanie Covington, co-director of the Centre for Gender and Justice in California, they brought a new programme to treat trauma through the lens of gender. The programme was based on two principles: first, that trauma drives women to commit crime, and second, that because women often experience gender-based violence (such as sexual assault and domestic violence), they require different approaches from men. The programme is now running in all 12 women's prisons in England.

The programme has three stages. Firstly, prison staff are trained to become *trauma informed*. All staff in the prisons were trained by Covington and Grosvenor: staff were taught about what trauma is, how it impacts women and how it can cause violent behaviour. The second stage is about becoming *trauma responsive*. In this phase, prison staff are taught to change their behaviour on the basis of what they have learned about trauma. For example, women who have experienced sexual violence can experience traumatic flashbacks and become violent as a result of being restrained by male prison staff. Alternative strategies that may avoid re-traumatising vulnerable women are taught, including de-escalating the situation without any physical contact. Lastly, the final stage involves developing *trauma-specific* services inside the prison. One such programme is 'Healing Trauma', a brief, gender-responsive intervention for women involved in the CJS (Covington and Russo, 2016). Healing Trauma comprises of six ninety-minute sessions in closed groups of up to ten women, peer-facilitated with support from specially-trained prison staff. It adopts a strengths-based approach aimed at empowering women to help them address their trauma, develop coping mechanisms to prevent violent outbursts, discover ways to thrive, to enjoy healthier relationships and happier lives.

Evaluations of Healing Trauma in the USA show the intervention to significantly improve symptoms of mental illness including depression, anxiety, PTSD, emotional regulation and aggression/hostility issues (Messina and Calhoun, 2018). Research on the impact of the work undertaken by One Small Thing in England was evaluated by Petrillo et al (2019) and, using a mixed methods approach, it found, like the USA, that the women reported significant reductions in symptoms of depression, anxiety, psychological distress, PTSD and trauma-related problems after completing the intervention. However, the results differed with the UK sample in terms of there being no significant differences in feelings of anger or aggression, nor changes in social connectedness or resilient coping. However, the data from the focus groups suggests the women did experience improved feelings of social connectedness and that Healing Trauma had taught them to cope with a range of stressors. Further work is required in this area, particularly in regard to understanding the longer-term impacts of the intervention (Walker, 2021).

Conclusion

This chapter has drawn together the recent work that has been undertaken with women who self-harm in prison. It has explored what has changed and what has stayed the same in this area since Pat Carlen's landmark book *Criminal Women* (1985). It is clear that, despite some positive changes, self-harm in women's prisons remains substantial and the challenges are immense, and with declining resources to manage such a vulnerable group, it appears that the situation is likely to get worse before it gets better.

It is proposed that the future direction of feminist criminology in this area should draw upon the strength of trauma-informed care and practice. However, developing a trauma-informed organisation in the CJS requires a commitment to incorporating trauma-informed services at multiple system levels. All departments within a prison each have to examine their policies and practices to develop trauma-informed services. Trauma-informed care requires a trusting, collaborative, safe and empowering environment that avoids dynamics that can re-activate trauma responses (Miller and Najavits, 2012; Bloom and Farragher, 2013; SAMHSA, 2014). All administrators and staff members in prison need to understand the impact and prevalence of trauma, and all screening and assessment processes, as well as services provided by the organisation that involve contact with individuals, should be trauma informed (SAMHSA, 2014). Furthermore, a core concept of a trauma-informed approach is acknowledging the different needs of men and women involved in the criminal system. To date, some positive steps have been taken for gender-specific programming, screening and assessment and organisational practices on women's needs in prison, however this still requires to be properly evaluated.

References

Abel, K., Shaw, J., Walker, T., Roberts, C., and Murphy, C. (2015) *Women Offenders Repeat Self-Harm Intervention Pilot II (WORSHIP II) (National Institute for Health Research for Patient Benefit (RfPB) Programme, Final Report Form)*, Manchester: University of Manchester.

Baranyi, G., Cassidy, M., Fazel, S., Priebe, S. and Mundt, A.P. (2018) 'Prevalence of posttraumatic stress disorder in prisoners', *Epidemiologic Reviews*, 40(1): 134–45.

Battle, C., Zlotnick, C., Najavits, L., Gutierrez, M. and Winsor, C. (2003) 'Post-traumatic stress disorder and substance use disorder among incarcerated women', in: P. Ouimette and P. J. Brown (eds) *Trauma and Substance Abuse: Causes, Consequences, and Treatment of Comorbid Disorders*, Washington, DC: American Psychological Association, pp 209–25.

Benjet C., Bromet E., Karam E. G., Kessler R. C., McLaughlin K. A., Ruscio A. M. and Koenen K. C. (2016) 'The epidemiology of traumatic event exposure worldwide: results from the World Mental Health Survey Consortium', *Psychological Medicine*, 46(2): 327–43.

Bloom, S. and Farragher, B. (2013) *Restoring Sanctuary: A New Operating System for Trauma-informed Systems of Care*, New York: Oxford University Press.

Bradley, A. (2017) 'Trauma-informed practice: exploring the role of adverse life experiences on the behaviour of offenders and the effectiveness of associated criminal justice strategies', Unpublished PhD thesis, University of Northumbria.

Braun, V. and Clarke, V. (2006) 'Using thematic analysis in psychology', *Qualitative Research in Psychology*, 3(2): 77–101.

Briere, J. and Gil, E. (1998) 'Self-mutilation in clinical and general population samples: prevalence, correlates, and functions', *American Journal of Orthopsychiatry*, 68(4): 609–20.

Brown, M., Comtois, K. and Linehan, M. (2002) 'Reasons for suicide attempts and non-suicidal self-injury in women with borderline personality disorder', *Journal of Abnormal Psychology*, 111(1): 198–202.

Carlen, P., Hicks, J., O'Dwyer, J., Christina, D. and Tchaikovsky, C. (1985) *Criminal Women*, London: Polity Press.

Chapman, A. L. and Dixon-Gordon, K. L. (2007) 'Emotional antecedents and consequences of deliberate self-harm and suicide attempts', *Suicide Life Threat Behaviour*, 37(5): 543–52. doi: 10.1521/suli.2007.37.5.543.

Corston, J. (2007) *The Corston Report: a review of women with particular vulnerabilities in the criminal justice system*, London: Home Office.

Covington, S. (2015) Becoming trauma-informed tool kit for criminal justice professionals. Available at: http://www.onesmallthing.org.uk/wp-content/uploads/2015/09/Becoming-Trauma-Informed-Tool-Kit-for-UK-2015.pdf [Accessed 21 September 2021].

Covington, S. and Russo, E. (2016) *Healing Trauma: A Brief Intervention for Women. Facilitator Guide* (2nd edn), Minnesota: Hazelden Publishing.

Dear, G., Thomson, D. and Hills, A. (2000) 'Self-harm in prison manipulators can also be suicide attempters', *Criminal Justice and Behavior*, 27(2): 160–75.

DeHart, D., Smith, H. and Kaminski, R. (2009) 'Institutional responses to self-injurious behavior among inmates', *Journal of Correctional Health Care*, 15(2): 129–41.

Department of Health (1999) *The national service framework for mental health: Modern standards and service models*, London: Department of Health.

Dixon-Gordon, K., Harrison, K., and Roesch, R. (2012) 'Non-suicidal self-injury within offender populations: a systematic review', *International Journal of Forensic Mental Health*, 11(1): 33–50.

Duperouzel, H. and Fish, R. (2010) 'Hurting no-one else's body but your own', *Journal of Applied Research in Intellectual Disabilities*, 23(6): 606–15.

Franklin, R. K. (1988) 'Deliberate self-harm: self-injurious behavior within a correctional mental health population', *Criminal Justice and Behavior*, 15: 210–18.

Gratz, K. (2001) 'Measurement of deliberate self-harm: Preliminary data on the deliberate self-harm inventory', *Journal of Psychopathology and Behavioral Assessment*, 23: 253–63.

Guarino, K., Soares, P., Konnath, K., Clervil, R. and Bassuk, E. (2009) *Trauma-informed organizational toolkit*, Rockville, MD: Center for Mental Health Services, Substance Abuse and Mental Health Services Administration, and the Daniels Fund, the National Child Traumatic Stress Network and the W.K. Kellogg Foundation.

Harris, M. and Fallot, R. (2001) 'Designing trauma-informed addictions services', *New Directions for Mental Health Services*, 89: 57–73.

Harris, T. (2015) *Changing prisons, saving lives: report of the independent review into self-inflicted deaths in custody of 18–24 year olds*, London: Her Majesty's Stationery Office.

Hawton, K., Linsell, L., Adeniji, T., Sariaslan, S. and Fazel, S. (2013) 'Self-harm in prisons in England and Wales: an epidemiological study of prevalence, risk factors, clustering, and subsequent suicide', *The Lancet*, 383(9923): 1147–54.

Herpertz, S., Sass, H. and Favazza, A. (1997) 'Impulsivity in self-mutilative behavior: Psychometric and biological findings', *Journal of Psychiatric Research*, 31(4): 451–65.

HM Prison Service (2001) *Prevention of suicide and self-harm in the prison service: an internal review*, London: HM Prison Service.

Humber, N., Hayes, A., Senior, J., Fahy, T. and Shaw, J. (2011) 'Identifying, monitoring and managing prisoners at risk of self-harm/suicide in England and Wales', *Journal of Forensic Psychiatry and Psychology*, 22(1): 22–51.

Jeglic, E. L., Vanderhoff, H. A. and Donovick, P. J. (2005) 'The function of self-harm in a forensic population', *Journal of Offender Therapy and Comparative Criminology*, 49(2): 131–42.

Kenning, C., Cooper, J., Short, V., Shaw, J., Abel, K. and Chew-Graham, C. (2010) 'Prison staff and women prisoner's views on self-injury; their implications for service delivery and development: a qualitative study', *Criminal Behaviour and Mental Health*, 20(4): 274–84.

Kidger, J., Heron, J., Lewis, G., Evans, J. and Gunnell, D. (2019) 'Adolescent self-harm and suicidal thoughts in the ALSPAC cohort: a self-report survey in England', *BMC Psychiatry*, 12: 69.

Liebling, A. (1993) 'Suicides in young prisoners: a summary', *Death Studies*, 17(5): 381–409.

Livingston, M. (1997) 'A review of the literature on self-injurious behaviour amongst prisoners', in G. Towl (ed.) *Suicide and Self-Injury in Prisons: Issues in Criminological and Legal Psychology*, 28, Leicester: British Psychological Society, pp 21–35.

Logan, C. and Taylor, J. (2019) 'Managing suicide and self-harm', in: D. Polaschek, A. Day and C. Hollin (eds) *International Handbook of Correctional Psychology*, London: Wiley, pp 224–45.

Marzano, L., Fazel, S., Rivlin, A. and Hawton, K. (2010) 'Psychiatric disorders in women prisoners who have engaged in near-lethal self-harm: a case-control study', *British Journal of Psychiatry*, 197(3): 219–26.

Marzano, L., Hawton, K., Rivlin, A. and Fazel, S. (2011) 'Psychosocial influences on prisoner suicide: a case-control study of near-lethal self-harm in women prisoners', *Social Science and Medicine*, 72(6): 874–83.

Marzano, L., Hawton, K. and Rivlin, A. (2016) 'Prevention of suicidal behavior in prisons', *Crisis*, 37(5): 323–34.

McHugh, M. and Towl, G. (1997) 'Organizational reactions and reflections on suicide and self-injury', in G. Towl (ed.) *Suicide and Self-injury in Prisons*, Leicester: British Psychological Society, pp 33–40.

McKenzie, K., Serfaty, M. and Crawford, M. (2003) 'Suicide in ethnic minority groups', *British Journal of Psychiatry*, 183(2): 100–101.

Messina, N. and Calhoun, S. (2018) *Healing trauma evaluation*. Year 1 findings, Simi Valley, CA: Envisioning Justice Solutions.

Miller, N. A. and Najavits, L. M. (2012) 'Creating trauma-informed correctional care: A balance of goals and environment', *European Journal of Psychotraumatology*, 3(1).

Miller, S. and Fritzon, K. (2007) 'Functional consistency across two behavioural modalities: fire-setting and self-harm in female special hospital patients', *Criminal Behaviour and Mental Health*, 17(1): 31–44.

Milligan R. and Andrews, B. (2005) 'Suicidal and other self-harming behaviour in offender women: The role of shame, anger and childhood abuse', *Legal and Criminological Psychology*, 10(1): 13–25.

Ministry of Justice (2013) *Guide to safety in custody statistics*, London: Ministry of Justice Statistics Bulletin.

Ministry of Justice (2019) *Statistics on women and the criminal justice system*, London: Ministry of Justice.

Nock, M. and Prinstein, M. (2004) 'A functional approach to the assessment of self-mutilative behavior', *Journal of Consulting and Clinical Psychology*, 72(5): 885–90.

Pattison, M. and Kahan, J. (1983) 'The deliberate self-harm syndrome', *Journal of Psychiatry*, 140(7): 867–72.

Petrillo, M., Thomas, M. and Hanspal, S. (2019) *Healing trauma: evaluation report*, Portsmouth: One Small Thing.

Powis, B. (2002) *Offenders' risk of serious harm: a literature review*, London: Home Office Research, Development and Statistics Directorate.

Pratt, D. (ed.) (2016) *The Prevention of Suicide in Prison: Cognitive Behavioural Approaches*, London: Routledge.

Prison Reform Trust (2018) *Prison: the facts. Bromley briefings Summer 2019*, London: Prison Reform Trust.

Rickford, D. and Edgar, K. (2005) *Troubled inside: responding to the mental health needs of men in prison*, London: Prison Reform Trust.

Royal College of Nursing (2010) *Prison Mental Health: Vision and Reality*, London: Royal College of Nursing.

SAMHSA (2014) SAMHSA's concept of trauma and guidance for a trauma-informed approach. Rockville, MD: Substance Abuse and Mental Health Services Administration. Available at: https://ncsacw.samhsa.gov/userfiles/files/SAMHSA_Trauma.pdf [Accessed 1 November 2021].

Samaritans (2011) *A history of the listener scheme and Samaritans' prison support*, Ewell: Samaritans.

Snow, L. (2002) 'Prisoners' motives for self-injury and attempted suicide', *British Journal of Forensic Practice*, 4(4): 18–29.

Stathopoulos, M. (2012) *Addressing Women's Victimisation Histories In Custodial Settings*, Melbourne: Australian Institute of Family Studies.

Suyemoto, K. (1998) 'The functions of self-mutilation', *Clinical Psychology Review*, 18(5): 531–54.

Sykes, G. (1958) *The Society of Captives: A Study of a Maximum Security Prison*, Princeton, NJ: Princeton University Press.

Towl, G. and Walker, T. (2015) 'Prisoner suicide', *Psychologist*, 28: 886–9.

Walker, T. (2015) 'Self-injury and suicide in prisoners', in G. Towl and D. Crighton (eds) *Forensic Psychology*, London: Wiley-Blackwell, pp 384–93.

Walker, T. (2021) 'Trauma informed care in the criminal justice system', in G. Towl and D. Crighton (eds) *Forensic Psychology* (3rd edn), London: Wiley-Blackwell, pp 735–54.

Walker, T. and Towl, G. (2016) *Preventing Self-injury and Suicide in Women's Prisons*, Hook: Waterside Press.

Walker, T., Shaw, J., Turpin, C., Reid, C. and Abel, K. (2017) 'The WORSHIP II study: a pilot of psychodynamic interpersonal therapy with women offenders who self-harm', *Journal of Forensic Psychiatry and Psychology*, 28(2): 158–71.

Walker, T., Shaw, J., Gibb, J., Turpin, C., Reid, C., Gutridge, K. and Abel, K. (2021) 'Lessons learnt from the narratives of women who self-harm in prison', *Crisis*, 42(4): 255–62.

Wolff, N. and Shi, J. (2012) 'Childhood and adult trauma experiences of incarcerated persons and their relationship to adult behavioral health problems and treatment', *International Journal of Environmental Research and Public Health*, 9(5): 1908–26.

Women in Prison (2019) Key facts. Available at: https://www.women inprison.org.uk/research/key-facts.php [Accessed 21 September 2021].

5

Criminal Mothers: The Persisting Pains of Maternal Imprisonment

Lucy Baldwin, with Mary Elwood and Cassie Brown[1]

Sadly, despite over 30 years of feminists and criminologists providing evidence of the repeated failure of the criminal justice system (CJS) to respond appropriately to female law breakers, very little has actually changed. The female prison population has continued to rise in tandem with supposedly progressive gender responsive reforms, and stubbornly remains between 3,000–4,000 as of 2021 (Baldwin and Epstein, 2017). Following the publication of the recent Female Offender Strategy (Ministry of Justice, 2018), the female-focused Farmer Report (2019) and the Joint Human Rights Committee report on maternal imprisonment (UK Parliament, 2019), there exists a cautious optimism that positive change is afoot, albeit in a limited capacity. It remains to be seen if these successive publications and their recommendations will enjoy any greater success than Corston (2007). Corston, in her review of 'vulnerable women in the criminal justice system', made 43 valid and sensible recommendations, the majority of which were accepted by government. However, over a decade later very little progress has been made in terms of their implementation, with only one recommendation fully actioned (Women in Prison, 2017). Indeed, it could be argued that with the implementation (and failure) of the Transforming Rehabilitation (TR) agenda, women law breakers are in a worse position than ever. Despite existing international sentencing guidelines suggesting the contrary, pregnant women and mothers of dependent children continue to be imprisoned for non-violent offences, most often offences that are rooted in poverty or trauma, or both (Penal Reform International, n.d.).

This chapter echoes the style of Carlen et al's (1985) seminal text which used the individual narratives of four women to explore and highlight the failures of the CJS. In the original *Criminal Women*, motherhood was only lightly visited, and mainly through Christina's narrative. Christina spoke about the tensions and struggles between 'criminality and motherhood', recalling that during her last sentence she could hear her son crying out to her, 'mummy, mummy'. Christina described being 'demented with grief' at their separation. When officers would not let Christina telephone him, she started 'smashing, crashing and fighting' and was placed in 'punishment', that is, solitary confinement (Carlen et al, 1985: 82). Personal narratives like Christina's (and Mary's and Cassie's presented in this chapter) highlight the importance of seeing and hearing women as individuals, rather than 'lumping' all women who come into contact with the CJS into one. Narratives around women in the CJS arguably often present only one perspective, with a narrow focus on their 'troubled backgrounds', the multiple challenges they face and their 'vulnerability' (Booth and Harriott, 2021). While it is very often true that many, if not most, women in the CJS have faced complex and multiple challenges and are vulnerable as a result, it is not true of *all* women, nor will all women experience their circumstances or the CJS in the same way (Rowe, 2011).

Discussions around gender and crime often highlight women's roles as mothers, not least because of an almost universal acceptance of what Baldwin calls 'a mothers code of conduct' (2017: 30), which informs perceptions of how women and mothers should, and importantly should not, behave. Significantly, this widely-accepted construction of motherhood ideology does not include criminality, drug and alcohol use or going to prison. Often, mothers attempting to mother in adverse circumstances – such as a life history of abuse or neglect, domestic abuse, poverty, unstable housing or substance misuse – feel like they are failing to meet impossible maternal standards (Boden et al, 2008; Baldwin, 2015, 2018). Thus, criminalised mothers who are often already facing individual and structural challenges which threaten their ability to mother to an 'accepted' standard, will, once criminalised, find themselves further at odds with the dominant 'good mother' script (Garcia, 2016).

When a woman, particularly a mother, is criminalised, there is still a sense that she is acting outside of her gender and role, that is, she is doubly deviant, often triply deviant if we are to include race and culture (O'Malley, 2018; Baldwin, 2021b). This perception is evidenced throughout criminal and social justice responses to women who come into contact with the CJS. Good mothering is deemed to be at odds with a criminal lifestyle, especially one that involves substance misuse, be that alcohol or drugs (Enos, 2001). Dominant motherhood ideology demands mothers adopt a selfless devotion to their children, meeting their every need through the absolute devotion of time, money, effort and emotion (Hays, 1996). Research suggests that such expectations of mothers, along with the assumption that motherhood is absolutely fulfilling, is fairly universal across class, cultures and ethnicity (O'Reilly, 2016). Idealised notions of motherhood make it challenging for mothers who are struggling with multiple identities or multiple realities (such as mental illness, addiction or domestic abuse) to seek help and support, not least because they fear the judgment of professionals that they are bad mothers, and ultimately they fear the risk of losing their children (Baldwin, 2015). It is clear this was a relevant factor in Mary's narrative below and is a reflection on the structural barriers to accessing support, more than a reflection of Mary's failure to access it.

Mothers in the author's doctoral study described how, from the moment they were criminalised, they struggled with balancing their good mother/criminal mother identities. Significantly, mothers in the study also described recognising that, not only did they struggle internally with their identity, but they were very aware that society judged them too (Baldwin, 2019). The mothers felt that there was a widely accepted perception that they could not be good mothers and break the law. Ultimately, becoming a criminal mother effectively and immediately excluded the mothers from 'good' motherhood and, furthermore, that the pursuit of a return to 'good' motherhood post-release became a primary focus (Baldwin, 2019).

This chapter illustrates the outcomes for two women who experienced maternal imprisonment. Mary, reflecting back on her life as a mother who broke the law, describes what she calls 'the inevitable destruction of my motherhood'. Mary details how the systems she found herself involved with failed her and robbed her not only of her own childhood, but her children's childhoods too. Mary reveals the lifelong impact maternal imprisonment has had on her and her sons, but also her absolute strength, resilience and determination to succeed and survive. Cassie's story, like many others, also includes reference to abuse, but significantly also highlights her strength and resilience, her determination to succeed, the interconnectedness of her maternal role and her desistance, as well as the importance of external support, formal and informal.

Rather than interrupting the following narratives with author commentary (as was the style of *Criminal Women*), this chapter presents Mary and Cassie's narratives uninterrupted by analysis or interpretation and as written by Mary and Cassie themselves. Please note that Mary and Cassie's life stories may be triggering and emotional.

Mary

I'm at a loss where to begin. I'm not sure where my story starts and finishes. I suppose when I was born would be a good place to start.

When I was born, I can't imagine that my mother loved me even then. I often think about babies that are planned and wanted; I think they must know, the babies I mean. I think they must feel loved even before they were born. I see pregnant mothers stroking their full bellies and talking, even singing to their baby, excited about their child's life to come. I genuinely can't imagine my mother ever having done that with me. I was unplanned, an inconvenience, an unwanted interruption of her life and her 'work'. I'm sure I would have gotten in the way of her work save for those perverts who like pregnant working girls. It makes me feel dirty even now knowing my mum must have been paid for her body to be used with me inside it. I feel like I must have absorbed some of that dirt, some of that shame. I've read that science says that unborn babies pick up on their mothers' moods so it stands to reason I must have picked up on some of what was going on. I know bonding can start before babies are born, so I guess so can indifference, and that's what I always felt my mother felt about me. Indifference – like it didn't matter if I was there or not. I know for certain I don't remember a single day where I felt loved by my mother, not one. It wasn't even as if I had a father to make up for the lack of love from her either. Neither me or her have any idea who my father even is. Some faceless nameless person who paid my mother to rent her body by the hour.

I used to fantasise that it was someone famous, that somehow, he would know I existed and would one day come and rescue me, take me away from the shit that was my life. To be fair I'd have settled for anyone, they didn't have to be famous. My mum did keep me though, for that I suppose I should be grateful. But again, sometimes I think about what my life would have been like if she hadn't. I might have been adopted by someone rich and normal and lived in Crouch End. I love words, maybe I could have got an education and been someone. I might have spent my time in libraries and theatres and had a brother called Charles!

Instead, I spent my childhood in a crummy bedsit, smelly, dark and dank, with two rooms, so I couldn't even escape her at home. If I wasn't trying to avoid seeing her 'at work' I was trying to avoid the men who came to her and who saw me as an added bonus, like a two for one offer in a supermarket. I try to convince myself my mother didn't plan that or take payment when I was used, or even that she didn't know when they used me to– but the older I got the harder that got to believe. Then I would try really hard to block those thoughts by doing stuff I shouldn't have even known about so young (self-harm and alcohol). But I guess she did know; I have to accept she did. I hope she felt like she got value for money!

I only really remember my mother as just being 'there', not absent, but not present either. Drunk more often than not and she was obsessed with her pills. I don't know what tablets they were, but I know she was stressed and strung out if she didn't have them – she would scream at me to find them – she would be hysterical. They definitely meant more to her than I did. I can't imagine her getting that stressed if she couldn't find me – I always felt like I was a burden, in the way, an irritation. So as soon as I was able to, I left. I left home just before I was 15, funnily enough I used to see all these posters about missing people all round London. Never saw a single one of me. I don't expect she even noticed I was gone. That was the last I saw her. I never went back. Why would I? I heard she died from the drink in the end – I knew it would be either her men, the drugs or the drink that killed her – she died her death how she lived her life, ugly and messy.

It's probably not surprising that I entered the world I did. I never have sold myself for sex, I'd never do that, not willingly anyway, but the drink got me too. In some ways I understand her a bit better now – maybe she used the drink to block it all out too – I get that. I would end up trusting men who would hurt me, ply me with drugs, try to get me on the game, knock me about. It was like I had a sign on my head saying, 'do this, treat me like a cunt, I'm used to it!'. I moved from pillar to post, sometimes to get away from men, sometimes because I was bored, sometimes because I just had no money to stay. Once because I was banned from my local off licence! Then I got pregnant. I felt like the happiest woman in the world. I was sad that, like me, my child wouldn't know its dad. I didn't know for sure who it was, but when they were older, I made something up, told my sons he was a good kind man who got run over buying me flowers – a dead dad is better than no dad. I was so happy to be pregnant, a child to love me, for me to love right back my own little family. But I worried all the time that the social would take my baby. I was ashamed I didn't know who the dad was, so I told them lies too but I think they knew. Then when I was about 6 months pregnant, I met a man, Ted, I thought he was going to be good and kind – I really liked him, I wanted us to be a family a proper family. But then one night when he was off his face, he raped me and beat me up, he told me I deserved it and I think I just figured he was right. I must have. Wasn't that what always happened?

After that he just got more and more controlling, nasty in fact – but I just accepted it as my lot – he put on a good front for the social [workers] so I didn't feel I could ask for help. Not that I would have anyway, I was too scared they'd take my son. So, in the end I did everything he asked, he wouldn't buy nappies or baby milk if I didn't do what he said … everything he said. So in the end I was 'moving things' for him, I never asked what, but I expected it was drugs. If I didn't do it, he would beat me up in front of my son and I didn't want him to be scared like I was, so I just did what he told me. To protect my son. So, I just fell into that lifestyle, it became normal to me. Then I got caught, he would have killed me if I'd grassed him up, so in court, I just pleaded guilty and accepted it. It was my first time in trouble, so I didn't think I'd go down. But I did, I was sent to jail. No warning just bam, off you go. My son had been taken into care when I was remanded, the judge said in court that my son was being 'properly cared for now' and I knew that was a dig at me. That he thought I didn't care for him properly and he was better off without me, and he was right. I was a shit mother; I'd hated my mother's life and yet I made all the same mistakes. I hated myself.

When I went to prison, I found out I was pregnant, they test everyone in reception, I'd had no idea. I didn't know how to feel. I was happy and sad, sad my baby would grow in prison, but happy because for a while anyway, I was safe. It was just me and him. I had the chance to be one of those mums who could stroke her bump and sing to her baby. I loved him before he even came because I had peace and space to love him. I wasn't worried about the next battering or paying bills or avoiding getting caught. Folk used to say 'aint you stressed about being pregnant in prison', but it was a lot less stressful than my life outside, so not at first no I wasn't. I knew it was another boy even before the scan, and I was glad. My world was no world for girls. In my world boys were safer. I was determined to be a better mother this time. To get my oldest one back and to be a proper mother, to cook and make biscuits and to take them to school – and be on time! In prison all I thought about was being a good mum, I was sure I could do it. I wanted it so much. For them. I got out when I was 7 months pregnant. I had been so scared he would be born early in prison. But there he was, my ex, Ted, waiting for me at the gate – to this day I don't know how he knew I was getting out. As soon as I saw him I lost hope. I was his meal ticket, of course he wasn't going to give up on me. He told me he had jobs for me, and I told him I wasn't going to do that no more, so he beat me black and blue. I thought I'd lose my baby he hurt me so bad but bless him he stayed put.

Then on it went. My life continued as before, only now it was worse. He even made me visit his mates in prison to take them drugs, pretending to be their girlfriends. That became my life. He said he was easier to smuggle because I was pregnant. I got supervised visits with my older boy and they were talking about giving me him back as long as I gave Ted up. I knew I had to for my sons. I was going to too, honestly after that last job, it was going to be my last job, and I was going to keep half the money and run. But I was drinking a bit again, I know it sounds crazy but I was so worried about losing my baby, and then losing both my sons forever, the only way I could cope with the anxiety and the worry was to just take the edge off with the drink. I had this one last job to do then I was leaving him, but I got caught taking drugs into prison didn't I. My solicitor told me I would not get remanded or jailtime, not with being so pregnant, I was due literally any day.

In court the Judge actually said, 'what kind of mother are you?' he actually said that. He said my child being in care was his best chance of having a 'stable life'. How could he even know that? He didn't know me; I was going to be such a good mum this time; I was determined to do it right this time. But in the blink of an eye, and because of him, Ted, that was it my chance to be good mum gone. I knew my son would be taken as soon as he was born. All I had left was to make the most of the couple of weeks I had left with him inside me. I must be only mum in the world who was delighted her baby was late. Every moment was precious and meant he was mine for longer, just me and him in our bubble – I barely even noticed I was in prison. But then the day came, the day he was born, the day they took him. I don't think it's right you know that they take them so quick – why couldn't I have had him a few days. Because I knew what was coming, I wasn't going to look at him or hold him at all. I was scared I wouldn't be able to cope – wouldn't be able to let him go. So, I'd told them to take him straight away. But when he was born, I changed my mind. I asked for him and I held him. He was so peaceful, he looked at me like he was studying me, pleading with me almost. I suppose that was just the guilt making me think that, but I felt like he was willing me to be better. I promised him I would be better, from now on. I promised him. I fed him. I felt good about that, like he would always have a bit of me with him. Silly I know. Then when he was sleeping, so he wouldn't know, I let them take him.

At first, I didn't cry, I remember just staring into space like I was frozen. I got up and went to the toilet and then I just broke down. I sobbed and sobbed and sobbed in that manky toilet. I felt broken, like I had nothing and no one, no purpose, no point, nothing. I'm ashamed to admit it now, but all I wanted at that point in time was some gear or some wine to numb the pain. The hurt was unbearable, and I just wanted it to go. I know not even half an hour had gone since I promised my boy I'd be better but, right at that moment in time, I just didn't know how to be, or even how I could be. My whole shitty life was passing before me and it was all rubbish, all of it. Now I'd lost both my boys and I just didn't know how I'd cope.

I was sent back to prison that night and locked in my cell. Thank god I wasn't alone, I had a pad mate, or I don't think I'd be here now. She knew how I'd be feeling god bless her and she had got gear ready for me to take, that probably sounds weird and sick, but it was the most caring thing she could have done. I took it gratefully. The rest of my sentence passed in a blur, a haze. I don't recall a single officer asking me how I was or how I was coping, other mothers did but not the screws. One actually told me that it was 'how it should be', that I 'deserved it' and 'prison was no place for babies anyway' – which I agreed with to be honest but that didn't help the pain. I remember thinking prison ain't no place for mothers either, but I didn't say it.

When I got out, I was determined to go straight, to be good. I was determined to get my boys back. Probation helped me get a job and I moved out of the hostel. I refused to have anything to do with my ex and moved towns so he couldn't find me. I stayed off the gear except for sleepers, but they were prescribed. Social services started to let me see my boys, supervised at first, then after 10 months I could see them on my own and then they came home. I was so so happy to have them home. We had two relatively uneventful years, just me and my boys. It was good, we were totally skint, but we had each other. Then I met him, Dean, and as usual when a man is in my life, it went to shit. At first, he was charming, lovely even, he loved the boys, they even started to call him dad. It was slow at first, but then it started, the jealousy, the control, the accusations. It got to the point where I'd even put the boys to bed early and go with them just to avoid him. I did everything I could to avoid pissing him off, but there was always something. Every time I thought I knew 'the rules' there was a new one. Eventually the slaps came, they turned to punches and then came the rest. He started asking me to move some parcels for him, again I never knew for sure what was in them, but I could guess. He said he'd hurt my boys if I didn't do as he said, so what choice did I have ? And I know he would have hurt them. He was a sadistic bastard. I refused one day, and he killed the boy's hamster, snapped its neck right in front of me and told me he would do the same to them. Its sounds mad now saying it to you but I believed him. After that he didn't even have to persuade me, I did whatever he asked. I couldn't leave, I had no family, no money, nowhere to go, no way to feed my kids. So I just took it and bit by bit I started drinking again, it was the only way to cope. I felt such a failure, I hated myself, I hated him, I hated my life, what my life had been, what it was shaping up to be, I hated everything. I remember my oldest son one day asking me why I fell over all the time and why I got so many bruises. My heart broke for him. I felt so guilty but weirdly I also remember feeling proud that he didn't know why, to me it meant I was doing something right. Sick I know. But that didn't last anyway.

I know they heard shouting, especially the oldest one, but I kidded myself they didn't really know anything. My oldest starting bullying the youngest though and now, with the benefit of hindsight, I know that's because of what he was seeing. Dean got worse and worse and I just disappeared, not literally (I wish), but the 'me' that I'd found in those two good years was gone. He would bring his mates round and I'd have to score for all of them and then one day he just told them they could have sex with me. I don't know to this day why I let them, why I didn't fight, why I didn't just leave – but I didn't. I just let them, and they paid him. I just got drunk after. That was it, I had come full circle, I was literally my mother. My worst fear. After that I spent my days in a haze of alcohol and drugs. I would manage to get the boys to school and then my day would disappear. I didn't do much else with them, I'm ashamed to say. I was a failure of a mother, I felt guilty when I was sober and it all hurt, so I just avoided being sober. Ironically, I think I now understood my mother even more.

Life would have just carried on like that I guess until one day I just 'snapped'. I'd dropped the boys off at school and came back to find a houseful, I knew what was coming. Afterwards, his 'friends' had just gone, four of them this time, all had taken their turn. He was asleep in the chair off his head on something. I don't really know what came over me or what happened. All I can remember is seeing the boys cricket bat leaning against the wall and I picked it up went behind the chair and hit him over the head with it. I can't remember how many times, but I know he was unconscious. I phoned the police and waited for them to come. I literally have no memory of this, but I was arrested and remanded. I pleaded guilty to GBH because my brief said if I didn't, they would go for attempted murder.

If I'd known that last night was to be the last time I put my boys to bed, I would have read them a story, I would have tucked them in. I didn't know I'd already taken them to school for the last time ever and I didn't even kiss them, that was all I could think about when I was remanded. They were taken into care and I tortured myself with how scared they must have been. To this day I don't even know who picked them up from school that day. I didn't think I could have hated myself more than I already did. I just existed from that day forward. Many times, in the prison sentence that came, I self-harmed, I tried to kill myself. I didn't feel I had anything to live for, but every time I was caught in time. I felt like nothing, no one ever really asked me why I did the things I did, but I don't know I would have told them anyway, they would have just said I deserved it. I got through my sentence somehow, but without seeing my boys at all. The social wouldn't bring them, said it was too far and not in their interests or something like that. My personal officer said to me I should just forget I ever had children because no way was I getting them back. So that was it,

I got out eventually, no money, no home, no job and no kids. What was even the point in trying to stay sober? In my view my destiny had been decided when I was born my mother's child. My fate was sealed.

So really the next ten years are a blur, in and out of prison drunk and sober, mostly drunk. Lots of short prison sentences for stupid things, sometimes just three weeks, I couldn't even tell you how many sentences of less than three months I've done but I know it's a lot. I felt like I was on a conveyor belt – the officers would laugh when I came back and say 'you again' – I felt like a joke, everything felt inevitable. There didn't seem to any point even trying without my kids, I didn't see my boys at all. My boys were in care, I had no fixed address most of the time so the social lost contact with me, not that I think they tried very hard anyway. I have to be honest and say I tried not to think about them, they were better off without me and really that part of my life was over. I didn't talk about them even. It was just too painful. What use was I as a mother anyway – no way would I have wanted them to see me like that, I'd seen my mother like that, and it wasn't pretty. So, I was happy imagining them with a good mum and dad in a nice area with a nice school and doing well, I even thought they would have their own rooms and TVs and bikes. All things I would never have been able to give them. They were in a much better place and I was glad. The only downside was I needed to drink to blot out the pain of it all, which mean robbing to pay for it. So that was my life year after year.

Then, on my last sentence, what changed it all was this one officer, young lass she was, but she asked me why I drank, she asked me about my life and if I had kids. No one in years and years had even mentioned my kids, and years and years longer since I spoke about my childhood. She asked me what I would want my boys to see if I ever saw them again, that made me want to do better. I didn't want them to be ashamed. She listened, she got me support, she got me counselling and drink support, and even made sure it would carry on when I was released. Without her I truly think I'd be dead now. Maybe the timing was just right, I was older and sick of the life I'd lived and was living, but I do think it was because she just gave me time. She wanted to understand. It was hard because I really was ashamed of me as a mum, but I knew that if I really wanted to stop drinking, I needed to face my demons, and being a shit mum like my mum was my biggest demon.

Anyway, to cut an even longer story short, I got help through my women's centre, I got clean, I got sober and I still am. It wasn't easy, but I did it. I got myself a little job in a supermarket and I love it and I volunteer at the women's centre every week. The staff at the centre, and the women and mothers I work with, all say I do a great job and

I know it helps the women to speak to someone who has gone through it and totally gets where they are coming from. I've been there years now. It helps me make sense of my experience too because I know I'm making a difference to them; I know that sounds big headed, but I am! I never thought I'd say this, but I'm dead proud of me! With my support worker's help, I found out where my boys where and after nearly 30 years apart we met. I can't tell you how amazing it was to see them, but oh my god the guilt. Turned out they hadn't had the good life I'd imagined all those years. They hadn't had a good time in care and had had several foster homes, some of them awful. Both of them have been in and out of prison and away from their kids too, which I know is my fault. The life they'd had, god I can't bear to think about it really. I had ruined my life, but the real tragedy is I ruined theirs. We are taking baby steps; we have a lot to catch up on. The boys are angry with me and rightly so, but we are getting there. I'm actually a granny too now, so exciting, one thing is for sure I know I will be a much better Nanny than I ever could have been a mum. I'll always be that mother that went to prison, but maybe it's not too late for me after all. (Mary)

Reading Mary's narrative, it is impossible not to recognise the many missed opportunities to offer the support that might have prevented Mary's criminalisation and imprisonment. In turn, this support might have mitigated the enduring harm caused not only to Mary but also to her children and grandchildren. Mary undoubtedly shows strength, resilience and determination, but in a relatively wealthy, contemporary society, should her journey have been this hard or this isolated? Mary's pathway through criminalisation and prison is not an unusual one, sadly neither is the lack of support. Clarke and Chadwick (2018) highlight that it is often individual women who themselves are punished despite society's failure to meet their needs and provide gendered support. Mary could and should have been supported at any number of points on her journey to prison, as a child and as an adult; instead, patriarchy, perceptions of and the reality of 'double deviancy' and oppression (Carlen, 1998) conspired to frustrate her attempts to mother through adversity or to secure the support she so desperately needed. Illustrating the power of kindness, trauma-informed practice and gendered responses to criminalisation, Mary was finally able to reconnect with her children, be supported away from her previous coping strategies (that had led to her offending) and look forward to being a grandmother. The tragedy is the excessive length of time it took, and the pain caused to her and her children in the process.

The chapter now hands over to Cassie, who also illustrates how her pathway into offending was triggered initially by abuse, but again reveals how her desistance was influenced by her desire to be and be seen as a 'good mum'. Cassie again demonstrates the resilience and ability of women and mothers to find agency in the face of multiple oppressions, and while fighting their way through the CJS (Carlen et al, 1985).

Cassie

Thanks for asking me to do this, I feel like it's a great opportunity for me to reflect on and show off about how far I've come. Yes, I went to prison and yes, I did drugs for a lot of years, but you know what? And I know it sounds weird, but I was still a good mum. I was the best mum I could be. I knew when I was going to be on a bender and always made sure my kids were safe at my mums. Everyone knew I took drugs and why, I was gang raped and it was a very public case in my town. I struggled to deal with it and drugs became my coping mechanism. But, and this is a big but, but I know my kids would tell you this, I'm a good mum. They stopped me from sliding all the way down, all the way in. They kept me far enough out of the scene that I never quite lost control. I wouldn't have no dealers at the house, and I was careful where I did drugs and who with, so nothing got back to my kids or my kids dads. It wasn't easy and at times I worried I wasn't being a good mum, but I also know how much I wanted to be. My mum was a good mum, is a good mum and I wanted my kids to have those memories too. So I made sure I took them to school, I was tidy, I was clean, always clean, they were well looked after, and we managed. We had fun, we had picnics, don't get me wrong it wasn't a fairy tale. We didn't have a lot of money, or fancy cars or holidays, but then neither did anyone else where I come from, but we did have, and still do have, love, and lots of it. My mum helped a lot, but really, I just managed, for them, because of them, my kids.

Then one day I just decided that was it, I wasn't going to take anything anymore, I'd had one really short spell in prison years before, and yes it was a nightmare, and yes it affected my kids, still does. I'd kept on with the women's centre to see my drugs worker ever since I'd been released, and I told her what happened. My daughter, who was about 10 by this time, well she found my stash. I will never forget it, I will never forget her questions, the disappointment in her face or my shame. From that day to this I've never touched anything, not even a headache tablet, and I swear on my kids' lives that's true. From that day I was determined to put it all behind me and to do I everything I could to get rid of that disappointment on my daughter's face. I was honest with her, I told her the truth and I told her why I used. You might think that's wrong because she was young, but I didn't want no more lies. I went to the centre and told my drugs worker what had happened and that I was done, she said to me 'Cassie', she said, 'I'm proud of you, I knew this day would come and now it has now we move forward'. She was right, I hadn't moved forward for years; I was stuck, and I didn't realise it. I started to volunteer at the women's centre, mainly at first to keep me busy – but then I loved it, I really loved helping the other women and I knew what life they were living so they trusted me. My drugs worker encouraged me to do a counselling course, they paid for it at the centre. I passed with flying colours and so then they encouraged me to do a degree. At first, I was like 'don't be bloody stupid a degree me'. But anyway eventually I did it, I loved being a student and I loved that my kids were proud of me. We used to all do our homework together at the dining table. It was funny. The kids found it hilarious, but I could see in their eyes they were proud of me. That meant everything to me. I even heard one of them bragging once that I was studying. It was nice, I was doing something they were proud of. It made me feel like I was being the mum I was supposed to be, a good mum. Most of all though, I gave them time, I was careful to make sure I was at school events, I took them swimming when I could afford it, I baked with them when I could, I still do, it's our thing. I literally am like supermum – only better! Anyway so yes, I do all that and now I work at the women's centre full time too. I'm knackered but I'm happy. I have a proper job and I know my work makes a difference to the lives of women, who are like I used to be. I tell them my story and it gives them hope. My kids are proud of me and I'm proud of me. I want to be able to show other women, other mothers, life can be good after prison, you can go to prison and still come out and be a good mum. I know because I've done it. (Cassie)

Discussion

Motherhood is underexplored in the original *Criminal Women* text, so it is impossible to know how much of a factor motherhood was in the lives of the women therein. More recently, motherhood in relation to criminology has attracted attention in the UK (Baldwin, 2015, 2017, 2018, 2019; Baldwin and Epstein, 2017; Lockwood, 2018; O'Malley, 2018; Masson, 2019; Abbott et al, 2020; Booth, 2020; Minson, 2020).

In *Criminal Women*, although not stated explicitly, Carlen implies that Christina's maternal role was a motivating factor, but also a source of pain. Further similarities between Christina and Mary are to be found in their shared experiences of negative relationships: relations with men that were unsafe and abusive, where each had used violence in self-defence or as a reaction to violence metered out to them. Yet, despite rarely being the perpetrators of domestic abuse, it is often the mothers who will come under scrutiny from social services for their 'failure to protect' (Barnes, 2015); rarer still are examples where mothers have been the abuser to their children.

In instances where mothers have killed their children, for example, Fiona Pilkington, Jael Mullings, Fiona Anderson and Charlotte Bevan, most often the tragedy comes after a long period of missed opportunities by multiple agencies to support mothers who were struggling with complex issues, and who were in dire need of support (see Baldwin, 2015: 23). All too often that support has not been forthcoming, whether due to cuts in services and limited resources, or because mothers were too afraid to ask for support; afraid of being judged bad mothers, seen as 'not coping' and, ultimately, the fear of losing their children. The failures of society to meet the needs of mothers, or to address the poverty and trauma which so often taints the lives of mothers who hurt or neglect their children, are rarely called to question in the courts or in the media. The focus lies on the failures of the mother who is held solely responsible, no blame is placed upon society for its failings. Mothers need to be able to ask for and be given support, and barriers to that support need to be reduced, at macro and micro levels. In such circumstances, many mothers would avoid criminalisation altogether. Baldwin argues,

> Many (if not most) women who are in prison, leaving prison or accessing services have 'complex needs' often as a result of multiple traumatic experiences – key to working positively with women throughout the criminal and social justice systems is aiming to promote an atmosphere of 'emotional safety'. (Baldwin, 2015: 36)

Understanding and recognising the significance of maternal expectation and maternal emotion – of the relationship between trauma and mothering in and through adversity – is key to helping to create this space of emotional safety. It is only there that criminalised mothers will be able to openly and honestly explore their feelings and experiences, not 'just' as women, but as mothers.

However, for criminalised mothers, this is often not an option, either because of failure to recognise their needs, the fear of unwanted intervention or because the mothers themselves do not want to initiate conversations that for them are so painful (and risky). In 'Motherhood disrupted', Baldwin (2018) reveals how the mothers in prison often refrain from speaking openly about their maternal emotions and their maternal role, experiences and emotions, despite them actually being a primary concern and focus. Baldwin's (2021b) doctoral research found this was particularly true for mothers imprisoned in closed conditions. Mothers in closed conditions knew each other less well and were often unaware of each other's maternal circumstances. Closed condition mothers described avoiding maternal conversations for fear of triggering a pain in themselves and in other mothers that was 'risky' and 'hard to control' once 'banged up and alone' in their cells. However, mothers in open conditions with more freedom to interact positively with other took great comfort from their supporting maternal conversations with each other. Rita called it the 'Mothers Club'. Rita stated that the mothers would actively seek each other out and found the support they got from each other important: 'just being mums and talking about life and everything … actually it was always about the kids' (Baldwin, 2021b: 198). Importantly, this is equally true for mothers who have lost care of their children. The environment, regimes and structure of the prison play a role in this, as do their interactions and relationships with staff.

There is no doubt that, for some of the women in Baldwin's study, prison had provided a temporary relief from domestic abuse, from anxieties related to living in poverty. Some women were able to access services they had not been able to access in the community (like drug and alcohol services and counselling). However, had gendered and appropriate support been available to mothers in the community, their prison experience would have arguably offered nothing by way of positivity. It is surely a failing of our society and our systems if anyone can fare better in prison than they do outside.

It is important to note that many positive interventions prison *can* offer are often impossible to access on a short sentence, and most women in prison (72 per cent) are serving sentences of less than 6 months. The mothers in Baldwin's doctoral research, most with lived experiences as complex as Mary's, experienced varied outcomes. All of the mothers felt that post-release support, especially related to their motherhood, was either lacking or, in most cases, completely absent. All of the mothers, some despite being decades post-release, described still feeling 'traumatised' by their imprisonment and the separation from their children. The impact of their imprisonment was experienced through their relationships with their children, grandchildren and wider family, but for many mothers a further significant impact was the impact on themselves. Specifically concerning her maternal identity and role, one woman noted: 'I will never be the same, none of us will ever be the same' (Karen). The guilt, shame, stigma and trauma mothers experienced post-prison was for some directly related to their desistance journey (like Mary).

Motherhood, spoiled identity and desistance: a complicated relationship

In more recent years, 'desistance' has been reconceptualised as a process rather than a static reaction to a developmental process (Stone, 2016: 956).

In relation to desistance, women's identities as mothers can and do play an important role in that process (Giordano et al, 2004; Rumgay, 2004). Baldwin's research demonstrates that a woman's identity as a mother remains important whether a mother's maternal role has been maintained or not, for example within mothers who have lost the care of their children (Baldwin, 2018, 2020, 2021b). Both Mary's and Cassie's narratives demonstrate the often-complicated relationship motherhood and maternal emotion can have with desistance. Mary initially demonstrates how the loss of her identity and role as a mother contributed to a path of resigned criminal activity. Conversely, Cassie, and later Mary, reveal how their motherhood became a motivator for desistance.

Cassie's narrative echoes many of the mothers in Baldwin's wider research. Her research with mothers and grandmothers after prison found they sought to demonstrate 'desistance' through the pursuit of idealised motherhood (that is, good motherhood/status). Many of the mothers felt that if they 'could just be good mother' (Tamika), and importantly be *seen* as good mothers, not only would that 'good mother' status override their ex-offender status, but it would also assist them in their abstinence from crime (or in the case of addicted mothers, the substance misuse that led to crime). Often, as mothers, the women were reluctant to give up any developing feelings of respectability and acceptance (in their own, their children and in society's eyes) as 'non-criminals'.

> 'Eventually I just changed my shit. I worked hard to leave that life behind me and the longer I was just a mum, and a good mum and not using and stuff, the further I felt away from the shit mother who didn't think of her kids .... Well I did, but everyone said I didn't. So ... I didn't want to go back, to that life, to prison, to any of it I just wanted to be a mum to my kids, to be a good mum.' (Tamika) (Baldwin, 2021b: 23)

Tamika goes on to say that, although to an extent she felt like she succeeded in leaving her 'old' identity behind, at least to the outside world, *internally* she felt her shame as a spoiled mother would never quite leave her:

> 'I know I look like I'm ok now, over it all, living a good life, and I am really, the kids don't mention that time often now and nor does my family, I have friends who don't even know I was in prison ... but I know. I know and sometimes when I'm on my own I cry. I feel so ashamed of what I used to be, and I know that will haunt me forever. I dread the kids ever asking me questions about that time because I'm ashamed and more than anything I don't want them to be ashamed of their mum.' (Tamika)

Similarly, another mother in Baldwin's study, Kady, described herself as 'tainted', and despite now thinking of herself as a good mother, she feels the 'shame' of her past. Kady's daughter was born while she was in custody; her daughter spent her first months in a prison mother and baby unit (MBU). Although her daughter was eight years old when interviewed, Kady had yet to tell her daughter this, and described never wanting to tell her that she had been 'born in prison':

> '...why would I want her to know that about herself, about me, she's got the most horrible birth story forever, I did that to her, me.' (Baldwin, 2021b: 228)

For mothers, the accepted notion of a 'spoiled identity' goes beyond that of an ex-prisoner (Goffman, 1963): post prison mothers also feel 'spoiled' as mothers (Baldwin, 2017). Stone (2016) argues that motherhood is an aspect of identity that occupies 'master status'; when women feel spoiled as mothers it can permeate their whole sense of self. Balwin's doctoral research found that, despite the importance mothers themselves attached to their maternal identity, 'structural barriers', external measures of good motherhood and impossibly high personal standards complicated mothers' efforts to maintain or resume their maternal role. As identified by Stone (2016), Sharpe (2015) and Brown and Bloom (2009), mothers also struggled to retain a positive sense of themselves as mothers. Stone (2016: 959) identifies that, particularly in the case of mothers who misuse substances, the 'powerful and stigmatising master narrative' of an addict challenges a mother's ability to release themself from their offending past and move successfully into a non-offending future. O'Malley and Devaney (2018) and Baldwin et al (2015) found that many addicted mothers worsened their addiction due to the 'shame' of their perceived 'failed' motherhood. This contributed to mothers' ability (or inability) to abstain from drugs and/or alcohol and ergo from the offending undertaken to fund their addiction (and often the addictions of male partners).

For some mothers, once they felt they had 'failed' at motherhood, they 'had nothing to go straight for', highlighting the long-term impact of child removal that is not always appreciated. Mary's narrative demonstrates powerfully how she once felt she had lost her role as a mother, that her maternal identity was so badly spoiled, she saw 'no point' in her either seeking support or desisting from offending. Yet, equally powerful are the points in Mary's narrative where she describes her boys and her motherhood as being her motivation to succeed: 'When I got out, I was determined to go straight, to be good. I was determined to get my boys back'. In seeking to motivate Mary to engage, Mary's prison officer used Mary's mother status as a hook: Mary told us that 'she asked me what I would want my boys to see if I ever saw them again, that made me want to do better. I didn't want them to be ashamed'. Imagining her sons meeting her again as adults and her desire to make them proud was the ultimate motivating factor for Mary to desist. There were, of course, additional factors such as maturity and access to appropriate support, but it was in seeking a return to what, for Mary, represented a positive maternal identity that she found the motivation to succeed in a way she previously felt she had failed. Or, as Mary states, 'I needed to face my demons and being a shit mum like my mum was my biggest demon'.

Tragically, with earlier support and perhaps an avoidance of criminalisation, Mary might have had the opportunity to mother her sons much earlier and not now have to rely on a 'second chance' via her grandchildren. Mary had been denied opportunities for support as a child and also as a young mother. Cassie's narrative reveals a similar experience, with motherhood eventually providing the hook and the motivation, importantly partnered with appropriate gender-specific support.

Like Baldwin, in her research with mothers after prison, Stone found that losing custody of children was perceived by mothers as the 'ultimate failure'. The removal of a child often coincides with removal of support, leaving now further traumatised mothers to struggle with their loss and their maternal emotions alone – which, unsurprisingly, can lead to mothers seeking to 'replace' their 'lost' child with another, but without the root causes of their substance misuse or trauma being addressed. Thus, the second child is often also withdrawn with the same 'justification' as the first. This cycle of removal of subsequent children can persist several times (Morriss, 2018). The loss of a positive maternal identity could and would send mothers into a 'downward spiral' of addiction, offending and/or self-destruction (Stone, 2016: 967). In Baldwin's study, Beth, a young mother of 19, was sent to prison when her child was only three months old; her baby was taken into care at her point of sentence. When released from prison, Beth felt her child 'didn't know her' and Beth was sure her child was being 'groomed for adoption' by social services and that they 'didn't want [her] to succeed'. Beth predicted in her interview that a return to drugs or suicide would be her 'best options' as she struggled to deal with her emotions as a 'failed mother' and the challenges of bonding with her daughter. She felt under enormous pressure to 'perform' as a mother for social services and felt they were placing undue pressure on her, without parallel support, and Beth felt unable to discuss her true feelings with social services. I later found out that, tragically, Beth had returned to substance misuse and had taken her own life just before her 21st birthday.

It is important that mothers receive the message that if mistakes are made, or external challenges forced on them make mothering impossible for a while, there is often hope. It is often possible to mother and mother well through challenges if mothers are supported appropriately, if their maternal identity and maternal selves are not allowed to fragment and fracture. Thus, the cycle of pregnancy, child removal and criminal activity persists, often multiple times. The aforementioned cycle is described by Stewart (2015) in her work with Claire a mother who had eight children previously removed but successfully managed to keep her ninth child (Tilly), after a support package was finally put in place in prison. Claire's experience yet again highlights the failure to recognise the needs of mothers facing multiple challenges in the community and a lack of resources to meet those needs. If Claire's last baby had been born outside of custody, it is very unlikely that social services would have afforded her the support or opportunity to keep her baby. It is tragic that Claire had to go to prison to access this support and for her child to begin her life on a prison MBU. Had Claire been appropriately supported much earlier, and importantly after the loss of her first child to care, eight children may not have ended up being removed from their birth mother, and Claire might have been spared the unimaginable pain of losing eight new-borns to the state.

Of course, there may well be instances where for whatever reason it is not safe or appropriate for mothers to retain care of their children. If separation is genuinely in the child's best interests, mothers need supporting through the process of understanding and accepting the decision to separate mother and child. Separating mothers need therapeutic support to deal with their maternal emotions, alongside appropriate practical and legal support, all of which is important to a mother's recovery and wellbeing (Baldwin, 2015; Barnes, 2015). Conversely, it is also important that, where mothers feel this decision should be challenged or is being made too soon, mothers are supported in questioning the decision to separate. We must always be accountable for decisions to separate mothers from their children and the long-terms harms mitigated against short term gain, even if to not separate would mean expensive and comprehensive support packages.

Conclusion

This chapter and the women's experiences discussed here highlight the frequency with which women – especially criminalised women and mothers – are consistently challenged and disadvantaged by structural inequality and limited access to services and support. Most women who enter the CJS are affected by social injustice in multiple ways.

The chapter highlights the often-central feature, and primary concern, of mothers in the CJS are their maternal role, their maternal emotions and their children – regardless of whether they have their children in their care or not. The chapter highlights the complicated relationship between motherhood and desistance. Reading Mary's and Cassie's narratives it is impossible not to recognise the many missed and lost opportunities to offer support and understanding. Such support that might have prevented the criminalisation and/or imprisonment of both mothers and importantly kept them safe, in turn mitigating the enduring harm caused to their children. Mary and Cassie undoubtedly show strength, resilience and determination, and in their different ways have 'survived' their challenges and the system that could have destroyed them. However, the personal cost to both women and their children has nonetheless been significant and lifelong.

The chapter also highlights the importance of trauma-informed, gender-specific tailored support for women. This support needs to be based on a strength-based ideology and which seeks to engage and empower women far beyond simply surveillance and enforcement. A gendered response to women in the CJS is essential, and women must be provided with opportunities, access to education and employment, encouragement, resources, access to childcare, emotional and financial support and a safe space. In order for this to be achieved, there must be a genuine, sufficient and permanent commitment to funding, targeted firstly at resources designed to divert women away from the CJS, and secondly at resources such as women's centres which are best able to support women in their rehabilitation.

Dee, a mother from Baldwin's research, sums up eloquently what is required of the CJS for women and mothers:

'It was awful, it was shit, it hurt, and I'm scarred, my life was chaotic and complicated before prison. My life as a mother in prison was broken. I've experienced more abuse in my life than most people do in a lifetime. I was an addict; I suffer from nightmares and trauma and depression. All of that is true, but don't just call me complex, don't just call me vulnerable. I'm strong but I want to be stronger. I'm free but I want to be freer. I've moved on but I want to go further ... I want society and services to support me not just label me, I want people to help me create chances for others not just give one to me, I don't want to be held back I want to be driven forwards.' (Dee) (Baldwin, 2021b: 316)

Despite their 'vulnerabilities' and the challenges they face, women in the CJS are so much more than this. Underrepresented in published research and reports about women in the CJS are their strength and resilience. Women like Mary and Cassie, who succeed and survive *despite* (sometimes because of) their lived experiences; women who not only survive their multiple realities but also survive among a system that does not recognise or meet their needs. This chapter sought to reinforce the message that there is no 'typical' narrative of women in prison, only individual stories. Where some women share similar characteristics and experiences, those characteristics and experiences are too often used to identify and label all women who come into contact with the CJS. Through their narratives, Mary and Cassie present a detailed reflection of individual strengths, successes and 'failures'. They demonstrate how individual women experience or interact with systems, which almost by design can systematically destroy women who break the law, arguably especially mothers (Baldwin, 2015; Lockwood, 2018). Rarely heard are the voices of women like Mary and Cassie who have, often against the odds, managed to continue to mother and/or to maintain a maternal identity, albeit often tainted and definitely externally and internally challenged (Baldwin, 2017, 2018). Similarly, less well represented in literature surrounding criminalised women are mothers, like Cassie and like Chris Tchaikovsky before her, who succeeded in forging a successful career in which they seek positive change, not just for themselves but for others facing a similar journey.[2]

Baldwin's studies (2018, 2021b) argue for the development of a matricentric feminist criminology, which would, in an ideal world, provide a lens to centre the experiences and voices of mothers in the CJS and engage women and mothers in the processes of change, seeking to mitigate the currently-felt harms. For serious and long-lasting change for women in the CJS, there must first be a commitment to improve social justice. Women who enter the CJS most often do so from a disadvantaged position and, despite the CJS doing little to improve their position, women most often survive, and through sheer determination go on to be their best selves. However, this should not be left to good fortune and opportunity – there needs to be a commitment to recognising and addressing structural inequality, poverty, the pandemic of abuse and violence and the lack of appropriate supportive resources, all of which impact on women so profoundly. It is nothing short of a disgrace and a tragedy that, despite over 30 years of evidence-based calls for change, this chapter and this collection are still summoning the same reforms and the same accountability of the judiciary, as called for by Carlen and Tchaikovsky in their concluding chapter of *Criminal Women* (Carlen et al, 1985). We are still hopeful that penological and sentencing reform will one day 'result in ever fewer or no women at all being given prison sentences' (Carlen et al, 1985: 186).

Author's note

The author of this chapter shares some of the 'expected' lived experiences of women who come into contact with the CJS. I grew up with violence and neglect, experienced child sexual abuse and attempted suicide, alongside experiencing rape and domestic abuse. I consider my teenage motherhood (pregnant at 16 and 18) my salvation (see chapter 1, Baldwin, 2015). Importantly, nay, vitally, I had professionals around me, who despite my troubled background and my expected future believed in me, supported me and encouraged me into education. Once, while living on benefits, and after I had lost my purse, I stole food for my children, but I wasn't caught. I am aware of how lucky I am to have not then been forever labelled or received into a system that would in all likelihood have led to very different outcomes for me and my children. Education gave me a passport into another world, one where I might access and share the 'power' of successful people. Education gave me the passport, but it was motherhood that gave me the motivation. I still made many of the mistakes 'expected' of me in terms of unsuitable partners and unhealthy coping strategies, but I survived; and through it all I continued to mother and to mother well. I am now a mother to three successful adults and five wonderful grandchildren. To this day, I find it strange when people make assumptions about my background and the supposed incongruence with my present self and life, which is part of the reason why for many years I wasn't always open about my past experiences or about how they shaped who I am and what I do. We professionals often invite speakers with 'lived experience' to events and who, rightly so, are warmly received and their bravery and candour appreciated. Yet, I have encountered discomfort, embarrassed silences and disapproval when I have discussed my lived experiences, something I write reflectively about in Baldwin (2021a). I find academia sometimes doesn't like to 'blur the lines', which perhaps raises questions about how we 'other' those whom we assume are different to 'us'.

Notes

[1] Mary Elwood and Cassie Brown are both mothers (who chose their own pseudonyms), originally from Baldwin's doctoral research, who wanted to take part in this additional piece of writing.
[2] One of the editors of the original *Criminal Women*, an ex-prisoner herself and founder of the national organisation 'Women in Prison', a feminist organisation that actively campaigns for and supports women in the CJS.

References

Abbott, L., Scott, T., Thomas, H. and Weston, K. (2020) 'Pregnancy and childbirth in English prisons: institutional ignominy and the pains of imprisonment', *Sociology of Health & Illness*, 42(3): 660–75.

Bachman, R., Kerrison, E. M., Paternoster, R., Smith, L. and O'Connell, D. (2016) 'The complex relationship between motherhood and desistance', *Women & Criminal Justice*, 26(3): 212–31.

Baldwin, L. (ed.) (2015) *Mothering Justice: Working with Mothers in Criminal and Social Justice Settings*, Hook: Waterside Press.

Baldwin, L. (2017) 'Tainted love: the impact of prison on maternal identity, explored by post prison reflections', *Prison Service Journal*, 233: 28–34.

Baldwin, L. (2018) 'Motherhood disrupted: reflections of post-prison mothers', *Emotion, Space and Society*, 26: 49–56.

Baldwin, L. (2019) 'Excluded from good motherhood: reflections of mothers after prison', in C. Byvelds and H. Jackson (eds) *Motherhood and Social Exclusion*, Ontario: Demeter Press, pp 94–104.

Baldwin, L. (2020) ' "A life sentence": the long-term impact of maternal imprisonment', in K. Lockwood (ed) *Mothering from the Inside: Research on Mothering and Imprisonment*, Bingley: Emerald Publishing, pp 85–102.

Baldwin, L. (2021a) 'Presence, voice and reflexivity in feminist and creative research: a personal and professional reflection', in I. Masson, L. Baldwin and N. Booth (eds) *Critical Reflections from the Women, Families, Crime and Justice Research Network*, Bristol, Policy Press, pp 173–97.

Baldwin, L. (2021b) 'Motherhood challenged: a feminist study exploring the persistent pains of maternal imprisonment', Doctoral thesis, Leicester: De Montfort University.

Baldwin, L., Atherton, S. and Thompson, C. (2015) 'Policing mothers', in L. Baldwin (ed) *Mothering Justice: Working with Mothers in Criminal and Social Justice Settings*, Hook: Waterside Press, pp 89–112.

Baldwin, L. and Epstein, R. (2017) *Short but not sweet: a study of the impact of custodial sentences on mothers and their children*, Leicester: De Montfort University.

Barnes, C. (2015) 'Damned if you do, damned if you don't: a social work perspective', in L. Baldwin (ed) *Mothering Justice: Working with Mothers in Criminal and Social Justice Settings*, Hook: Waterside Press, pp 65–88.

Boden, J. M., Fergusson, D. M. and Horwood, L. J. (2008) 'Early motherhood and subsequent life outcomes', *Journal of Child Psychology and Psychiatry and Allied Disciplines*, 49(2): 151–60.

Booth, N. (2020) *Maternal Imprisonment and Family Life: From the Caregiver's Perspective*, Bristol: Policy Press.

Brown, M. and Bloom, B. (2009) 'Re-entry and renegotiating motherhood: maternal identity and success on parole', *Crime & Delinquency*, 55(2): 313–36.

Carlen, P. (1998) *Sledgehammer: Women's Imprisonment at the Millennium*, Basingstoke: Palgrave Macmillan.

Carlen, P., Hicks, J., O 'Dwyer, J., Christina, D. and Tchaikovsky, C. (1985) *Criminal Women*, Cambridge: Polity Press.

Clarke, B. and Chadwick, K. (2018) 'From troubled women to failing institutions: the necessary narrative shift for the decarceration of women post Corston', in L. Moore, P. Scraton and A. Wahidin (eds) (2018) *Women's Imprisonment and the Case for Abolition: Critical Reflections of Corston Ten Years On*, London: Routledge, pp 51–70.

Corston, J. (2007) *The Corston Report: a review of women with particular vulnerabilities in the criminal justice system*, London: Home Office.

Enos, S. (2001) *Mothering from the Inside: Parenting in a Women's Prison*, Albany: State University of New York Press.

Farmer Report (2019) *Importance of strengthening female offenders' family and other relationships to prevent reoffending and reduce intergenerational crime*, Available at: https://www.gov.uk/government/publications/farmer-review-for-women [Accessed 22 September 2021].

Garcia, J. (2016) 'Understanding the lives of mothers after incarceration: moving beyond socially constructed definitions of motherhood', *Sociology Compass*, 10(1): 3–11.

Giordano, P. C., Cernkovich, S. A. and Rudolph, J. L. (2002) 'Gender, crime, and desistance: toward a theory of cognitive transformation', *American Journal of Sociology*, 107(4): 990–1064.

Goffman, I. (1963) *Stigma: Notes on the Management of Spoiled Identity*, London: Prentice Hall.

Hays, S. (1996) *The Cultural Contradictions of Motherhood*, New Haven, CT: Yale University Press.

Hays, S. (2003) *Flat Broke with Children: Women in the Age of Welfare Reform*, New York: Oxford University Press.

Lockwood, K. (2018) 'Disrupted mothering: narratives of mothers in prison', in *Marginalized Mothers, Mothering from the Margins*, Bingley: Emerald Publishing Limited, pp 157–73.

Minson, S. (2020) *Maternal Sentencing and the Rights of the Child*, London: Palgrave Macmillan.

MoJ (Ministry of Justice) (2018) 'The female offender strategy'. Available at: https://www.gov.uk/government/publications/female-offender-strategy [Accessed 22 September 2021].

MoJ (Ministry of Jusice) (2020) *Outcomes by Offence Tool 2019*, London: MoJ.

Morriss, L. (2018) 'Haunted futures: the stigma of being a mother living apart from her child(ren) as a result of state-ordered court removal', *The Sociological Review*, 66(4): 816–31.

O'Malley, S. (2018) 'The experience of imprisonment for incarcerated mothers and their children in Ireland', Doctoral thesis, Galway: National University of Ireland.

O'Malley, S. and Devaney, C. (2016) 'Maintaining the mother–child relationship within the Irish prison system: the practitioner perspective', *Child Care in Practice*, 22(1): 20–34.

O'Reilly, A. (2016) *Matricentric Feminism, Theory, Activism and Practice*, Ontario: Demeter Press.

Penal Reform International (nd) 'UN Bangkok rules'. Available at: https://www.penalreform.org/issues/women/bangkok-rules-2/ [Accessed 22 September 2021].

Prison Reform Trust (2019) *Why Focus on Reducing Women's Imprisonment?*, London: Prison Reform Trust.

Renzetti, C. M. (2013) *Feminist Criminology*, Abingdon: Routledge.

Rowe, A. (2011) 'Narratives of self and identity in women's prisons: stigma and the struggle for self-definition in penal regimes', *Punishment & Society*, 13(5): 571–91.

Rukeyser, M. (2006) 'Käthe Kollwitz', *The Collected Poems of Muriel Rukeyser*, Pittsburgh: University of Pittsburgh Press.

Rumgay, J. (2004) 'Scripts for safer survival: pathways out of female crime', *The Howard Journal of Criminal Justice*, 43(4): 405–19.

Sharpe, G. (2015) 'Precarious identities: "Young" motherhood, desistance and stigma', *Criminology and Criminal Justice*, 15(4): 407–22.

Stewart, P. (2015) 'A psychodynamic understanding of mothers and babies in prison', in L. Baldwin (ed) *Mothering Justice: Working with Mothers in Criminal and Social Justice Settings*, Hook: Waterside Press, pp 167–84.

Stone, R. (2016) 'Desistance and identity repair: redemption narratives as resistance to stigma', *British Journal of Criminology*, 56(5): 956–75.

Women in Prison (2017) *Corston+10: The Corston Report 10 years on. How far have we come on the road to reform for women affected by the criminal justice system?*, London: Women in Prison.

6

'The World Split Open': Writing, Teaching and Learning with Women in Prison

Hannah King, Kate O'Brien and Fiona Measham, with Verity-Fee, Phoenix, Iris and Angel

Verity-Fee, Phoenix, Iris and Angel are white, working-class women who are, or who have been, locked out of sight from society in a women's prison in England. They are just four of the women we have had the privilege of collaborating with over the past five years as part of the work we do delivering a prison education programme called the Inside-Out Prison Exchange Programme[1]. Our collaborative work and writing in this book is organised into two connected chapters. Chapter 6 is about context. Drawing on our experiences of writing, teaching and learning *with* women in prison, this chapter outlines the prison-based teaching programme that brought us together and explores our theoretical and conceptual approach. Much of our thinking about the punishment of women and prisons is born out of our many conversations with incarcerated women who have taken part in classes or with whom we have worked over the years. In Chapter 7, we go on to provide a critical reflection of our varied epistemologies on the imprisonment of women. We make no excuses for writing in an emotive way, and, in places, exposing our 'uncomfortable' and contradictory perspectives. On the contrary – this is first and foremost a feminist project and as such we celebrate subjectivity and individual experience (Reinharz, 1992), which are particularly impossible to ignore in a prison environment (Liebling, 1999). Chapter 7, is also co-authored with Verity-Fee, Phoenix, Iris and Angel but their names appear before ours in the authorship order, partly because their writings and prison journeys take centre stage.[2] Through their poetry and creative writing, the chapter that follows provides a platform for their voices and complex experiences to be heard. We include short biographies as a way to contextualise their written pieces, which, when read together, we hope conveys a sense of their journey through prison.

We came to know each other through the Inside-Out Prison Exchange Programme, a prison-based education programme that brings academics and outside university students into prison to learn alongside, and as equals with, women and men detained inside prison. We provide and draw upon a range of texts as part of the programme. However, finding texts that prioritise and forefront women's voices in prison is surprisingly difficult. The few examples that we have are written from the American context. One key UK text that we consistently work with on our Inside-Out programme is Pat Carlen's co-authored seminal book *Criminal Women*. Despite being published in 1985, we find that it powerfully resonates with the people we work with who are incarcerated in English women's prisons today. *Criminal Women* provided the original inspiration for this book and for our journey in writing with women in prison. This chapter and the next are our contribution to readdressing the balance in academic writing about prisons, which tends to be concerned predominantly with the male prison estate and men in prison. Furthermore, we forefront women's voices in the English prison system. This is particularly important to us because of how we work through the powerful ethos of Inside-Out and our commitment to supporting women.

Inspired by the work of Carlen et al, both chapters are structured around the contributions of the four women – short poems and prose pieces – that they wrote four years ago for a writing project that did not come to fruition. Before writing this book, we had an opportunity to revisit the pieces with the women and explore with them their reflections on their earlier autobiographical works, and the wider contexts to their experiences and their journeys through the criminal justice system (CJS). In forefronting the voices of these four women, it shines a cold light on the stark realities and experiences of so many women who find themselves locked up in the English prison system, and in particular, their experiences of childhood trauma and the prolonged violence and abuse inflicted on them in their lives, predominantly by men. Because of this content, this chapter and the chapter that follows come with a trigger warning.

The Inside-Out Prison Exchange Programme and Think Tanks

> Through dialogue our aim is to make the walls that separate us permeable. (Pompa, 2013)

The Inside-Out Prison Exchange Programme is an innovative model of prison education that fosters a transformative collective learning experience underpinned by a critical pedagogy. It is designed to break down barriers and prejudices and provide university (Outside) students and incarcerated (Inside) students with a unique opportunity to study together as equals. The programme was founded in 1997 by Lori Pompa, a Temple University criminologist, working collaboratively with a group of incarcerated men at Graterford State Correctional Institution to address racial injustice in the US CJS (Pompa, 2013). With the initial idea stemming from a man serving a life sentence in a US prison, a key feature of this programme is that all Inside-Out instructors receive a week's intensive residential training, including a number of days inside a prison being taught by incarcerated Inside students, using the distinctive dialogic critical pedagogy of Inside-Out. Over the following two decades, the programme expanded across North America, Europe and Australia, and Lori Pompa's work was recognised with an American Society of Criminology Lifetime Achievement Award for Teaching in 2016.

The roots of the Inside-Out educational approach lie within the critical pedagogy of Freire (2000), bell hooks (1994) and the teaching practice advocated by Palmer (2007). Their works argue that students should not be 'objects that teachers do something to', rather, teachers should listen, ask questions, welcome students' insights and encourage them to always learn more. Inside-Out is education in its truest form, embracing both possible interpretations of the word 'education' – drawing on its Latin roots in 'educare', to lead or to train, and 'educere', to draw out from within – and creating an environment whereby Inside and Outside students together creatively explore issues of crime and criminal justice. Thus, teaching Inside-Out involves engaging in the process that bell hooks calls 'teaching to transgress', that is, allowing students to understand experientially the ways in which every day and commonplace environments are shaped by inequalities (O'Brien et al, 2021).

Most classes take place within the prison walls. Readings, assessments and discussions prioritise the collective building of knowledge through dialogue. Students sit in a large circle and in alternate seats, so each Outside student sits next to an Inside student. This seating arrangement makes a powerful statement about our common humanity and fosters a shared sense of equity, equality and inclusion: students have an equal voice and stake in the learning process. The circle provides a space of liberation, not only because both Inside and Outside students regularly say that they become so absorbed in classroom dialogue that they 'forget' where they are, but a place where each student is recognised for their unique contribution. Using community-building exercises, we grapple with issues together and – in contrast to the didactic approach of traditional higher education pedagogy – everyone is empowered to be both teacher and learner, creating knowledge together. Crucially, this approach enables us, as facilitators, to expose and then break down barriers and prejudices.

The concept of 'walls' is employed as a powerful metaphor in Inside-Out to convey its purpose and the challenge of our existing CJS. Inside-Out is about walls, some of which are made of bricks – 'but all are held in place by the mortar of fear and ignorance. We fear what we don't know—in others, in the world, even in ourselves. So, we build walls, thinking we can keep ourselves safe from whatever we imagine is threatening us. It is a dangerous delusion' (Pompa, 2013: 133). Inside-Out moves through and beyond the walls through facilitating an interaction between people on both sides of the prison walls. The aim, therefore, is that through participation in the programme the walls that separate us can begin to crumble: 'The hope is that, in time, through this exchange, these walls—between us, around us, and within us—will become increasingly permeable and, eventually, extinct—one idea, one person, one brick at a time. All of our lives depend on it.' (Pompa, 2013: 133).

The Durham University Inside-Out Prison Exchange Programme was established in 2014 and runs undergraduate and postgraduate level programmes at two men's and one women's prison each year. Both female and male university outside students participate in the programme at the men's and women's prisons. As is part of the Inside-Out ethos of continuing education, representation and empowerment after the programme is completed, Think Tanks were established at the women's prison and one of the men's prisons in 2015. The Think Tanks consist of inside students who successfully completed the programme, meeting monthly with Inside-Out instructors to support the programme and other projects within the prison. Together, the Think Tanks form Durham Inside-Out Collective.

A strong sense of collective identity and community spirit has developed within the groups, as each Think Tank focuses on change – the essence of education – as we work with the human capacity to develop and become more (Freire, 2000). We have also supported and trained both the women's and men's Think Tank members to become university teaching assistants, co-develop the curriculum and co-facilitate the Inside-Out programme with us. Collaboration and co-production are integral to the united way in which we work together. Furthermore, the Think Tank in the women's prison, along with the wider prison population, includes a diversely gendered membership that includes transgender men and women.[3] It is with this Think Tank that in 2020 we trained members in participatory action research methods and have been developing and supporting a number of projects including exploring housing and homelessness upon release; parental rights in prison; and specialist sexual violence counselling services in prison.

Origins of this writing project – 'the world split open'

What would happen if one woman told the truth about her life? The world would split open. (Rukeyser, 2006 [1968])

This is a line by the Jewish feminist poet Muriel Rukeyser from one of her biographical poems about the artist Käthe Kollwitz, whose own work centred on women and the impact of poverty, hunger and war on the working class. This powerful line was the basis of a women's writing project that took place in the USA in 2016. Think Tank members were invited to contribute to the project: an anthology of writings from women's prisons. This creative writing project was one of the first projects we developed with the Think Tank and included a session with a creative writing tutor. Unfortunately, the anthology never came to fruition. Given the regularity of the experiences of disappointment, rejection and betrayal for many women in prison, it was important to us that we honour our commitment to publishing their work. Collectively, we decided to incorporate their poetry and creative writing into these chapters. Their words have power in their own right, but in this chapter we are positioning them within the broader context of women's experiences within the CJS.

The creative writing process took place over several months and ensuring that the women were properly supported throughout this was important. Our Inside-Out experience has taught us that Inside students are generally well rehearsed in reflective thinking, which is often revealed in the reflective essays they write for their assignments. We have found that women Inside students more openly and regularly share and reflect upon the traumatic experiences they have faced, which brings a deeper emotional dimension to our work in the women's prison. We were acutely aware that this writing project could unearth deeply personal and moving stories. We worked closely with our training and education lead in the prison, and she helped us put in place wraparound support following our sessions.

Muriel Rukeyser was a poet of the personal and the political. Her work is often described as feminist, articulating 'the thoughts and feelings of the unnoticed and excluded' (Anna Herzog, *The Women's Review of Books*), giving 'voice to the repressed, particularly to the lives of women and the marginalized' (Lee Upton, *Belles Lettres*). Her fascination with Kollwitz is thus perhaps unsurprising. Much of Kollwitz's work focused on women and the working class, particularly during the First World War. Her powerful depictions of the pain endured by mothers and the plight of people incarcerated in prison feel particularly pertinent to this project.

Figure 6.1: *The Prisoners*

Source: Kollwitz (1908): Honolulu Museum of Art

Figure 6.2: *The Mothers*

Source: Kollwitz (1919): Metropolitan Museum of Art, Museum Accession, transferred from library, 1962

Figure 6.3: *Mother with Dead Child*

Source: Kollwitz (1903): https://commons.wikimedia.org/wiki/Kthe_Kollwitz

The line from Rukeyser's poem hit a chord with all of us and the four women passionately set about writing to that sentiment, writing about their own lives. The pieces of writing they produced are presented in the next chapter.

Reflections on our approach: women, prisons and violence(s)

Our work with women and men in prison is informed by intersectional feminist and critical criminological perspectives.[4] Although women represent less than 5 per cent of those incarcerated in England and Wales, their rates of imprisonment have multiplied significantly faster than men's and they are subjected to longer sentences for commensurate offences (Prison Reform Trust, 2020). As this book attests, there is plentiful research into the distinct vulnerability and gender-specific needs of criminalised women. This has led campaigners, such as the Prison Reform Trust, Women in Prison and Sisters Uncut to call for the decarceration of women. The crisis in English women's prisons has continued unabated since Baroness Corston's seminal review of women with additional vulnerabilities in the CJS (2007). A decade later and just 2 of her 43 recommendations – to develop 'a distinct, radically different, visibly-led, strategic, proportionate, holistic, woman-centred, integrated approach' – had been fully implemented (Women in Prison, 2017).

The majority of women in prison (80 per cent) are incarcerated for non-violent offences, two thirds of sentences are less than six months and over half of those remanded in custody do not then go on to receive a custodial sentence (Women in Prison, 2020). These remarkable figures suggest that the CJS in England and Wales simply does not know what to do with women who may (or may not) have offended. The majority of female offenders experience a vast array of social problems, often related to social and economic marginalisation, and in recent decades we have seen the increasing criminalisation of female poverty, along with the increasing feminisation of poverty, reflected in prison sentencing. An issue of concern for feminist criminologists in the 1980s (see Glendinning and Millar, 1987; Carlen, 1988), this has been exacerbated by successive doggedly punitive governments and more recently by austerity and welfare reforms. Baldwin and Epstein (2017) found that the bedroom tax, benefits caps and Universal Credit system were all direct reasons for some women's offending, such as shoplifting baby bottles, nappies and food. Often first offences, these regularly resulted in short prison sentences with dire consequences for their children. Current Ministry of Justice data shows that almost a third of women's convictions are for not paying the TV license fee of £157.50 and that women are ten times more likely to be convicted for this offence than men (MoJ, 2020).

Prisons are a 'key function in the maintenance of blatantly unequal societies' used to punish the poor and marginalised (Scott, 2013: 313). Prisons act as a warehouse for society's 'undeserving' and 'undesirable'; a place to lock away the poorest and most marginalised, with little chance of 'rehabilitation'. Wacquant (2016) argues that social welfare and penal policies have become inextricably linked, with welfare revamped as 'workfare' and 'prisonfare' stripping any pretensions of rehabilitative dimensions of prison. This 'single organisational mesh' is flung at the same clientele, the poor – the dispossessed and dishonoured (Wacquant, 2016: 114). King et al (2021) argue that 'citizens of the UK are more likely to suffer from the effects of welfare reforms and austerity measures, imposed upon them by their own government, than they are from pandemics, terrorist attacks or environmental or climate related disasters.' The gendered nature of this oppression becomes particularly stark when we look at the criminalisation of women's poverty, violence against women and girls (at both the personal and state level) and women's experiences in prison.

The reasons for women's offending, as we will explore through Verity-Fee, Iris, Phoenix and Angel's poetry and creative writing pieces, are complex, multi-dimensional and, for most, bound in a web of patriarchal violence. The disproportionate use of prison for women can be seen as a consequence of community deficits (most recently exacerbated by austerity in the UK) and as structural violence. Structural violence is caused by institutionalised inequalities that create harm by preventing people from meeting their basic needs (Cooper and Whyte, 2018). It is systemic, silent, naturalised and built into structures of power in a way that ensure it is imposed on victims with impunity: indirect and with no identifiable perpetrator. This structural violence and oppression results from the coalescence and interactions of the inequitable identities, statuses and stratum known as intersectionality (Crenshaw, 1989) and that include race/ethnicity, sex/gender, social class, age, sexuality and (dis)ability. Within this context, the CJS responsibilises those subjected to its iron reach, reserving its harshest condemnation for women. We see this most powerfully in Phoenix's creative writing in the next chapter. Research demonstrates that female perpetrators of crime receive longer sentences than their male counterparts for similar offences (Prison Reform Trust, 2019). This connects to Carlen's (1988) notion that women are considered by the CJS to be doubly deviant – offending against the law and offending against their femininity, resulting in double jeopardy (harsher social judgement and harsher sentences). Bosworth (1999: 96) further argues that the penal power exercised in women's prisons is 'legitimated by, and therefore reliant on, a particular construction of (docile, feminine) subjectivity.' Consequently, it is not just expressions of agency and autonomy that are treated as resistance, but non-normative ways of being too.

It is arguable that all women who have been through the prison system have been 'responsibilised', that is, they have been expected to wholly and individually take responsibility for their actions (and are often forced to) and reminded about it on a daily basis. Indeed, their very release may depend on this. Yet, at no point has the system taken responsibility for the structural violence it has inflicted upon them through the state, before they went to prison, during prison and now that some of them have left prison. Responsibility is all too often imposed 'by those who wish to deny or escape their own responsibilities, upon those who are not responsible for their condition and do not have causal powers that responsibility attributes to them' (Rose and Lentzos, 2017: 8). With many of the women we meet in prison, it is the abdication of responsibility by the state and society that leads us to question why they are in prison in the first place. As we reveal in the next chapter, for Verity-Fee, Phoenix and Angel, both state and society abdicated responsibility for them as children and women only to demand they take responsibility as women in prison.

Women's prisons are arguably the most brutal representation of the gendered nature of this structural violence (see Moore and Scraton, 2014). In 1978, Smart and Smart argued that '[t]he social control of women assumes many forms, it may be internal or external, implicit or explicit, private or public, ideological or repressive' (1978: 9). Anglin (1998: 147) explains that to 'speak of "gendered structures of violence" is not to suggest that women are always the victims, but instead to call attention to the differential effects of coercive processes on women and men, girls and boys.' Focusing on the differential effects of structural violence on women is key to understanding state punishment, and ultimately to dismantling the prison system. Abolition is not just about getting rid of the CJS or prisons, but is about eradicating the conditions under which prison became the solution to the problems (Gilmore, 2007). This necessarily includes the structures and processes which perpetuate structural violence, in all its intersectional forms (including racialised, gendered and class-based). It is perhaps useful to remind ourselves of Audre Lorde's (2007) comment that there 'are no single issue struggles, because we do not lead single issue lives'. Women in prison and those we work with have multidimensional identities which are impacted in nuanced ways by structural violence enacted through the prison system. They are subjected to its highly-gendered nature through the CJS and the women's prison estate. Moore and Scraton (2014) argue that prison is a space that harms all women; a gendered, violent institution in which power and control serve to perpetuate and replicate the challenges and inequalities faced by women in wider society. In the next chapter we breathe life into these arguments by forefronting the voices of Verity-Fee, Phoenix, Iris and Angel through their creative writing pieces and accompanying biographies. In doing so, we seek to advance theoretical understandings of women and prison, particularly within the UK context, through women's voices and experiences.

Prisons and their regimes have 'been shaped by some of the most repressive, discriminatory and usually outdated ideologies of womanhood and femininity that have been prevalent in society at large' (Carlen and Worrall, 2004: 2). For centuries, female offenders have been characterised as 'essentially mad, bad, or sad, or caring or neglectful mothers' (Gelsthorpe, 2004: 84) and indeed a key aim of the feminist criminology project for academics like Carlen and Smart has been to dismantle these longstanding stereotypes. Consequently, women in prison 'have not only been physically secured by all the hardware and disciplinary control paraphernalia of the men's establishments, they have, in addition, been psychologically interpellated (if not always constrained) by the triple disciplines of feminisation, domesticisation and medicalisation' (Carlen and Worrall, 2004: 2). As Davis (2001: 7) argues, 'state-sanctioned punishment is informed by patriarchal structures and ideologies that have tended to produce historical assumptions of female criminality linked to ideas about the violation of social norms defining a woman's place.' Furthermore, we can see that patriarchal structural violence in the private realm – domestic violence – is replicated in the public realm through women's prisons. Over half of the women in prison have experienced some form of intimate partner and/or sexual violence (Prison Reform Trust, 2020) and, for some, this has dominated their lives since childhood. The prison system can be seen as an oppressive apparatus that extends the violent control that many women have experienced from the private to the public sphere. These two modes of gendered punishment are facilitated and enacted by the patriarchal state; both are built upon oppression, coercion, the stripping of freedom and asserting of control over women's bodies. All four women speak to these arguments in their creative writing in the next chapter, none more so than Verity-Fee.

Turning the gaze to women's prisons globally highlights their retention of oppressive patriarchal practices, which essentially remain hidden from the public, such as strip-searching and sexual abuse (Willingham, 2011). These are not unique to women's prisons, as the countless high-profile media cases involving men and powerful institutions attest. Prison (in)justice is thus an important feminist issue and the call for abolition of women's prisons is unsurprising. In the meantime, however, those currently in prison should not be subjected to ever-worsening conditions while campaigners move towards future decarceration and abolition (Davis, 2001; Moore and Scraton, 2014; Moore et al, 2017). Academics like Gilmore (2007) and organisations such as Abolitionist Futures (https://abolitionistfutures.com/) argue for 'non-reformist reforms'. These involve enacting changes that will shrink the system and redirect resources into actions and systems that will actually keep women safe, for example housing, violence against women and girls (VAWG) organisations, mental health support, the redistribution of resources, anti-racism and so forth, all of which are needed to undo the structures that cause the harm.

While we can see prison as an institution of structural violence, patriarchally enforced upon women, we also cannot ignore that the women we work with sometimes describe and experience prison as a place of safety. Angel's story, as we will see in the next chapter, is testament to this observation. Indeed, some of the members of our Think Tanks have been released only to return to prison within weeks, with mixed feelings of both relief and resentment. We continue to grapple with this uncomfortable tension ourselves, exploring its dimensions in the biographies presented in the next chapter. Wacquant (2002: 388) recognises that the prison may act 'counterintuitively and within limits, as a stabilizing and restorative force for relations already deeply frayed by the pressures of life and labour at the bottom of the social edifice.' While prison usually results in feelings of powerlessness, frustration, sadness and disconnection (see Moore and Scraton, 2014), it can also trigger feelings of safety, security and even familiarity (Bradley and Davino, 2002; Prison Reform Trust, 2014). However, the feminist abolitionist calls of Angela Davis and others remind us that, if we addressed patriarchal violence against women (both structural and interpersonal), they would not need the respite of either prisons or refuges for their safety. Indeed, we would not need prisons for women at all.

Concluding thoughts

We write this chapter with a reflective, feminist critical criminological voice mindful of the 'disrupting and revolutionising' potential of writing, teaching and learning together with our Inside-Out students and colleagues (Potter, 2015). We bring an intersectional perspective to our work too, one which recognises that structural distinctions are interconnected and therefore that power structures and their influence over the CJS cannot be understood without a consideration of this intersectionality. We are also mindful that we are white women from working class and middle class backgrounds with different levels of opportunity and privilege, operating in education and criminal justice systems where being Black and minoritised brings enormous additional deprivations, inequalities and discrimination. Therefore, while these chapters are silent on the Black and minoritised experience of the CJS, we recognise that the women represented here have had very different experiences of the prison system to their Black and minoritsed incarcerated sisters, and we recognise structural violence in relation to race, as well as gender and class (see Collins, 2019). We are alert to Crenshaw's continued plea for the urgency of intersectionality, of the need to bear witness to and confront the painful realities of everyday violence and humiliation faced by Black women across colour, age, gender expression, sexuality and ability (Crenshaw, 2016).

We embark on our work with women in prison as critical feminist social researchers, which involves 'being there' and 'bearing witness, gathering testimonies, sharing experiences, garnering the view from below' (Scraton, 2007: 5). Michelle Fine, often in collaboration with peer researchers, some of whom are incarcerated, has written and spoken frequently on this issue, on the importance of bearing witness and documenting circuits of dispossession and privilege within a context of state violence, particularly towards people in prison (see Fine et al, 2003). She argues (2006: 83) that 'in a world of diasporic oppressions and flares of resistance, social research [can] provoke greater awareness of injustice and contribute to social movements more intimately.' However, she recognises that this collaborative work is often built on fragile solidarities. These solidarities require us to be open to, and sit with, the uncomfortable, complex and sometimes contradictory spaces that are inevitable within this type of work. Relatedly, we find ourselves constantly grappling with the tension of abolitionist beliefs, while essentially working inside the system in order to facilitate the Inside-Out programme and our collective work with the Think Tanks.

Our monthly meetings in the prison library are both joyful and painful. We drink tea, share food and invariably spend our first hour together catching up on recent news and gossip from the wings, complimenting each other on new hairstyles and clothes, discussing recent TV programmes we have watched and talking about past and future family visits. For us, it is always a pleasure to be able to stop, sit and converse with inspiring, brave and insightful men and women, and free from the distraction of mobile phones. We enjoy each other's company immensely. It is impossible not to feel present and in the moment during these sessions. It is evident from how they arrive in the room and take their place at the table that this is a space where they can be themselves, 'feel normal' and momentarily step out of the chaos and noise that fills the wings and corridors outside the library. When we get to work, our conversations can go deep and, at times, we feel helpless and hopeless. For example, when we learned about Tracy's release from prison. Tracy was a member of the Think Tank who was released from prison with nowhere to live. She was subjected to a horrific sexual assault in a makeshift bed she had made in a supermarket carpark. With no other options available to her, she breached her license conditions as a route back to prison and a return to a place that for Tracy was warmer and safer than the violence she experienced on the street. Over the years, there have been many similar conversations and episodes that have made us feel powerless and ill-equipped to respond adequately.

Many of the conversations that we have are incredibly difficult to participate in and hearing their stories can be hard and painful. The challenge and impact of dealing with and reflecting on emotions within research has been largely neglected by academia. Clarke et al (2017: 277) acknowledge from their extensive collaborative work on criminalisation and injustice that the critical social research process 'is messy and complex, involving emotion and intuition' and is full of 'dilemmas and contradictions'. We often feel helpless and hopeless but know that this work is crucial and that it is not enough to standby and do nothing. To borrow from Leonard Cohen, we must work within the cracks (of this broken system) for that is how the light gets in. As academics, we occupy a privileged position 'in bearing witness to the experiences of others and to state institutional processes and practices' (Clarke et al, 2017: 268). We have a duty to expose the many injustices that define state institutions, such as prisons, and to share and communicate this knowledge.

Ignacio Martin-Baro (1994: 189) argues that established power structures in El Salvador have produced a collective lie that is ideologically compatible with the interests of the dominant class, with three consequences: 'the country's most serious problems have been systematically hidden from view; the social interests and forces at play have been distorted; and people have internalized the alienating discourse as part of their personal and social identity.' We believe this holds true for the UK as well. He argues that critical social researchers must uncover these collective lies and unearth untold stories to increase critical consciousness and shape a new collective identity (Martin-Baro, 1994). Scraton (2016: 7) further argues that 'critical social research bears witness to systemic abuse, harnesses official discourse of formal inspections, and provides empirical, alternative accounts to those carefully orchestrated by prison managers and state departments. It projects the "personal troubles" of the incarcerated to the wider stage of societal "public issues". Yet, it should not be limited to an elaborate academic critique only directed inwards towards mainstream social sciences.' One option available to us, and our way of doing this, is to forefront and platform the voices of those locked within the prison system. We also share Clarke et al's (2017: 277) notion of a longer-term commitment to a case or issue, which is 'underpinned by our positionality – a recognition of injustice, a rejection of the processes and discourses driven by the State; and a desire to intervene.' Indeed, our commitment to Inside-Out and working with women (and men) in prison continues. The chapter that follows, Chapter 7, positions Verity-Fee, Phoenix, Iris and Angel centre stage. Their poetry and creative writing pieces, together with extended biographies that were written in collaboration with them, add texture, nuance and complexity to the theoretical ideas and concepts we have outlined in this chapter. Thus, by foregrounding the voices of incarcerated women and their varied 'lived experiences', we are enriching theoretical approaches that explain women's imprisonment in the UK as structural violence, patriarchal violence or both.

Notes

[1] https://www.insideoutcenter.org/

[2] The women's names have been changed throughout to ensure anonymity and confidentiality, but we recognise here their individual and collective contributions to these chapters and to the wider Inside-Out programme. The continuing and gendered nature of stigma and oppression faced by those in the CJS means that they are unable to use their names as authors of these chapters.

[3] The prison system in England and Wales operates a policy (HMPPS, 2020) whereby a transgender individual is usually incarcerated in a prison corresponding to their legal gender, or subject to an application to a case board, the gender that they identity if different, or other factors such as safety, risk and lived experience. Consequently, prisons contain people who are transitioning and have transitioned, with or without gender reassignment surgery, against a backdrop of two centuries of a highly segregated binary UK prison estate divided on the basis of sexual rather than gender identity. The relevance of this to these chapters is that firstly, we note that the women's prison Inside-Out Think Tank contained members identifying as women and men, including those who had transitioned from female to male and male to female identities. Secondly, the seemingly contradictory framing of prisons as places of punishment and of safety, discussed further in the next chapter, was particularly salient to the transgender prison population.

[4] In particular, the work of Kimberle Krenshaw, bell hooks, Angela Davis, Pat Carlen and Loraine Gelsthorpe.

References

Anglin, M. K. (1998) 'Feminist perspectives of structural violence', *Identities*, 5(2): 145–51.

Baldwin, L. and Epstein, R. (2017) *Short but not sweet: a study of the impact of short custodial sentences on mothers and their children*, Leicester: De Montfort University.

Bosworth, M. (1999) *Engendering Resistance: Agency and Power in Women's Prisons*, London: Routledge.

Bradley, R. G. and Davino, K. M. (2002) 'Women's perceptions of the prison environment: when prison is "the safest place I've ever been"', *Psychology of Women Quarterly*, 26(4): 351–59.

Carlen, P. (1988) *Women, Crime and Poverty*, London: Open University Press.

Carlen, P. and Worrall, A. (2004) *Analysing Women's Imprisonment*, London: Willan.

Clarke, R., Chadwick, K. and Williams, P. (2017) 'Critical social research as a "site of resistance": reflections on relationships, power and positionality', *Justice, Power and Resistance*, 1(2): 261–82.

Collins, P. H. (2019) *Intersectionality as Critical Social Theory*, Durham, NC: Duke University Press.

Cooper, V. and Whyte, D. (2018) 'Grenfell, austerity and institutional violence', *Sociological Research Online*, October, pp 1–10.

Corston, J. (2007) *The Corston Report – Review of Women with Particular Vulnerabilities in the Criminal Justice System*, London: Home Office.

Crenshaw, K. (1989) 'Demarginalizing the intersection of race and sex: a black feminist critique of antidiscrimination doctrine, feminist theory and antiracist politics', *University of Chicago Legal Forum*, 1989(1): Article 8.

Crenshaw, K. (2016) 'The urgency of intersectionality', *TEDWomen*. Available at: https://www.ted.com/talks/kimberle_crenshaw_the_urgency_of_intersectionality [Accessed 22 September 2021].

Davis, A. (2001) 'Public imprisonment and private violence – reflections on the hidden punishment of women', in M. R. Waller and J. Rycenga (eds) *Frontline Feminisms: Women, War and Resistance*, London: Routledge, pp 2–17.

Davis, A. (2003) *Are Prisons Obsolete?*, New York: Seven Stories Press.

Fine, M. (2006) 'Bearing witness: methods for researching oppression and resistance – a textbook for critical research', *Social Justice Research*, 19(1): 83–108.

Fine, M., Torre, M. E., Boudin, K., Bowen, I., Clark, J., Hylton, D. and Upegui, D. (2003) 'Participatory action research: within and beyond bars', in P. Camic, J. E. Rhodes and L. Yardley (eds) *Qualitative Research in Psychology: Expanding Perspectives in Methodology and Design*, Washington, DC: American Psychological Association, pp 173–98.

Freire, P. (2000) *Pedagogy of the Oppressed*, New York: Continuum International Publishing Group.

Gelsthorpe, L. (2004) 'Back to basics in crime control – weaving in women', *Critical Review of International Social and Political Philosophy*, 7(2): 76–103.

Gilmore, R. W. (2007) *Golden Gulag: Prisons, Surplus, Crisis, and Opposition in Globalizing California*, Berkeley: University of California Press.

Glendinning, C. and Millar, J. (1987) *Women and Poverty in Britain*, Hemel Hempstead: Harvester Wheatsheaf.

HMPPS (Her Majesty's Prison and Probation Service) (2020) 'The care and management of individuals who are transgender: operational guidance'. Available at: https://www.gov.uk/government/publications/the-care-and-management-of-individuals-who-are-transgender [Accessed 22 September 2021].

Herzog, A. (nd) *The Women's Review of Books*. Available at: https://www.poetryfoundation.org/poets/muriel-rukeyser [Accessed 22 September 2021].

hooks, bell (1994) *Teaching to Transgress – Education as the Practice of Freedom*, London: Routledge.

King, H., Crossley, S. and Smith, R. (2021) 'Responsibility, resilience and symbolic power', *The Sociological Review*, 69(5): 920–36.

Liebling, A. (1999) 'Doing research in prison: breaking the silence', *Theoretical Criminology*, 3(2): 147–73.

Lorde, A. (2007) 'Learning from the 60s', in *Sister Outsider: Essays & Speeches by Audre Lorde*, Berkeley, CA: Crossing Press, pp 86–96.

Martin-Baro, I. (1994) *Writings for a Liberation Psychology*, Cambridge, MA: Harvard University Press.

MoJ (2020) *Outcomes by Offence Tool 2019*, London: MoJ.

Moore, L. and Scraton, P. (2014) *The Incarceration of Women: Punishing Bodies, Breaking Spirits*, London: Palgrave Macmillan.

Moore, L., Scraton, P. and Wahidin, A. (eds) (2017) *Women's Imprisonment and the Case for Abolition: Critical Reflections on Corston Ten Years On*, London: Routledge.

Palmer, P. (2007) *The Courage to Teach Guide for Reflection and Renewal*, Hoboken, NJ: John Wiley & Sons.

Pompa, L. (2013) 'One brick at a time: the power and possibility of dialogue across the prison wall', *The Prison Journal*, 93(2): 127–34.

Potter, H. (2015) *Intersectionality and Criminology: Disrupting and Revolutionizing Studies of Crime*, Abingdon: Routledge.

Prison Reform Trust (2014) *A Place of Safety?* [Online] Available at: http://www.prisonreformtrust.org.uk/ProjectsResearch/Mentalhealth/TroubledInside/Aplaceofsafety [Accessed 22 September 2021].

Prison Reform Trust (2019) *Why Focus on Reducing Women's Imprisonment?*, London: Prison Reform Trust.

Prison Reform Trust (2020) *Bromley Briefings Prison Factfile*, [Online] Available at: http://www.prisonreformtrust.org.uk/Publications/Factfile [Accessed 22 September 2021].

Reinharz, S. (1992) *Feminist Methods in Social Research*, New York: Oxford University Press.

Rose, N. and Lentzos, F. (2017) 'Making us resilient: responsible citizens for uncertain times', in S. Trnka and C. Trundle (eds) *Competing Responsibilities: The Politics and Ethics of Contemporary Life*, Durham, NC: Duke University Press, pp 27–48.

Scott, D. (2013) 'Unequalled in pain', in: D. Scott (ed.) *Why Prison?*, Cambridge: Cambridge University Press, pp 301–24.

Scraton, P. (2007) *Power Conflict and Criminalisation*, London: Routledge.

Scraton, P. (2016) 'Bearing witness to the "pain of others": researching power, violence and resistance in a women's prison', *International Journal for Crime, Justice and Social Democracy*, 5(1): 5–20.

Smart, C. and Smart, B. (1978) *Women, Sexuality and Social Control*, London: Routledge and Kegan Paul.

Upton, L. (nd) *Belles Lettres*. Available at: https://www.poetryfoundation.org/poets/muriel-rukeyser [Accessed 22 September 2021].

Wacquant, L. (2002) 'The curious eclipse of prison ethnography in the age of mass incarceration', *Ethnography,* 3(4): 371–97.

Wacquant, L. (2016) 'Bourdieu, Foucault and the penal state in the neoliberal era', in D. Zamora and M. C. Behrent (eds) *Foucault and Neoliberalism,* Malden, MA: Polity Press, pp 114–33.

Willingham, B. (2011) 'Black women's prison narratives and the intersection of race, gender and sexuality in US prisons', *Critical Survey,* 23(3): 55–66.

Women in Prison (2017) *Corston+10 – The Corston Report ten years on,* London: Women in Prison.

Women in Prison (2020) 'Key facts, Women in Prison', [Online]. Available at: https://www.womeninprison.org.uk/campaigns/key-facts [Accessed 22 September 2021].

7

Women's Biographies
through Prison

Verity-Fee, Phoenix, Iris and Angel,
with Hannah King, Kate O'Brien and Fiona Measham

Four incarcerated women were involved in the project. They are each strong, kind and thoughtful and, like all of us, have flaws (Fine and Torre, 2006). After several years delivering prison education and working within the prison estate, we have learned not to judge or romanticise the women we work with. We understand that some people detained in prison have committed serious crimes. However, we approach our work with a strong sense of humanity, of seeing the humanity in all of us. We also approach our work from the standpoint that people, no matter who they are, should not be defined by the worst thing they have done in their lives. The Inside-Out programme focuses on mutual engagement, learning through dialogue and critical thinking. Inside-Out does not 'research' or objectify the inside students who participate in the programme and does not scrutinise their individual offences. All students are known only by a first name or chosen nickname and past offences – of inside or, for that matter, outside students – are not known to the class. Similarly, the Inside-Out Think Tank members that we write with here are serving diverse sentences for diverse offences, but the specifics of those offences are unimportant and not the focus of our work together.

Through a process of working and writing together, the women originally wrote their contributions as part of the 'World Split Open' creative writing project discussed in Chapter 6. However, we have continued to work together since, and during that time have been privy to their experiences within, journeys through, and for one of the women, out of the prison system. We revisited these writings with them and asked them to reflect on who they felt they were at the time of writing, how they feel about that writing now and who they are today. Verity-Fee, Phoenix, Iris and Angel have all contributed to, read and given feedback on this chapter, providing us with the details they wanted including or omitting from their biographies. Two of the women wanted to choose their own pseudonym.

Key themes run through the writing. Given the structural violence inflicted upon women outside and inside prison, outlined in Chapter 6, it is perhaps unsurprising that each of the women represented in this chapter have experienced violence and abuse at some point in their lives and are all from white working-class backgrounds. Three of the writings shine a light on the various ways in which violence and abuse have continued to haunt and shape their experiences and sense of self.

Their words also evoke a sense of anger: an anger at having been let down by the state and wider society and an anger at subsequently being punished by that same state and society. All of the women have been, through the prison system, 'responsibilised' – expected to wholly and individually take responsibility for their actions and are reminded of this on a daily basis. There is also a sense that, whatever they do, it will never be enough. This leads to moments of despair but also ensures that anger still burns within them. There is also the recurrent theme of relationships. We all experience complex relationships, especially with those we care for and love the most. However, very few of us have to experience how these relationships are impacted by prison. Many of the women we work with are mothers and the rupturing of motherhood is a painful experience for so many women in prison. For some, it means the end of their physical presence as mothers, temporarily, while they are in prison. For others, it means a permanent end to their relationship and contact with their children. As mothers, they feel that rupturing deeply and it continues to impact upon them.

Verity-Fee

Verity-Fee is currently in prison serving her longest sentence yet, after countless, usually short, sentences. She is labelled by the system as a 'revolving door prisoner', a term that she sometimes wryly uses herself. Her experience of hundreds of convictions over two decades is a stark reminder of the problem of short sentences, which are often the result of addiction, vulnerability, mental health, multiple deprivation and even homelessness as opposed to the severity of the crime. Nearly half of women leaving prison return within a year. The number is higher (61 per cent) if the sentence was under 12 months and for women like Verity-Fee, who have been to prison more than 10 times, the figure is higher again at 78 per cent (Women in Prison, 2020). As Verity-Fee's writing demonstrates, her biography and prison journey are punctuated by a long history of surviving violence, abuse, drugs and self-harm. When we first met, Verity-Fee was at possibly the most positive point she had experienced during any of her sentences. She was successfully coming towards the end of a drug treatment programme for heroin addiction, 'getting clean', feeling 'in control', was beginning to have some contact with key familial relationships outside, had finished the relationship with her violent (outside) partner and felt good about herself and her future. She threw herself into the Inside-Out programme. Throughout, she was always honest, critical and keen to learn; to explore, challenge and support her peers. She acted as a particularly important peer mentor to some of the most vulnerable members of the group. She wrote this piece shortly after completing the programme, in 'a good place' and with clear hopes for after her release.

Hearing her words when she first read this piece to us was harrowing. The violence conveyed, which continues to haunt her, is the first of many episodes of sexual violence that Verity-Fee has experienced and recounted to us. Her writing also reflects societally ingrained victim-blaming narratives of sexual violence, as she frames her experience of childhood rape as her own fault. These are experiences recounted by so many women in prison. Over 70 per cent of women in prison have experienced domestic violence and over 50 per cent have experienced childhood abuse (Women in Prison, 2020). Hence, at times, prison has the capacity to be a place of respite and safety from the violence women experience outside (Bradley and Davino, 2002; Baldwin and Epstein, 2015). However, prison has also been a site of violence and abuse (physically and structurally) for Verity-Fee. Her experiences lay bare the tension in seeing prison as a 'safe space' for some women at the same time as being a place of repression, re-victimisation and compounding abuse.

The prison environment can exacerbate the traumas already experienced by many women. Patriarchal systems of power and control are fundamental to domestic violence and this dimension is replicated through the prison system, a powerful institution that prioritises patriarchal violence over and above reform and rehabilitation (Davis, 2003). Verity-Fee's experiences evidence the tangled web of complex relationships for women who move in and out of prison and how both worlds can collide, often with violent consequences. Some of her relationships inside have mutated and become problematic on the outside and vice versa. These relationships, and experiences of violence inside and outside of prison, are frequently intertwined with drug use. Compared with men, women entering prison are significantly more likely to be serving sentences not for drug supply, but for offences relating to their own (and their partner's) drug and alcohol use, with BAME female foreign nationals particularly over-represented (for drug courier/low level trafficking offences) (Joseph, 2006). This was certainly the case for Verity-Fee, who talked often about her addictions and how these were woven into her relationships with men and involvement in theft and handling stolen goods. It was important to Verity-Fee that she was known as a 'shoplifter' and not 'a prostitute' – a theme that often entered the Inside-Out classroom and opened up fascinating discussions about women's identities, morality, respectability and stigma.

Over half of the women entering prison report needing help with a drug problem and over two thirds report mental health problems (PRT, 2019). Within the chaos and unpredictability of prison life, some women need to feel in control of something, or some aspect of themselves. This is how anorexia and self-harm became interwoven into Verity-Fee's biography. Like many women in prison, Verity-Fee uses self-harm as a way to express herself, feel in control and cope in prison. She describes self-harm as a way to deal with her situation and feelings. The main reasons for women's self-harm in prison include histories of sexual abuse and trauma and their guilt and distress at separation from their children and mental illness (Corston, 2007). Over a third of women in prison are reported to self-harm and almost half have attempted suicide at some point in their lifetime (Women in Prison, 2020). Self-harm and deaths in custody (including suicide) have risen dramatically in recent years, yet the historic lack of governmental concern about suicide in prison continues (Walker and Towl, 2016). Although this current sentence may provide Verity-Fee with the opportunity to receive desperately-needed support, confronting a life filled with such trauma, it can sometimes also feel too difficult and too much to ask.

Verity-Fee has been released and returned several times since we first met. Each time we see her it is devastating to see that she has returned, as we always hope that she will 'make it', but we cannot hide our joy at seeing her again. Whatever is happening in her life, she's always there with a warm smile and good humour. Most recently we have been speaking to Verity-Fee at what is a particularly difficult time for her, as her mother is terminally ill. She knows that she will not be able to go out to visit her before she dies or to attend the funeral. As her writing demonstrates, her relationship with her mother has been complex and difficult, but as Verity-Fee says, 'she's still my mam and I love her'. This also intersects with her own experiences as a mother, especially as she no longer has contact with her children. Almost two thirds of women in prison have children under the age of 18 (PRT, 2018). However, this is only an estimation as this data is not formally collected – another demonstration of the government's lack of concern for women in prison, or their children. Kincaid et al (2019) estimate there to be 312,000 children of people in prison in England and Wales, 20,000 of whom have mothers in prison. Furthermore, only 5 per cent of children remain in their own home following maternal imprisonment and 45 per cent of people in prison lose contact with their family while in prison (DBIS et al, 2014). This gives an indication of the enormity of the impact of maternal imprisonment (Minson, 2019). We have touched on the subject of motherhood above, and Verity-Fee illustrates how this situation continues to 'eat her up inside'. As we write this, she is not in a good place. Addiction has taken hold again and she herself feels there is no point in tackling this until she has worked through her mother's death and what happens next. However, she is also using this time for reflection. She still has great ambitions and ideas, including writing a blog from inside prison, inspired by the writings of Erwin James for the *Guardian* (James, 2003). Right now, she is using writing as her favoured medium to express herself.

On reading her original piece, the emotional response is raw and visible. She feels complicated – proud about having written her piece, but angry and confused at how you can feel proud for writing about something 'so horrific and so wrong'. We encourage her to continue with her writing, seeing its positive impact upon her, and she has since shared some of her more recent writing, all reflective pieces cataloguing horrifying experiences of sexual violence and abuse, interwoven with a complex relationship with drugs. In all of Verity-Fee's writing, she writes 'as it is'. It is the simplicity that she brings to such highly-emotive experiences that make them feel as raw today as when she experienced them. Engaging in Inside-Out (which requires the submission of reflective essays for assessment purposes) and this creative writing project has opened the door for Verity-Fee to writing and expressing her creative nature and this is something that she continues today. A victim of our patriarchal state, Verity-Fee continues to try to be upbeat especially in supporting those around her, mostly those who are even less fortunate and more vulnerable than herself.

Verity-Fee's writing

I was approaching my twelfth birthday and had recently been told the man I believed to be my birth father wasn't. This information broke my heart, talking about it took the breath out of my body.

I grew up calling Bill 'dad'. I was closer to him than my mam. It was my 'dad' who I turned to with school problems, teenage trouble and fights with mam. It made my blood boil that I'd been lied to my whole life and that's when I decided to meet my biological father 'John', a decision that would turn my world upside down.

The process happened quickly. My mam somehow contacted him and within two weeks I was sat in a local pub with my mam staring into a stranger's face trying to look for similarities. Straight away I noticed we had the same nose. I sat there in silence while my mam and John talked. To this day I can't remember the conversation. All I know is that it was agreed I would see him once a week, on Saturdays to begin with. My dad asked about the meeting when we got home. I went to watch TV while my mam gave my dad the details. Later that day my dad said something to me which I will never forget, 'no matter what I'm your dad. I changed your nappies, I picked you up when you fell, I clothed and fed you. I love you and you'll always be my daughter', he was crying. I was happy it was hurting him. I wanted it to hurt him. He had lied to me my whole life and I wanted him to feel the pain I was feeling.

Over the next few months I went to see John at his bedsit every Saturday. We gradually got to know one another. He was a strict Hindu, had no other kids, all his family lived in Trinidad, the country where he was born and had worked as a waiter. Although it was very boring, I went week after week knowing it was hurting my parents.

Some months later I arrived home after playing netball and was told by my dad that I would not be allowed to see my biological father again. I asked why and was told it was for my own good and that's all he would say. I tried to protest but, in my dad's opinion, the discussion was over. I wasn't going to let my dad stop me from seeing John so I met him on the sly, without my parents knowing.

On another day I arrived home from school excited about an under 18s disco. I had a huge argument with my mother because one of her friends had seen me out with John. She was trying to stop me from going to the disco. I was very angry. I sneaked out while she was cooking. I ran to John's bedsit and decided to get ready there.

John opened the door and looked happy to see me. He let me in and I realised straight away he was drunk. This was unusual because he didn't drink due to his religion. I told him about the argument I had with my mam. He said he was more than happy for me to get ready at his place which I did. I had a drink with him and felt all grown-up – having a drink while getting ready for a night out with my friends felt good.

Once I was ready I looked in the mirror and liked what I saw. I turned to John and he looked at me with disgust. He said I brought shame on him and with that he punched me square in my face and took me clean off my feet. He jumped on me reigning punch after punch into my head and face. As he was doing this he was screaming 'you're just like your mam'. Next, the man who I share my blood with, violently took my virginity and raped me a total of three times over the next couple of hours.

'I changed your nappies, I picked you up when you fell, I clothed and fed you, I love you and you'll always be my daughter' kept going over and over in my mind. I wanted my dad to help me.

Eventually I talked John into letting me go home. I promised I wouldn't tell anyone. I told him it was my fault and he wasn't to blame.

In autopilot I walked to my best friend's house and told her what had just happened. She broke down and told her mam.

I just wanted to go home, go in the shower and go to bed but I had my mam and two police officers in front of me telling me I'd be going to the Rape Crisis building to give a statement, be medically examined and, 'I'm not to worry'. I thought, 'not to worry' – I was terrified. My mam was holding my hand so hard I thought it would fall off. Me and my mam got into the back of the car. I caught sight of my reflection and noticed I had a black eye. This upset me. Once I started crying I couldn't stop. I was crying for myself, my mam and my dad. When we arrived at the crisis centre I was introduced to a woman called Tracey who explained she needed my clothes. I took them off and they were placed in evidence bags. I was given a white tracksuit to put on. I then lay on a bed and was examined by a doctor. They took swabs and photos of my injuries. I remember feeling embarrassed as my mam looked on. My dad had arrived by now. The doctor then asked to speak to my mam. I don't know what the doctor said to her but she screamed so high it gave me goose bumps. I heard my dad sobbing and saying 'calm down, Verity-Fee will hear you, she'll be scared.' He was right, I was scared. In fact, I was terrified and I just wanted to go home. I was asked to give another statement and then we were allowed to go home.

I think I was in shock. I couldn't believe it was a few hours ago that I was getting ready to go to an under 18s disco and now I was travelling home after being medically examined. It was as if I was living a nightmare. I wished it was a nightmare I could wake up from but it wasn't.

I was angry at myself for allowing this to happen. Why did I continue to see him? Why did I even want to meet him? Why didn't I listen to my dad? Why didn't I put up more of a fight? Why has this happened to me? I wanted to hurt my mam and dad so I had allowed myself to be raped.

That man had taken my virginity and innocence. He also took away my childhood, my trust in others and my life away from me. I was angry at everyone for this happening to me. We finally went to court and although the medical evidence was blatantly clear, John made me give evidence. He was found guilty and given a nine-year sentence. At the time I was pleased but I now know it wasn't long enough.

That night changed my life. I went off the rails and left school with no qualifications. I started getting into trouble with the police, spending time with the wrong crowd and pregnant at 14 years old. I've ended up losing my children through drug abuse, and in and out of prison. I no longer speak to my mam and dad.

My dad has custody of my children, which I'm happy about, but I'm still angry. During the trial I found out that they were keeping things from me. John put the car tyres down and was found sleeping in our shed twice but my mam and dad kept all this from me and I asked them why they didn't tell me.

'To protect you' was their answer. Well that plan didn't work did it?

Phoenix

The definition of a phoenix, a bird in classical mythology that rises from the ashes, very much sums up Phoenix and her journey through the prison system. We first met Phoenix four months into her prison sentence when she was incredibly shy and withdrawn. Now in her thirties, she has been on a tremendous journey of self-discovery and self-development, and we now have the privilege of working with her outside prison following her recent release. Phoenix was but a shadow of herself when she came inside and described Inside-Out as an awakening. The programme, relationships and community enabled her to begin to reflect and see the value in herself and her confidence grew immeasurably, particularly in the first few months. However, low self-esteem and anxiety continue to be difficult to deal with, including outside of the prison walls. Prison has given Phoenix access to a range of services and opportunities that she would have been unlikely to have encountered on the outside. She has grasped these, working hard to make the most of her time inside and also to 'work' on herself. From mental health programmes and domestic abuse courses, to mentoring (as both mentor and mentee) and working up to an Open University Foundation Programme. Prison for Phoenix, as for many women, has served as an escape route from an abusive relationship which had 'knocked everything out' of her. Reflecting on how lost she was back then, so low that thoughts of overdosing and suicide engulfed her, Phoenix doesn't recognise the person who first entered prison. Her journey can be seen as a positive one, ascending to the highest positions of responsibility and privilege within the prison. While she is grateful for the opportunities and proud of what she has achieved, not least educationally, this picture masks a more complex reality. Again, we see here the tension in viewing prison as a 'safe' space for support and development. The failure of community support and the provision of alternatives to custody plays a fundamental role in this (Baldwin and Epstein, 2015).

Prison could be considered a strange place within which healing or recovery might take place, symbolising both freedom and containment for many incarcerated women, through the combination of being a place of potential refuge, ultimately, within a locked cage. Bradley and Davino's (2002) study of women's perceptions of the prison environment found that 38.5 per cent of women consider prison to be safer than other places and, for some, the safest place they'd ever been. Even for women such as Phoenix, who has in some ways benefitted from prison, her perception of the prison environment is incredibly complex and difficult. Self-reflection and the types of 'self-work' expected from the prison are incredibly hard work, involving deep emotional labour. Engaging with some of these life experiences is even tougher within prison, complicated by the physical environment and relationships with your jailors. How can you approach and begin to understand the violence and abuse that has been inflicted upon you when you reside in an institution that replicates that violence and those controlling relationships? How do you understand and learn how to be assertive in a system that shuts you down and punishes you when you try to have a voice? These are the challenges that women in prison face on a daily basis. After release, this distressing conundrum continues. How can you be assertive and try to be true to yourself after leaving a place that institutionalised and broke you? How do you develop a positive understanding and view of yourself once back outside in a society that continues to judge you? How do you move forward with labels and sanctions tied around you wherever you go and whatever you do, like a leash just waiting to tug you back inside? In some ways, Phoenix is thriving now, and yet the wounds of prison need persistent attention and represent a daily battle for her to overcome.

When Phoenix reflected on writing her poem, she talked about the anger that rages inside her and the injustice of the prison system. Although she feels that she is a considerably different person today, to the young, scared woman who wrote the poem four years ago, that anger still burns inside her, as does a longing for justice. The injustice that she feels extends through her experience, not just of the initial sentencing experience (reflected on in the poem) but of her entire journey through the CJS. It continues to haunt her and follow her now that she's outside the confines of prison. Reflecting on that journey, Phoenix said 'I've done everything they've asked of me. I've achieved more than I could ever have possibly imagined when I first wrote the poem. I've worked hard in different roles, studied hard and supported others [through mentoring and Inside-Out]. Whatever I do, it's never enough. The prison and the system always demand more.' The final blow was delivered two weeks before her release when her sheltered accommodation offer was withdrawn and she was expected to be released homeless. Feeling that everything she'd achieved was pointless and completely let down by the system, she was then re-issued her accommodation place the day before her departure. This illustrates the intense rollercoaster of emotions produced by a system that 'picks you up and pulls you down in a heartbeat'.

This is the lived experience of the structural violence of prison, of a responsibilising system that abdicates its responsibility to its citizens. When she reflected on the poem again after having been released, Phoenix reiterated this: 'Now that I'm outside again, I've done everything that's been asked of me – in my accommodation, volunteering, relationships that I'm building – but whatever I do it's never enough. Now I'm no longer in prison, the system still demands of me and now so too does society, but it's never enough.' This is where her anger comes from. This is the sense of injustice. Her poem and her experiences reflect the ability of the state and society to judge and condemn. They reflect a state-sanctioned system of structural violence, gendered in its nature, that treats women differently and more harshly than men (Davis, 2001). Her unfolding experience on the outside demonstrates how that system maintains its grip even after the sentence has been served. Despite acting as a space for growth, prison (and its aftermath) is often about survival. As Mandela (1994: 340–1) argued, the 'challenge for every prisoner … is how to survive prison intact, how to emerge from a prison undiminished, how to conserve and even replenish one's beliefs.'

Despite our closeness, there are still some topics that are too painful to talk about and to share (including with others in prison). One of those is motherhood. The co-authors – as mothers and daughters, as mothers with daughters – occasionally have shared snippets of our family experiences, but this is difficult territory to navigate and discuss. The silences are powerful and convey a pool of pain too deep to penetrate. Through her prison journey, Phoenix has maintained some family relationships and recently, has positively reconnected with others, but she no longer has access to her children. This is an issue that is too painful to talk about, to us or her friends in prison. Even within informal support networks, women carefully manage their discussions and emotions to minimise further harm to each other in terms of their maternal pain (Baldwin, 2018). There is too great a risk for this unspoken anguish to 'bubble up and consume you'. This is yet another highly-gendered experience, with mothers facing the double punishment of imprisonment and losing their children, an aspect of gendered state intervention that can be conceptualised as a continuum of structural violence towards women (and their children). Phoenix is also a spiritual woman, having found religion in prison, and this has helped her deal with this pain. With the help of an inspiring deacon, the prison chapel became a place of respite and comfort, as well as a place of educational stimulation, as the location for Inside-Out classes. Eventually baptised as a Roman Catholic, religion provided a source of guidance and answers. Outside, Pheonix is yet to find a church where she feels comfortable and considers this as a missing piece of the jigsaw since her release. Despite her experiences and her anger at what she has been put through, Phoenix is an incredibly positive woman. Her grounded attitude of 'you just have to get on with it' has seen her flourish inside and now outside prison, overcoming every obstacle put in her way. She continually seeks and sees the best in people.

Phoenix's writing

<u>You Don't Know Me!</u>
I'm sitting in the dock
Waiting for my fate
12 strangers have a decision to make
Everything's a blur,
I can't concentrate.

It's up to 12 strangers to decide my future
That doesn't seem fair.
All they do is sit and stare.
My mind's in overdrive
I'm trying to read their faces.
Trying to guess the decision they'll make
Hoping they won't make a mistake.

My future is in their hands,
They will never be able to understand!
I fight for my freedom,
I tell the truth,
Hoping the jury will just cut
Me loose.

There's a tight feeling inside my heart,
I can't bear the thought of my family
Being torn apart.

How can 12 strangers decide what's true?
They don't know what kind of person I am.
They'll never be able to understand!
The strangers in the court room don't know all the fears I have,
All they know is what the prosecution
Think are the facts.

I'm listening to all their sly tactics.
They keep looking over at me
To see if I can hack it.

They don't know what happened that day.
Who are they to decide my future?
Who are they to have a say?
Why should they have the power to take everything away?

They don't know what I've been through.
They don't know my nature.
They just listen to all the rubbish
And start to hate ya.

Who are they to judge?
They haven't walked in my shoes.
If only they could look inside and see all my scars.
See the damage this nightmare has put me through,
Understand how hard it's been
Not letting this nightmare tear me in two.

I can see my family looking on
I know for them I have to stay strong.
They are going through all this heartache and pain.
The strangers in the court room are just looking for someone
to blame.

My fate's been made in the blink of an eye.
I can't take in what they're saying.
I fall to my knees and cry.
I look at my mum without a chance to say goodbye.

Surely this can't be my fate.
This can't be real, please tell me it's fake!
I pinch myself to make sure I'm awake.

I'm thinking of everything I will be missing.
They haven't got a clue that they've just made
The wrong decision!

I'm not letting this time break me.
I need to stay strong to prove
My innocence when I'm set free.

My friends and family know the real me.

I will prove you all wrong,
I hope you feel guilty for what you've done.
I will continue to believe in myself.
I will fight for justice!

They can incarcerate me, they can turn the key.

I know I'm not guilty, inside I'm truly free.

I know that my story will get told.
When I prove my innocence I will write it BIG AND BOLD!

I will never get back the days that have been taken away.
I know the people who made the decision to lock me away,
Will be sat reading my story someday.

"She was telling the truth" they will say
"we never should have taken her freedom away"
"we should have listened to her that day,
We shouldn't have taken her freedom away."

One day I know my door will be open.
I am going to make sure my words are spoken.
I'm stronger now than ever before
I won't always be locked behind a door.

I REFUSE TO BE BROKEN ANYMORE

Iris

Iris is serving a life sentence for a first offence. In many ways, she epitomises the opposite of the stereotypes of women in prison. Now in her 60s, we first met Iris a few years into her sentence, by which point she had already come to be seen by her peers as a 'mother hen' of the prison, a role she has taken to well. However, navigating a life sentence is incredibly difficult and demands different coping mechanisms to the other women whose biographies are shared here. Although Iris' is a very different story and journey, some of the themes run through her experiences, including sadness, anger and experiences of abuse, though in Iris' case of a different nature. Iris, like Phoenix and Angel, threw herself into prison life and is an active member – and often leader – of numerous groups and activities. Empathic and supportive of others, she is viewed by many in the prison as a motherly figure. Warm and friendly with everyone, it is most often those who are younger and more vulnerable than herself that she casts a protective arm around. A proud wife and mother on the outside, she has carried that mothering instinct with her inside. Unlike others, Iris happily talks about motherhood and being a wife. Her continued regular family support from outside, enabled through visits and letters, are her rock inside. Keeping busy and supporting others are an integral part of Iris' identity but have taken on an even greater significance in enabling her to see out her sentence. Over the years, she has surprised herself and achieved, particularly educationally, much more than she could ever have imagined. She has risen to positions of responsibility within the prison and is widely respected and liked by other women and staff alike. Long periods of boredom need to be filled, and 'keeping busy', though seemingly a sensible tactic, can be exhausting. For this reason, and after several years of active participation in Inside-Out, Iris is currently taking a break from the Think Tank, although we continue to see and meet with her.

Iris wrote her piece when she first came into prison, before the 'World Split Open' project, but decided to use it for that purpose, feeling it spoke to Rukeyser's sentiment. When she reflected on what she wrote, she said she could see and hear the fear and bewilderment in her writing and while, to a certain extent, that initial fear has subsided, the prison system still scares her. She says that she's still not used to prison, 'you never get used to it, and you shouldn't, because that's when you let your guard down and things can go wrong'. That fear of the system and what it can do to you never goes away. Lempert (2016) has described life imprisonment as 'a death penalty by erosion', with a 'soul-crushing impact' on women. Serving a life sentence is a wholly different experience, which again is highly gendered. From the minimal research into life imprisonment (Cohen and Taylor, 1972) and just a few studies of women lifers (Crewe et al, 2017), we know that prison life varies considerably for this group, particularly the challenges of serving life sentences, managing the sentence, issues of identity, change and the future, and social and relational life within and beyond the prison. Women experience the pains and problems of long-term imprisonment and ageing within the prison estate with significantly greater severity than men (Crewe et al, 2017). For women, coming to terms with a life sentence is similar to the 'stages of grief' and the 'existential death' of a life sentence is not dissimilar to learning to live with a terminal illness (Jose-Kampfner, 1990: 110).

One of the most traumatic factors for women serving life sentences is the 'stripping of the mother role' (Crewe et al, 2017). To a certain extent, Iris has circumvented the restrictions to fulfilling 'traditional' maternal role obligations that most women face when entering prison (Owen, 1998) by embodying a motherly role to others within the prison. As a lifer and motherly figure, Iris has garnered much respect from her peers. She is adept at navigating the system and its processes and has earned the privilege of residing in the 'open' wing. Other women, particularly younger women, look up to her as a role model, admiring the apparent ease with which she is managing a life sentence. Iris is always quick to support others, but who will look after her? As friends get released and generally don't keep their promise of staying in contact, who is left to look after the lifers? Unlike most men and women serving life sentences, Iris has maintained familial contact. Her husband visits weekly, and she has re-established contact with her son and grandson, aspects of her life which she is very proud of and readily discusses. The usual impacts of dislocation from loved ones have not impacted on her in the same way and, unlike for most women lifers, she and her family have actively nurtured their relationship. This crucially provides an unusual element of stability and control in her life.

Over time, Iris has learned how to navigate relationships inside. However, prison is an intense greenhouse of emotions that can change rapidly. The culture within women's prisons, combined with the pressures that inmates face, mean that relationships and friendships are under constant threat from gossiping, bitching and backstabbing (Rowe, 2011). Through the emotionally claustrophobic environment and pain of losing friendships, she has learned not to let people get too close and to be guarded about what she shares and with whom. The lack of emotional privacy in prison can be exhausting. The emotional dimensions of private life and relationships are public currency in prison. While men generally experience this as emotionally repressive, keeping their feelings private, for women the emotional intensity can be suffocating (Crewe et al, 2017). This, often coupled with histories of abuse, results in a generalised sense of mistrust for women in prison, who are fearful of being let down. This is compounded by the prison environment, which itself reproduces the dynamics of abuse and sense of powerlessness (Girshick, 2003). There is rarely any silence; a constant cacophony of shouting, laughter, wails, alarms and the trauma of others. It is difficult in this environment to think and find peace, and mental health problems are rife across the women's estate. At the same time, there is an expectation to complete all of the 'self-work' demanded by the system, which also impacts upon parole, appeals and length of time served. Iris has undergone multiple knockbacks, particularly in relation to her conviction. She described her appeal process as 'like somebody dangling a bit of string, giving you the tiniest bit of hope, then pulling it away'. The effort of putting yourself back together within such a chaotic and oppressive environment takes its toll, particularly on women's mental health. For women serving life sentences, there is also a much higher tendency (than for men) to ruminate on their offences, leading to acute guilt and self-hatred, reflected in more severe psychological and emotional experiences in prison (Crewe et al, 2017). Ultimately, the experience of female lifers, subjected to additional deprivations and debasements, are often more acutely painful and problematic than for their more numerous male counterparts (Crewe et al, 2017)

Iris' writing

My life before prison was very normal, I met my husband at 16, got married at 21, had two boys, worked all my life from leaving school, so just a regular home-making housewife. Due to a mixture of unfortunate and bizarre circumstances, I found myself in prison at 57 with a life sentence in my back pocket. To say it was a shock is an understatement. Fortunately, or maybe not, I do not actually remember coming into prison, or the following three months, I was undoubtedly in shock. I know now that my head was mashed for want of a description and I was effectively a train wreck. It has taken three long years to sort myself out mentally with the aid of two programmes, Dialectical Behaviour Therapy (DBT) and Thinking Skills Programme (TSP).[1] These two programmes complement each other and I found them extremely beneficial to me. I took the time to evaluate myself and realised that I had changed dramatically before prison but I just didn't realise that fact. I wanted to do for myself and my sanity anything it took course wise to get me back to the person that I used to be. I was not doing these programmes to tick boxes for people, they were for my benefit alone. I am pleased to say that I now look and feel like my old self, my husband, family and friends have travelled this journey with me every step and have watched my transition back to my old self. It has now been five years since I came into prison and I have devoted my time in here to myself to a certain degree. I have found and discovered more about me than I ever knew, I found myself, basically being a wife, mother, housewife, took up all of my time and I lost my identity, now this time is mine and I intend to explore and exploit it for my benefit. Looking back over the past five years, I have come through culture shock, mental strengthening and self-analysis and become a stronger person for the experience and I look forward to more discoveries and hidden talents inside of me that are lying as yet un-awakened.

Ain't That the Truth
You come through the gates
And you hear that last click
You see all the bars
It makes you feel sick

You get to reception
They take your details
You're sitting there shaking
And biting your nails

They give you a fob card
With number and name
That's when you realise
This isn't a game

You're given a room
A bed and some bars
And if you're real lucky
You may see the stars

You're living your life
In a 4 by 4 cell
What have you done
To be living this hell?

If you do the crime
You must do the time
That's what the law says
So you count off the days

We've all broken the law
There's a price to be paid
The judge passed the sentence
His decision was made

Some of us know that
In hell we will burn
But if you've got brains
You'll never return

Angel

Angel is in her late twenties at the time of writing. She has a gentle and warm nature, and is thoughtful, insightful and one of the brightest women we work with. She is driven by a desire to help others and is most proud of the work she does as a prison listener, a respected and highly regarded role that involves being trained by the Samaritans to provide in-cell emotional support to others who are incarcerated. During her sentence, she has worked hard to earn the highest level of privileges. Angel was part of the first cohort to take Inside-Out for the first time at the women's prison in the spring of 2016. A founding member of the Think Tank, she continued to work with us up until her transfer to an open prison in late 2019. Angel taught us, and others via her role as an Inside-Out teaching assistant, so much about prison culture and prison life from a woman's perspective. As we sketch out below, Angel also challenges us to rethink much of what we believe about the prison system and the inherent harms prison inflicts on women inside. Like all the women we work with, Angel taught us to listen deeply and without judgement to the various and often conflicting stories of incarceration for women (Fine and Torre, 2006; Fleetwood, 2014). In contrast to many other women we collaborate with on the inside, Angel had many positive stories to share about prison life. She talked often and with conviction about prison being a place for her to heal, to feel safe and to grow. For some women, prison can be a relatively safe environment and the perception of safety often varies depending on previous experiences of interpersonal violence in childhood and adulthood (Bradley and Davino, 2002: 351). As her writing demonstrates, this was clearly the case for Angel. As critical criminologists and feminist scholars, we continue to find it challenging to theorise and explain Angel's prison journey because of this.

Angel is serving a 13-year sentence for an offence she was convicted of when she was 18 years of age and, like Verity-Fee, she has had to navigate prison life as a young woman. A defining aspect of Angel's prison experience has been her friendships with other women. She has talked at length about prison culture, 'the lasses' and how emotionally volatile relationships in prison can be. In particular, Angel's tendency to gravitate towards women much older than her has been an important aspect of her prison journey. From our first encounters with her in the prison classroom, it seemed to us that Angel's relationships with older women were positive and meaningful to her. She found a mother figure in them, a source of support, guidance and comfort. These are women, including Iris, who over the years have played an important role in helping to build Angel's confidence and self-worth. Iris and others supported Angel to take the brave steps to follow a path of personal growth via education. However, it was the woman Angel speaks of as her 'mother' on the outside who encouraged Angel to pursue academic studies: in her words, 'she encouraged me to see that education was the path for me and that it would open so many doors in my life'.

It is not uncommon for some women on the inside, particularly younger women, to develop pseudo-familial kinship relationships and view other women as sisters and mothers, though these are rarely seen as formal or structured family roles (Greer, 2000). Although emotional support is generally readily available within women's prisons, emotions can be omnipresent to the point of being overwhelming (Greer, 2002). Close relationships are constantly threatened by 'relationship talk', 'bitching', 'gossiping' and 'backstabbing' (Crewe et al, 2017). As with the other women in this chapter, Angel learned this difficult dimension through the loss of a close friendship. Unsurprisingly, in women's prisons, there is a fear of forming close relationships with other women because of the emotional risks involved (Greer, 2000), and 'the element of distrust is *always* present' Girschick (1999: 84).

It is not surprising that Angel has been nurtured by and found sustenance in her relationships with older women in prison. Her early years were defined by neglect and abuse inflicted on her by her birth mother and coping with many years in and out of the care system. Angel is not alone in her childhood experience – in England 53 per cent of women in prison experienced abuse as a child, compared with 20 per cent of the general population, and 31 per cent were taken into care as a child, compared with just 2 per cent of the general population (PRT, 2019). Angel's poem speaks powerfully to these early years, her relationship with her birth mother and the various traumas she endured as a child. In our conversations with her and in her various writings, Angel spoke about prison as a place where she could develop positive and meaningful relationships with women for the first time in her life. She has valued the consistency and security of prison and has developed deep and meaningful friendships, although these are also more painful when they go wrong. For Angel, prison represents a 'safe haven' away from sexual and domestic violence and toxic relationships. In her words, 'there might be people in prison who would want to manipulate you but it's a much safer place than outside'. This casts light on the extent and severity of abuse experienced by so many women on the outside that they consequently view prison as a safe place (Bradley and Davino, 2002). Wacquant (2002: 388) sees that the prison may act 'counterintuitively and within limits, as a stabilising and restorative force for relations already deeply frayed by the pressures of life and labour at the bottom of the social edifice'. Angel also talked about prison as 'saving her' and providing her with opportunities that she could never have dreamed of on the outside.

When Angel began her sentence at the age of 18, she could barely read or write, a fact she is always open about. When she was transferred to an open prison in 2019, Angel had not only completed prison-based qualifications in numeracy and literacy to the highest level available to her at that time, but she had also successfully completed an Open University BA degree in Arts and Humanities. This journey is extraordinary. A remarkable achievement on many levels, not only in going from being illiterate to graduating in a handful of years, but because she had to overcome the many unique challenges that accompany studying in prison; including accessing funding for HE courses in the first place, having little if any access to online resources, lacking (decent) pens and paper and the unimaginable challenges of trying to think and write in a space that offers limited privacy, can be unpredictable, chaotic and very noisy (Coates, 2016). Angel is quite rightly very proud of this achievement.

In the eight years before Angel was transferred to an open prison, she had secured a number of 'trusted prisoner' roles in the prison: a Shannon Trust mentor, a prisoner information desk (PID) worker and the role of listener. The latter was the role she found most rewarding and fulfilling, which has influenced her plans to pursue a career in counselling upon release. Ironically, the severe prison service cuts under austerity have led to increased and more diverse 'work' opportunities as some responsibilities have been transferred from officers to people detained in prison. In 2017–18, over 12,000 men and women worked across the prison estate for a total of 17 million hours for £4–£20 per week (PRT, 2019). Angel's mentoring and listener roles involve skilled and significant emotional labour. She never divulged the details but, where appropriate and relevant, she would share her insights and reflect on her work as a listener; for example, how she sometimes had to help women having flashbacks, 'talk down' women from self-harming, help women unable to sleep, or who were hallucinating, after taking controlled or prescription drugs. Always with care and respect to her peers, Angel revealed in conversations with us, the deep emotional, psychological and also physical wounds that so many women in the prison system sustain and endure. Despite her conviction in her own positive journey in prison, she remains critical of the society that has seen her locked away and of the daily damage inflicted by the system on others around her.

Angel's writing

Do you See What I See?

Do you see a child or a woman?
Do you see the pain and misery built up over many years?
The fear behind closed doors, what is it that awaits the child being physically abused by a drug addict mother,
The cane or perhaps the belt buckle, whatever came first was taken with sorrow and loneliness.

Do you see that frightened child within me or that young woman screaming in a crowded room?
Do you see the hopes and dreams that once were there?

Do you see the loss and longing in her eyes?
Or do you see a mere prisoner that has done no wrong?

What is it you actually see when you look at me?

I would enquire you to look beyond what you may have heard.
Past the mask I allow to be seen.
Look past the potential aversion.

I am so much more than what you see!!
I am still a child wanting to be loved,
Someone who would like to be happy,
I am also still lost and trying to find my way
But most of all I am but 26.

I am scarred from passed relationships.
Bang there was the fist,
The physical and mental abuse that followed the sorrow and despair.
I am scarred from childhood treatments too.

Do you see them in me?

I hate the way it makes me feel.
I hate the way you look down on me.
I hate the labels once given or even some today.
I hate the ignoramuses that think they know best
And I hate the way you glance at me.

But underneath all that I hate the way you just assume without asking why
Or even wanting to know what really happened.
I wish things were different but they're not.
I also wish time would take its toll.
Most of all do you see, I wish it was me instead of him.

If only it was all different.
People say 'God works in mysterious ways'
This is my path to walk, and walk alone I shall
Carrying the guilt of all past mistakes
To maybe one day have the victory warranted,
To show all those doubters the innocence in me.
To finally be free in order to live life for the first time
Alone or otherwise
Where will I be?

Conclusion

As these biographies and writings show, the lives and experiences of women in prison are diverse but consistently framed by patriarchal oppression. The short biographies cannot do justice to these four incredibly strong and complex women. Their intersectional identities are reflected in their intersectional lives and experiences of prison – none of us lead 'single-issue lives' (Lorde, 2007). Their multifaceted and often contradictory experiences of prison challenge the idea that the power of prisons, over women and their bodies, is absolute. The women's determined sense of self and survival are testament to this; at some point they have all looked us in the eye and said 'I refuse to be broken.' While none of them have had whole-heartedly negative experiences of the

CJS or prison, this sentiment speaks to the belief that prisons are mechanisms designed to 'break human beings' (Davis, 2001). All four of the women see the positives of their experiences of prison – mostly of making the most of (limited) educational opportunities, of building, what they hope will be, lasting friendships and in some cases of the safety of prison. Yet, these positives refract the gaze back onto society and the structural violence that framed their lives before prison, thus enabling prison to be seen as a relatively safe place. This view of prisons, as potential places of safety, continues to challenge our feminist and critical criminological standpoint on the harm of the prison system. These positive experiences are not glimmers of the potential of prisons but a powerful reminder of the pervasive nature of structural violence framing women's lives inside and outside of the prison walls.

Some of the key themes interwoven through the four women's prison narratives speak strongly to family and motherhood and violence and abuse. Their experiences shed light on the complexities of understanding the impacts of long-term severe violent victimisation and coercive control. Consequently, prison is experienced as both freedom and containment, as sanctuary and structural violence. For three of the women, their children have been removed from them. The hope of one day being able to re-engage with their children is intertwined throughout their narratives. Within the women's estate, motherhood remains one of the main sources of joy and pain. Despite these stories, what we are greeted with every time we meet these women is smiles, friendship and laughter. It is likely that you, the reader, will have many more questions bubbling up about the crimes these women committed and their alleged innocence. We want to reiterate that the offences they committed are not important to your understanding of their experience of prison. First and foremost, they are women, they are mothers, they are daughters, they are friends. We, as a collective, as seven women co-authors, hope that in these short pages, you, the reader, have had a glimpse into the lived experiences of the diverse women who are subjected to the prison system, a fleeting kaleidoscopic view of all its raw complexity. 'It is in collectivities that we find reservoirs of hope and optimism' (Davis, 2016: 49).

Notes

[1] DBT is a type of psychotherapy which attempts to promote effective and reduce unhelpful behaviours. It is often used to treat Borderline Personality Disorder. TSP is a cognitive skills programme which addresses how people who have committed offences think and behaviour associated with their offending.

References

Baldwin, L. (2018) 'Motherhood disrupted: reflections of post prison mothers', *Emotion Space and Society*, 26: 49–56.

Baldwin, L. and Epstein, R. (2015) 'Short but not sweet: exploring the impact of short sentences on mothers', *European Journal of Parental Imprisonment*, Winter edition: 20–23.

Bradley, R.G. and Davino, K.M. (2002) 'Women's perceptions of the prison environment: when prison is "the safest place I've ever been"', *Psychology of Women Quarterly*, 26(4): 351–59.

Coates, Dame S. (2016) *Unlocking potential: a review of education in prison*, London: Ministry of Justice.

Cohen, S. and Taylor, L. (1972) *Psychological Survival – The Experience of Long-Term Imprisonment*, London: Pelican.

Corston, J. (2007) *The Corston Report: a review of women with particular vulnerabilities in the criminal justice system*, London: Home Office.

Crewe, B., Hulley, S. and Wright, S. (2017) 'The gendered pains of life imprisonment', *British Journal of Criminology*, 57(6): 1359–78.

Davis, A. (2003) *Are Prisons Obsolete?* New York: Seven Stories Press.

Davis, A. (2016) *Freedom is a Constant Struggle*, Chicago: Haymarket Books.

DBIS (Department for Business, Innovation and Skills), National Offender Management Service (NOMS), Policis, Kingston University and Toynbee Hall (2014) *Parenting and Relationship Support Programmes for Offenders and Their Families*, London: Policis.

Fine, M. and Torre, M.E. (2006) 'Intimate details: participatory action research in prison', *Action Research*, 4(3): 253–69.

Fleetwood, J. (2014) *Drug Mules – Women in the International Cocaine Trade*, London: Palgrave Macmillan.

Girshick, L.B. (1999) *No Safe Haven: Stories of Women in Prison*, Boston, MA: Northeastern University Press.

Girshick, L.B. (2003) 'Abused women and incarceration', in B. Zaitzow and J. Thomas (eds) *Women in Prison: Gender and Social Control*, Boulder, CO: Lynne Rienner Publishers, pp 95–117.

Greer, K.R. (2002) 'Walking an emotional tightrope: managing emotions in a women's prison', *Symbolic Interaction*, 25(1): 117–39.

Greer, K.R. (2000) 'The changing nature of interpersonal relationships in a women's prison', *The Prison Journal*, 80(4): 442–68.

James, E. (2003) *A Life Inside: A Prisoner's Notebook*, London: Atlantic Books.

Jose-Kampfner, C. (1990) 'Coming to terms with existential death: an analysis of women's adaptation to life in prison', *Social Justice*, 17(2): 110–25.

Joseph, J. (2006) 'Drug offences, gender, ethnicity, and nationality: women in prison in England and Wales', *The Prison Journal*, 86(1): 140–57.

Kincaid, S., Roberts, M. and Kane, E. (2019) *Children of prisoners: fixing a broken system*, Nottingham: Crest Advisory and University of Nottingham.

Lempert, L. (2016) *Women Doing Life: Gender, Punishment and the Struggle for Identity*, New York: New York University Press.

Lorde, A. (2007) 'Learning from the 60s', in *Sister Outsider: Essays & Speeches by Audre Lorde*, Berkeley, CA: Crossing Press.

Mandela, N. (1994) *Long Walk to Freedom: The Autobiography of Nelson Mandela*, Boston, MA: Little Brown.

Minson, S. (2019) 'Direct harms and social consequences: an analysis of the impact of maternal imprisonment on dependent children in England and Wales', *Criminology & Criminal Justice*, 19(5): 519–36.

Owen, B. (1998) *'In the Mix': Struggle and Survival in a Women's Prison*, New York: State University of New York Press.

Prison Reform Trust (2018) *'What about me?' The impact on children when mothers are involved in the criminal justice system*, London: Prison Reform Trust.

PRT (Prison Reform Trust) (2019) *Bromley briefings prison factfile*, Winter 2019, London: PRT.

Rowe, A. (2011) 'Narratives of self and identity in women's prisons: stigma and the struggle for self-definition in penal regimes', *Punishment and Society*, 13(5): 571–91.

Wacquant, L. (2002) *Prisons of Poverty*, Minneapolis: University of Minnesota Press.

Walker, T. and Towl, G. (2016) *Preventing Self-injury and Suicide in Women's Prisons*, Hook: Waterside Press.

Women in Prison (2020) 'Key facts, Women in Prison', [Online]. Available at: https://www.womeninprison.org.uk/campaigns/key-facts [Accessed 22 September 2021].

Afterword

No one should underestimate the impact of *Criminal Women*, published in 1985, not least because it emerged at a time when, although there was *some* awakening of interest in the misfortunes of women in conflict with the law and enmeshed in the criminal justice system (CJS), there was by no means proper recognition of the need for gender-sensitive or gender-responsive policies and practices. The book was powerful; the women's stories of their experiences of pathways into crime and experiences of the CJS and allied agencies harrowing.

In some ways, the intervening years between then and now have led to two steps forwards and three steps backwards in penal policy and practices. We have witnessed the development of community centres or services for women following the *Together Women* initiative taken by the Labour Government in the early 2000s, building on best practice developed by small-scale projects such as the 218 Centre in Scotland and the Asha Centre in England and Wales, and leading to the creation of over 40 such community centres for women at risk and women caught up in the CJS. Often, these have served as places of hope and of refuge for women, where there has been genuine care, constructive dialogue and steps forwards and away from crime and the CJS. At the same time, we have seen such centres falter and collapse through a lack of funding. In 2018, we saw a Conservative Government Female Offender Strategy which appears to recognise the need for early interventions. These interventions include practical help and increased diversion from the CJS, community solutions which revolve around the concept of 'whole system approaches' and holistic support, including support for those subject to domestic abuse, all to ensure that fewer women end up in custody. A third strand of developments in the 2018 Female Offender Strategy concerns the need for 'better custody' (improving safety, health and wellbeing, contact with children and families and helping women more effectively in relation to education and employment, for instance). A UK government policy, *Concordat on women in or at risk of contact with the Criminal Justice System*, across different agencies emerged in December 2020 to endorse the chief aims of the Female Offender Strategy. This was heartening. Then, January 2021 brought news of the creation of 500 extra places in women's prisons. We are still waiting to hear what the rationale for this is, given that academics, campaigners, policy-makers and practitioners alike have all pointed to the fact that women's crimes tend to be on the lower end of the scale of seriousness, property-related rather than violent, and that too many women receive short prison sentences. We argue that diversion or a community sentence (with use of a gender-informed community centre or services where available) would make far more sense and be far more meaningful and effective for women in conflict with the law. Policy and practice are riddled with paradoxes and inconsistencies.

But there have been consistent messages from women themselves; it is just that we have been slow to learn from them. The stories woven into this edited collection of essays, inspired and led by a group of feminist scholars involved in *The Criminal Women Voice, Justice and Recognition Network*, are harrowing, insightful, thoughtful and add fuel to the arguments for radical change and a clear mission. It is absolutely right that women's stories and experiences be placed centre stage. The book should be essential reading for all politicians, policymakers and sentencers.

Loraine Gelsthorpe, 2021

Index

Page numbers in **bold** refer to tables; page numbers in *italics* refer to figures; 'n' after a page number indicates the endnote number.